Big Band Jazz in Black West Virginia, 1930–1942

Big Band Jazz in Black West Virginia, 1930–1942

Christopher Wilkinson

University Press of Mississippi / Jackson

American Made Music Series
Advisory Board

David Evans, General Editor
Barry Jean Ancelet
Edward A. Berlin
Joyce J. Bolden
Rob Bowman
Susan C. Cook
Curtis Ellison
William Ferris

John Edward Hasse
Kip Lornell
Bill Malone
Eddie S. Meadows
Manuel H. Peña
David Sanjek
Wayne D. Shirley
Robert Walser

www.upress.state.ms.us

The University Press of Mississippi is a member of the Association of American University Presses.

Copyright © 2012 by University Press of Mississippi
All rights reserved
Manufactured in the United States of America

First printing 2012

∞

Library of Congress Cataloging-in-Publication Data

Wilkinson, Christopher, 1946–
Big band jazz in black West Virginia, 1930-1942 / Christopher Wilkinson.
p. cm. — (American made music series)
Includes bibliographical references and index.
ISBN 978-1-61703-168-7 (cloth) — ISBN 978-1-61703-169-4 (ebook) 1. Jazz—West Virginia—1931–1940—History and criticism. 2. African American coal miners—West Virginia—Social life and customs—20th century. I. Title.
ML3508.7.W5W55 2012
781.65089'960730754—dc23   2011020889

British Library Cataloging-in-Publication Data available

To Carroll Wetzel Wilkinson,

Samuel Wilkinson, Bobbi Nesbitt,

Alexis Wilkinson, Jack Wilkinson,

and especially to the memory of my mother,

Jule Porter Wilkinson

Their patience and support made this book possible.

Contents

ix   Preface

3   Introduction: Coal, Railroads, and the Establishment of African American Life in West Virginia

PART ONE   The Economic Foundation of Big Band Dance Music in the Mountain State

35   **CHAPTER ONE**   From the Coal Face to the Dance Floor: Black Miners as Patrons of Big Bands

48   **CHAPTER TWO**   Validating Herbert Hall's Contention: Paul Barnes's Gig Book

PART TWO   Big Bands in Black West Virginia: 1929–1935

61   **CHAPTER THREE**   Newspapers and Radio Bring the World of the Big Bands to Black West Virginia

68   **CHAPTER FOUR**   Local and Territory Bands in the Emerging Culture of Big Band Jazz and Dance Music in the Mountain State

86   **CHAPTER FIVE**   Big Band Jazz Comes to the Mountain State: 1929–1933

102   **CHAPTER SIX**   Comparative Prosperity Arrives, September 1933–April 1935

PART THREE West Virginia in the Swing Era, 1935–1942

125   CHAPTER SEVEN   The Place of the Mountain State on the Road Traveled by the Big Bands

140   CHAPTER EIGHT   The Big Bands' Audience in the Mountain State

148   CHAPTER NINE   The Dance Repertory Played in the Coal Fields

165   CHAPTER TEN   The Party Winds Down

179   Notes

185   Works Cited

191   Index

Preface

Mention the state of West Virginia to many devotees of American music, and they would probably envision small ensembles of white musicians playing fiddles, guitars, banjos, and upright (that is, string) basses. Occasionally, a hammer dulcimer might be part of the sonic mix of such string bands, but no keyboards, rarely drums. Depending on a group's preferred style or that of a particular piece, the music might be labeled old timey or traditional, bluegrass or country. The repertory could range from fiddle tunes of long ancestry and gospel hymns of the early twentieth century to songs by bluegrass masters, who began to define this style after World War II and brought it to prominence by the end of the 1950s, and more recent music by the singer/songwriters who call Nashville, Tennessee, home.

Such perceptions of this musical culture are overly simple. Most obviously, current technology has made an enormous variety of musical styles accessible to West Virginians, who may choose to engage with almost any musical tradition found in the world. Less obvious may be the fact that, despite what may seem at present to be a kind of stylistic and racial homogeneity within the musical culture native to the Mountain State, its musical past was more complicated.

The place of big band jazz in West Virginia during the 1930s and early 1940s has not been studied until now, nor, for that matter, has West Virginia's place in the history of big band jazz of that time. These intertwined perspectives reveal a great deal not previously known about how this music was imported to the state from the major northern cities that were home to the leading bands of the period. While one encounters passing descriptions of the tours dance bands made during the Swing Era, until now those tours have not been closely examined from the perspective of the audience to be found along the routes the bands followed. Who were they? In a time of economic crisis, how did they acquire the financial resources to attend dances with great regularity? Where did the dances take place? Who organized them? How did word get out that a band was going to be performing in a particular location?

This study addresses not only these questions but also others more fundamental. How did there come to be so many African Americans living in West Virginia? What brought them to the Mountain State, and why did they stay? How did they become part of the national audience for big band jazz, and how did they stay up to date with its latest developments? What sort of music did they like to hear during a dance, and how did the bands satisfy those preferences? In what ways, if any, does the reception of this music in West Virginia enlarge previous understandings of the connections between a band, its style and repertory, and the audiences it encountered while touring the country?

The answers to these questions (and others as well) emerged as evidence presented itself in the newspaper record and in the scholarly literature on an array of subjects. In addition to the larger history of jazz in the 1930s, equally important are the parallel histories of the coal industry and the labor it required, of state politics and racial policy, and of the formation of a black musical culture in West Virginia prior to the arrival of the big bands. Finally, a number of African American informants, all of whom had resided in the coal fields of the state during the 1930s, provided invaluable insight into life in the state's black communities and the place of music in that life.

As evidence accumulated, answers to the questions cited previously began to present themselves. As I will show, during the 1930s West Virginia provided a unique economic and social environment in which African American music could flourish. There were two reasons for this. First, West Virginia's coal industry responded positively and proactively to the Roosevelt administration's New Deal legislation that created the National Recovery Administration (NRA), resulting in high levels of comparatively well-paid employment. Second, West Virginia had from the early 1870s forward guaranteed blacks' voting rights, and their relatively large numbers assured sufficient influence upon state policies to guarantee a freedom of action not found in adjacent southern states. This included creating their own cultural environment without interference.

The economic conditions created by the policies of the NRA and, after it was ruled unconstitutional, subsequent legislation intended to maintain many of its policies enabled black coal miners in the state to earn wages not only considerably higher than those earned by sharecroppers and other African American agricultural workers in the Deep South, but substantially more than those of blacks working in the heavy industries of the

North as well. Thus they had more discretionary income at their disposal than did black folk in surrounding states and further south.

Though the styles of big band jazz and dance music so admired by African American Mountaineers originated principally in the black communities of northern cities (of which the most prominent was New York), black West Virginians were almost as well informed about this music as anyone living in one of those urban areas. This was due in part to the fact that they read the coverage of black music in one of the leading black newspapers of the time, the *Pittsburgh Courier*, and like most Americans they listened to live performances of this music on the radio. Black West Virginians were knowledgeable about the styles of individual bands, had very strong preferences for one style of dance music or another, and their spectrum of tastes was broad.

I have concluded that, beyond its entertainment value, the principal reason for the popularity of big band jazz and dance music among African American Mountaineers was that it served as a source of racial identity and pride. Unlike the music of many of their white neighbors that was embedded within the folk traditions of the central Appalachians and was thus a marker of *place*, the music of black dance orchestras was a marker of *race*, more particularly of racial pride and achievement. It provided occasions in which black West Virginians could socialize in their own company and on their own terms without fear of either intrusion by or criticism from the majority population of the state. Moreover, it was modern in style, urban in origin, and sophisticated in content: the antithesis of the folk traditions brought into the Mountain State by black immigrants from states further south as well as those traditions that many associate with white Mountaineers even today.

The study is organized in three broad sections preceded by an introduction with a substantial discussion of four developments predating the 1930s that were key to the establishment of the culture of big band jazz in the Mountain State: its geological history; the construction by thousands of African American men of the three railroads that served the southern coal fields; the musical life of black Mountaineers before the years of the Great Depression; the nature and consequences of public policies (both state and national) that determined the quality of life and the level of economic prosperity for black West Virginians before and during the 1930s.

Following the introduction, Part I, in two chapters, is devoted to an examination of the close economic connection between the work of the thousands of black miners in the state's coal fields and their enthusiastic attendance at dances for which leading dance bands provided the music, including those led by Count Basie, Cab Calloway, Duke Ellington, Erskine Hawkins, Andy Kirk, and the most frequent visitor of all, Jimmie Lunceford.

Part II looks closely at the period from the start of the Great Depression to the year 1935, by which time black West Virginians were participating with great enthusiasm in the Swing Era. It is in this section that the role of newspapers and radio in bringing big band music to the attention of black Mountaineers is analyzed and the place of local and territory bands in introducing the music to this audience is documented. Also discussed are the earliest documented performances by bands based in New York who would become icons of big band jazz in the latter part of the 1930s. The final topic in this section concerns the evidence of the comparative prosperity enjoyed by black Mountaineers following the implementation of New Deal policies as reflected in a dramatic increase in the number of public dances, many of which attracted many hundreds of fans, some traveling great distances to attend.

Part III looks at the period from 1935 to 1942 from three perspectives. The first examines the connection between the bands and their New York–based managers and entrepreneurs in the Mountain State who organized and promoted dances, arranged for venues in which those dances would occur, and booked the bands to perform. Chief among the latter group was George Morton, who was associated with one of the leading managers of black bands in New York, Joe Glaser, and who was the principal figure in the cultivation of big band jazz in the southern coal field in the second half of the 1930s.

The second perspective concerns the demography of the audience for this music: who they were, where they resided, what they did for a living. Relying on census data as well as the memories of my informants, I discuss the place of both middle- and working-class black Mountaineers in the cultivation of big band dance music.

Finally, I take up the complex issue of the repertory of music played by the touring bands at the numerous dances for which they were engaged. There is unmistakable evidence of a diversity of tastes in dance music: those who were adamant in their preference for hot, swinging jazz, and others as strongly in favor of sweet styles. As I will show, the two audiences were not defined by class. Equally apparent is that whatever their place in jazz history might be, all of the black bands were prepared to perform arrangements running along the spectrum of style from sweet to hot and did so with great regularity.

The final chapter discusses the principal forces that by the summer of 1942 brought to a close the lively engagement with big bands that black Mountaineers had enjoyed for a number of years: the increasing mechanization of mining operations, which led to reductions in the labor force starting with black miners; and wartime policies concerning rationing of rubber and petroleum, materials vital to the war effort.

The chapter concludes with an examination of several issues embedded within the history of this musical culture. I discuss the reasons why this culture flourished in West Virginia to an extent not to be observed in states lying to its east, west, or south. This is followed by reflections on the meaning of the dances themselves as social occasions within the African American world of the Mountain State. The available evidence of white Mountaineers' interest in the music of the black bands, and how that interest was accommodated in a state that by custom, though not by law, required the racial segregation of dances is another topic of discussion. I propose reasons why middle- and working-class black Mountaineers embraced a broad range of musical styles that might seem otherwise inexplicable, with particular attention to why those living in coal company towns might find a musical style associated with Guy Lombardo's Royal Canadians to be particularly appealing. Finally, I consider the patterns of immigration to West Virginia that established the significant black presence in the coalfield counties beginning in the early 1870s and the departure of many black Mountaineers beginning in the late 1930s and accelerating in the decade to come. Whereas their arrival was part of the larger movement of African Americans in search of a new life following Emancipation in 1865, in migrating out of the state beginning just before World War II, black West Virginians might be said to have joined the Great Migration that defined much of African American history in the first half of the twentieth century. Unlike those who made their way from the economically and racially hostile southern states to northern cities with a realistic prospect of a better life, for black Mountaineers who were deprived of well-paying jobs in the mines as well as the benefits of life in a rural setting, that trip did not promise improvement in their condition but rather a decline in quality of life.

This study is a revelation of the unexpected. Who would associate West Virginia with black history in general or with jazz history more particularly? At the same time, it serves as an introduction to big band jazz seen not from the perspective of its creators or from that of the cities that many of those musicians called home, but from that of an audience for this music that resided far from New York, Chicago, or Kansas City. Who constituted that audience, and the connections between their daily lives and jazz in the Swing Era, are the focus of this book. Their story reveals much about the reception of jazz throughout African America.

◆ ◆ ◆

A project such as this is the result of invaluable assistance from many individuals to whom I am extremely grateful and for whom my words of thanks are barely adequate. I must begin by thanking the wonderful and generous black Mountaineers who welcomed me into their homes and shared with me their recollections of life before World War II. They include June Glover of Williamson in Mingo County, West Virginia, who put me in touch with friends of hers from throughout the southern coalfields: Mr. and Mrs. E. Ray Williams of Welch, McDowell County; Thomas Mack of Bluefield, Mercer County; and Mrs. John Flippen and her son Bryan, both now residing in Florida but for whom Beckley, Raleigh County, was home. I must also thank Joel Beeson of the Perley Isaac Reed School of Journalism, West Virginia University, for facilitating a wonderful conversation with another group of black West Virginians: Marcus Cranford of Morgantown, Monongalia County; Hughie Mills, formerly of Charleston, Kanawaha Country; and John Watson, formerly of McDowell County. James Roderick of Cumberland, Maryland, introduced me to Lester Clifford of Piedmont, Mineral County, with whom I had two informative conversations in the summer of 2001. My first conversation took place in May 2000, with the late Geraldine and Horace Belmear of Morgantown, whose recollections gave me the first clues of the breadth and depth of this musical culture.

It goes almost without saying that historical research of any sort is beholden to the expertise of librarians and library staff members. The West Virginia and Regional History Collection of the West Virginia University Library provided a goldmine of information and documents thanks to Harold Forbes, Kevin Fredette, and Christy Venham. Catherine Rakowski and Frank Tovar prepared a number of the photographs and other documents that appear in this book from that archive. Christine Chang facilitated my examination of several important government documents. The creation of maps and the final preparation of all of the illustrations was ably handled by Sue Crist, manager of design in the University Relations department of West Virginia University.

A particular word of thanks is due Ellen Ressmeyer, Archivist at the Drain-Jordan Library of West Virginia State University in Institute, West Virginia. Over a period of several years she painstakingly collected as many issues as she could locate of the student newspaper, the *Yellow Jacket*, from the period when West Virginia State College, as it was formerly known, was one of the principal black colleges in the nation. Thanks to her efforts, it was possible to reconstruct the social and musical life of this institution in a time of racial segregation. In too many instances, racial integration in the state in the mid-1950s was quickly followed by the destruction of documents that would have told the story of African American higher education with great precision. Her work ensured that not all of that story was lost.

Bruce Boyd Raeburn and the late Richard B. Allen of the William Ransom Hogan Jazz Archive of Tulane University also aided in my research. It was Dick Allen who drew my attention to the whereabouts of the professional diary maintained by Paul Barnes during the period of his performing in King Oliver's dance band in the mid-1930s, and it was Bruce Raeburn who encouraged my research and provided access to that gig book following Allen's death.

I am grateful to Professor Alex Albright of East Carolina University for sharing information from Mose McQuitty's route book concerning tent shows in the southern coalfields.

On two separate occasions, in 2002 and 2005, the West Virginia Humanities Council awarded me research fellowships that facilitated my work, as did smaller development grants awarded by West Virginia University and its College of Creative Arts. This support facilitated my travels to the southern coal fields and the opportunity to meet those individuals who became my informants.

I wish to thank the readers of portions of this study as it was developing. Professor John Renton of the Department of Geology and Geography, Eberly College of Arts and Sciences at West Virginia University, ensured that my synopsis of the relevant geological history of the state was accurate. Charles K. Cannon, Professor Emeritus of English at Coe College, Cedar Rapids, Iowa, read a number of the early chapters and offered very useful comments on both argumentation and style. To the readers at work on behalf of the University Press of Mississippi I owe many thanks for their very useful and highly constructive criticism of the book.

Of all of the readers of this work as it was progressing, I must single out Jule P. Wilkinson, my late mother, for particular comment. A professional editor for many years, she brought to the task of reading early drafts of various chapters a keen sense of style. Having a personal interest in the music under discussion, she also provided the perspective of an extremely intelligent lay reader of a subject of great interest. The result is a text that is far better than would otherwise have been the case.

In the final analysis, of course, the strengths of this study are very much a testament to the help I received from those previously mentioned. Whatever shortcomings that remain are my own responsibility.

I am also grateful for the support and, above all, the patience shown by Craig Gill, my editor at the University Press of Mississippi. I also thank Anne Stascavage, Managing Editor at the Press, for her assistance in preparing the manuscript for publication, as well as other members of her staff who contributed their efforts to the cause.

In conclusion, I must thank my family that now extends over three generations for its interest and support. My wife, Carroll, endured the most. My son Sam, his wife Bobbi Nesbitt, their children Alexis and Jack observed what was going on from a greater distance. Even so, they provided the encouragement so essential to a project that has taken more than a decade to complete. One could not ask for more.

Big Band Jazz in Black West Virginia, 1930–1942

Introduction
*Coal, Railroads, and the Establishment
of African American Life in West Virginia*

"Well, all the bands were goin' through West Virginia because the mines were in operation, and everyone, you know, was employed." Jazz clarinetist and saxophonist Herbert Hall made this observation on February 23, 1980, in the course of an interview with Sterlin Holmesly, a journalist with the *San Antonio Express News*. Hall recounted details of his life including his years as a member of a dance band that the New Orleans–born trumpet player Don Albert formed in October 1929, and broke up in the summer of 1940. While exploring Hall's memories of his years with Albert's band, Holmesly took up the subject of its tours; there were twelve during the almost eleven-year history of the band. Holmesly started reciting the names of various states, asking Hall if the band had played in any of them. Arkansas? Yes. Tennessee? Yes. Kentucky? Yes. Virginia? Yes. West Virginia? In response, Hall made the statement quoted above.

One does not associate the idea that "everyone was employed" with the Great Depression; massive, persistent unemployment was one of the defining characteristics of that period. One does not associate West Virginia with the comparative prosperity that steady employment might bring, particularly in a period of the nation's history when so many were in desperate economic straits. It was certainly not that way in the spring of 1960 when John F. Kennedy traveled to the Mountain State during his presidential campaign and drew attention to the seemingly endemic poverty of the coal fields and, by doing so, unwittingly created an image of the state that has endured to this day. That there had been a black population of sufficient size to attract dance bands to the Mountain State in the 1930s, let alone one that would produce on many occasions hundreds of people eager to dance to the music of those bands seems equally improbable. Finally, that the economic foundation of this musical culture was coal mining, a dangerous occupation carried out by workers regularly subject to unsafe working conditions and economic exploitation, may also strain credulity.

Hall's recollections have proven to be accurate. The extent of interest in big band jazz and dance music in the Mountain State is demonstrated by the fact that, between April 1930 and August 1942, newspapers published in West Virginia as well as the *Pittsburgh Courier* documented a total of 256 public dances presented by various dance bands for black Mountaineers. Most took place in the months of February, April, July, November, and December. April was the "dancing-est" month, perhaps because the constraints of the Lenten season were past but equally likely because winter was giving way to spring, and travel was easier.

That same coverage included numerous references to the exceptionally large numbers of attendees, of which the following are representative. Noble Sissle's band reportedly drew 1,000 to a dance at the National Guard armory in Charleston in March 1934 (*PC* 3.31.34, 3). The following September, Jimmie Lunceford's Orchestra attracted a crowd of almost 700 for a dance in Fairmont, the first of nineteen engagements he would play in West Virginia between 1934 and 1942 (*PC* 9.29.34, 2/7). In 1936 Andy Kirk and his Twelve Clouds of Joy had advance ticket sales of over 600 for his debut in Fairmont (*PC* 10.24.36, 2/7). In September 1940 a crowd "estimated at close to 4,000 people turned out . . . recently at Charleston's auditorium to hear Joan Lunceford and her orchestra," according to a report in the *Pittsburgh Courier* (*PC* 9.28.40, 20).

Hall's association of this lively culture of big band jazz and dance music with an active mining industry is corroborated most convincingly by a diary kept by Paul Barnes, who for several months was a clarinetist/saxophonist in Joe "King" Oliver's dance band. As will be discussed in detail in chapter 3, Barnes's "gig book" listed, among other items of information, the money paid to each player at the end of each of the band's engagements between October 1934 and the end of June 1935. In that period, the band played a total of 151 dances, twenty-two of which were held in various communities within the Mountain State. Barnes's gig book documents the fact that engagements in West Virginia paid Oliver's musicians almost twice as much as those played in neighboring states to the east and west and a third more than those played further south. All of the available evidence indicates that many other black bands including those mentioned above did at least as well, if not better.

The musical culture upon which this study is focused was ultimately dependent upon enormous deposits of high-quality bituminous coal in the Mountain State (the existence of which became known a few years after it achieved statehood on June 20, 1863, in the midst of the Civil War). Understanding the history of the development of the coal industry in West Virginia is key to understanding why the state later proved to be so attractive to touring black dance bands in the 1930s.

In his study of coal mining, David Alan Corbin summarized the impact of America's post–Civil War industrialization on what would become the southern coalfields of the Mountain State.

> At the end of the 1870s, southern West Virginia was a relatively isolated, underpopulated, agrarian region, occupied by subsistence farmers, hunters, and family clans like the Hatfields and McCoys. The rise of the coal industry in the next decade, however, transformed the area economically, politically, and socially into both an industrialized region and an economic colony. The growth of the coal industry gave the coal operators a dominance in the state government over southern West Virginia until the New Deal. It also broke down the traditional mountain culture, introduced new values, and brought in tens of thousands of southern blacks and Europeans to mix with the native population in the confines of the company town. By 1921 southern West Virginia was a heavily populated, industrial economy dependent upon coal production and linked to national and international markets (Corbin, 1981, 1).

The migration of African Americans was shaped by the growth of the coal industry during the period Corbin discussed. According to Thomas E. Posey, in 1860, 18,371 slaves and 2,773 free blacks resided in six counties that, with the exception of Kanawha County, were located in what would become the eastern region of the new state where agriculture was the principal activity (Posey 1935, 5). By 1870 the official number of black residents had declined to 17,980 as many moved away following Emancipation, but by 1880 almost 26,000 African Americans resided in the Mountain State, some having returned from temporary residence elsewhere, others migrating from adjacent states. Ten years later that number had increased to 32,690, and by 1900 it had reached just under 45,000. Over the next forty years it continued to grow to 64,178 (1910), 86,345 (1920), 114,893 (1930), peaking in 1940 at 117,754 or 6.2 percent of the state's total population of 1,901,974 (*Sixteenth Census of the United States 1940* 1941. *Population: Second Series*, Table 4, 10).[1]

Fig. I.1. The Northern (Fairmont) and Southern Coalfields with those counties highlighted that had significant African American populations during the 1930s. County seats are also identified. (West Virginia University–University Relations–Design)

That this growth in the black population was linked to the coal industry is also documented by census data that consistently show that throughout the first four decades of the twentieth century the vast majority of African American Mountaineers resided in just two regions of the state. Some lived and worked in three of the six counties that made up the northern coal field, known locally as the Fairmont Field—Harrison, Marion, and Monongalia. In far greater numbers, black West Virginians resided in six counties embraced by the far larger southern fields, a dramatic shift from the antebellum distribution of the black population that had reflected their work as farmers and farm workers (see Fig. 1.1). Kanawha, McDowell, and Raleigh counties were home to three-quarters of the state's black population. African Americans constituted one-quarter of McDowell County's population according to both the 1930 and 1940 censuses (*Sixteenth Census of the United States 1940. Population: Second Series*, Table 21, 40–43).

The significant black employment in the coal industry was also documented in tables, entitled "Nationalities of Persons Employed at the Mines and Coke Ovens by Counties," that regularly were included in the annual reports of the state's Department of Mines until 1933. These data show that not only did blacks regularly constitute the second largest "nationality" after "native-born Whites," but that they worked in greatest numbers in the southern counties.[2] They, their families, and other African Americans employed on the railroads and elsewhere in the coalfields constituted the source of the large audiences for big band jazz and dance music in the Mountain State during the Great Depression.

This introduction examines four developments that account for the presence of so many blacks in the Mountain State and their creation of a lively musical culture that would come to embrace the big bands: the formation of the enormous reserve of high quality bituminous coal for which there was a continuing demand; the role of black Mountaineers in building the railroads that would ship that coal to its many markets both in the United States and abroad and that would remain the second major employer of African American Mountaineers until the 1940s; the nature and extent of blacks' political and economic power not to be found in Kentucky, Virginia, or other states lying further south having substantial black populations, and the benefits of that power served to attract still more black immigrants to the state.

The final topic concerns a development that did not occur until the first one hundred days of the presidency of Franklin Delano Roosevelt: an agreement forged in 1933 by Roosevelt's administration between West Virginia's coal companies and the United Mine Workers of America that led to a period of stability and growth in the coal industry that would prove exceptional in its history and a marked contrast to the state of the economy in many other parts of the country during most of the 1930s. As a consequence, from late in 1933 to the middle of 1942 black Mountaineers enjoyed a higher level of economic prosperity than was typical of African America. Their comparatively good fortune was reflected in part by their frequent attendance at dances for which the music was provided by black dance bands.

The Formation of West Virginia's Coalfields

Understanding the importance of coal mining to this culture raises the question, how did so much of this mineral come to underlie so much of

West Virginia in the first place? By way of background, the surface of the earth is broken into a number of "plates," many consisting of portions of both the visible land and of the adjacent ocean floor. Of the numerous plates covering the earth's surface, our concern is with the North American plate, which, like the others, has been moving around the planet since it first formed.

The formation of West Virginia's coal deposits began in the Pennsylvanian or Upper Carboniferous Period around 323 million years ago, when the North American plate was located close to the equator, not unlike Indonesia today. For thirty million years or so, climatic conditions were right for the formation of the coalfields now located in the Mountain State as well as in eastern Kentucky, eastern Ohio, and southwestern Pennsylvania because of the North American plate's location.

The coast of the North American plate was then characterized by swamps lush with tropical vegetation. In *Annals of the Former World*, John McPhee explained what happened to initiate the formation of the coalfields:

> The freshwater swamp forests stood beside the nervously hanging coastline of a saltwater bay, just as Sumatran swamps now stand beside the Straits of Malacca and Bornean everglades beside the Java Sea. This was when glacial cycles elsewhere in the world were causing sea level to oscillate with geologic rapidity, and so the swamps pursued the shoreline as the sea went down, and marine limestone buried the swamps as the sea returned. In just one of these cycles, the shoreline would move as much as five hundred miles.... There were so many such cycles at close intervals in Pennsylvanian time that Pennsylvanian [and West Virginian] rock sequences are often striped like regimental ties—the signature of glaciers half the world away. (McPhee 1998, 246)

Thereafter, over millions of years the North American plate with its load of carboniferous material moved north, colliding at least twice with adjacent plates and acquiring some portion of their material in the process. The second collision, 248 million years ago, involved the North American and African plates in what geologists refer to as the Alleghenian Orogeny (Byerly and Renton 2006, 5). Those plates "came together not head-on but like scissors closing from the north, folding and faulting their conjoining boundaries to make the Atlas Mountains [of Morocco] and the Appalachian chain" (McPhee 1998, 126). Gradually, the carboniferous material, buried for millions of years under thousands of feet of newer rock, was compressed and heated by the plates' collision, hardening into the bituminous coal found in great quantity in the Mountain State.

The force of the collision also elevated to altitudes comparable to those of the Himalayas today the sequences of rock that McPhee suggested resembled the stripes of a regimental tie, the black "stripes" being the coal. Erosion over the next 150 million years then washed away the highest elevations. Around 65 million years ago, for reasons not fully understood (though plate tectonics was apparently not involved), another uplifting of much of what is now the eastern United States began. Subsequent erosion created the terrain of West Virginia we know today (Byerly and Renton 2006, 6).

Reflecting the impact of this geological history, West Virginia is divided into two regions. To the east lies a series of ridges and valleys running from southwest to northeast: a major portion of the Allegheny Mountains—the central Appalachians by another name. To the west is the heavily eroded Allegheny plateau—"dissected" is the geologist's term—that extends from the westernmost ridge of the Alleghenies across the state and into eastern Kentucky and eastern Ohio.

The plateau presents itself as a series of seemingly innumerable ridges running in all directions separating V-shaped valleys carved over millennia by small streams. The sides of many of these valleys have angles of 35 to 40 degrees, some so deep that the sun rarely reaches the bottom and then only in the height of summer, and many so narrow that the bottom land can barely accommodate a single-lane road, a single railroad track, and a single line of houses. The rail line would have served one or more coal mines; the houses, built and owned by one of the mining companies, would have housed its employees—among them black miners and their families, the audiences for the touring big bands during the 1930s.

The erosion that created those valleys also exposed one coal seam after another, making them easy to mine at first. As Joseph T. Lambie observed in his study of the Norfolk & Western Railway, the rough terrain

> that impeded agriculture favored mining by exposure of the coal beds on every hillside. In nine-tenths of the area the veins are either horizontal or gently sloping—a condition that permits drift or slope mining, which is much more economical than the shaft mining of most of the bituminous regions to the northward. There is usually enough incline in the seams to provide good drainage and make

hauling easy.... Over most of the field the strata are strong enough to provide stable roofs in the mines, so that the minimum of timbering is required.... And a major factor in their favor was the thickness of the seams. Through a large area the Pocahontas Number Three seam runs from six to twelve feet. (Lambie 1954, 40–41)

The Role of Blacks in Building West Virginia's Industrial Infrastructure

Before West Virginia's coal could impress consumers with its extraordinary quality, it had to be shipped out of the state to the ports and industries of the Eastern Seaboard and to the steel mills and factories of the Midwest. Building railroads and starting up mines began more or less simultaneously in the early 1870s for one principal reason: the railroads' financiers made certain to purchase vast portions of the southern coalfields even as their engineers were surveying the routes by which the coal would be exported to other parts of the country as well as abroad. By leasing the rights to mine portions of their land holdings to various companies, the railroads created a captive market for themselves as the sole means of transport of the coal mined on their property. Thus they were paid twice: once for the coal and again for transporting it.

Prior to the Civil War, only one railroad passed through any of the counties that would become part of West Virginia: the Baltimore & Ohio which ran to Wheeling and Parkersburg on the Ohio River, passing through the heart of what would become the northern coalfield and thus being a major force in the development of the resources unearthed there. In the forty years between 1869 and 1909, three railroads were constructed that turned southern West Virginia, to quote David Corbin, "into both an industrialized region and an economic colony" (Corbin 1981, 1). In order of completion, they were the Chesapeake & Ohio Railway, the Norfolk & Western Railway, and the Virginian Railway. Their importance to this study is due to the fact that each was built by thousands of black laborers who migrated to the state in pursuit of jobs and who would remain to work on the railroads or in the mines they served.

Construction of the Chesapeake & Ohio was financed by a group of New York capitalists led by Collis Potter Huntington, who had acquired control of the railroad in 1867. Having been a major player in the construction of the western portion of the first transcontinental railroad,

Huntington's intention was create a coast-to-coast trunk line, though he was hardly indifferent to the profits to be made from transporting West Virginia coal for shorter distances.

Despite the otherwise formidable challenges of the mountainous terrain of West Virginia, acquisition of land in four connected river valleys provided the C&O with a right-of-way with easy grades, something any construction engineer would regard as ideal. From the east, the first of these valleys was that of the Greenbrier River. The second began where the Greenbrier flowed into the New River at Hinton. Further downstream, the New was joined by the Gauley River to become the Kanawha River. West of Charleston, the rail line left the Kanawha and entered the Teays Valley, a geological oddity in that the river that had created it had been captured by the Kanawha at some point in the distant past; thus the Teays Valley is a river valley minus the river.

Of the four divisions into which Huntington divided the railroad, the New River Division presented the greatest construction challenge. Ironically named, the New River is among the planet's oldest, rising in North Carolina, east of the mountains that it traverses in its westward course, and cutting a deep and narrow gorge for more than a hundred miles through some of the highest ridges of the Alleghenies. Though the absence of any roads through that canyon posed significant logistical problems for both surveyors of the right-of-way and construction workers who subsequently created the roadbed and laid the rails, "the New River Gorge offered the only practical route across the mountains, since the natural fall of the river provided easy grades over the most difficult terrain" (Eller 1973, 38). For our purposes, equally important is that the New River provided ready access to coal, for the valley it created exposed numerous coal seams, the sites for future mines.

West of the New River, in the Kanawha Division, the route passed through still other coal deposits in Fayette and Kanawha counties. Surveying these in 1872, a geologist named Thomas S. Ridgway concluded that "the amount of coal available from West Virginia is incalculably large; sufficient, allowing for a normal ration of increase in consumption, to supply the Western markets for a thousand years to come" (Ridgway 1872, 387–88).

The ultimate destination of the C&O was Holderby's Landing, near the confluence of the Big Sandy and Ohio rivers where Kentucky, Ohio, and West Virginia meet. Huntington instructed his brother-in-law, Delos W. Emmons, to acquire five thousand acres on which to construct the railroad's western terminus. The community that formed adjacent to this facility was later named Huntington and would become the largest city on the Ohio River between Cincinnati and Pittsburgh and a regular destination for black dance bands in the 1930s (Eller 1973, 42).

That African American laborers built the C&O was noted in 1873 by the journalist Jedidiah Hotchkiss, who wrote frequently about the potential wealth to be found in West Virginia's coalfields (Williams 2002, 183–84). In 1872 he traveled the length of the newly completed C&O and summarized his observations in a two-part essay that appeared in *Scribner's Monthly* in December 1872, and January 1873, entitled "New Ways in the Old Dominion: The Chesapeake and Ohio Railroad" illustrated by one or more commercial artists who accompanied him. The second part of this essay drew attention to those who had built the railroad:

> Our artists were surprised to find negroes so generally employed as road-builders. They have proved in fact to be fine laborers, both as track-makers, and for mining, blasting, and all the other work of railroad building. They lived in shanties along the road, wherever their work lay; and as is usual with the negroes, they were musical, as well as orderly and sober. . . . They save money—the contractors reported this very generally; they have not the habit of drinking whisky; and on the work itself, as they took their chance with the white workmen, so they were treated with absolute equality, not the slightest bullying being allowed or attempted. . . . The contractors had but one complaint to make—that the colored men *would* go "home" for Christmas. Home to them meant Eastern Virginia and we were told that many of them returned joyfully to the old plantations where formerly they were slaves and where . . . they are still made welcome on holidays. (Hotchkiss 1873, 289)

At the conclusion of his text, Hotchkiss discussed the contributions of black workers, revealing both their numbers and their places of origin, information helpful to an understanding of the initial growth of the black population of the Mountain State:

> Nor is the construction of such a road without what may be called wholesome political results. In the first place it was built almost entirely by the labor of negroes, who here proved themselves admirable and trustworthy workmen; sober, equal to the severest toil, and

winning the good opinion of everyone. In the work they learned self-dependence, became more intelligent, were drawn away from their homes, and thus had the advantage of travel and of seeing a new life. These blacks, of whom *five thousand were employed* on the road, all formerly *slaves in Eastern Virginia*, will be the better citizens for this experience. (Hotchkiss 1873, 292 [emphasis added])

Not only was Virginia the home to many of these workers; it would continue to be the birthplace of the greatest number of African American immigrants to the Mountain State, at least up to the time of the 1930 census (Trotter 1990, 75–76). As the railroad was built and mines opened along it, the black population of West Virginia steadily rose.

Once the main line of the C&O was completed, there was still work to do. As Hotchkiss noted, "[a]t many points you will notice preparations for building short branch lines within three or five miles of the main line. It is a well-ascertained fact that coal can be mined at a profit within five miles of the line of the Chesapeake and Ohio Railroad" (Hotchkiss 1873, 289). Just as they constructed the main line, blacks built those branch lines which over time extended further up the side valleys of the New and Kanawha rivers as the market for coal increased and mining operations proliferated.[3]

After the railroad was finished, African Americans continued to work as brakemen and firemen on trains and as laborers in the shops that maintained the equipment (Taylor 1926, 115). Others were maintenance-of-way workers: the gangs of laborers who maintained the rail lines themselves. It will be recalled that Hotchkiss had noted the musicality of the blacks building the railroad. Both then and into the twentieth century, a varied repertory of railroad work songs made track work go more smoothly along the ten-mile stretch of right-of-way for which each crew was responsible (Clifford 2001).[4] The songs of those "track liners" also became an important component of the musical culture of black Mountaineers.

Completion of the C&O was followed by work on a second railroad that eventually stretched across the lower portion of the southern coalfields from the Virginia line to the Ohio River: the Norfolk & Western. The driving force behind it was Frederick J. Kimball, who envisaged a railroad devoted almost exclusively to the transportation of coal. He had made certain that allies acquired title to as much as possible of the Pocahontas coalfield situated on Great Flat Top Mountain, south of the New River and north of the Big Sandy River, the latter constituting a portion of the boundary between Kentucky and West Virginia. Thus, even before it was built, the N&W had created a market for its services (Lambie 1954, 19–24).

Originally, the N&W was to terminate at the eastern edge of the Pocahontas field, from which coal could be shipped to the railroad's tidewater port at Lambert's Point near Norfolk. Kimball assumed that another of the numerous railroad companies being incorporated during the 1880s would take up the challenge of reaching from the Ohio River east into the developing coalfields, after which his railroad could be linked with it. Not until 1886 was it apparent that no other company would take up the challenge, and not until 1889 was the route that today traverses Mercer, MacDowell, and Mingo counties determined. Only in 1892 was the entire route finished from the mouth of the Chesapeake Bay to the Ohio River (Lambie 1954, 123–25). As James Laing reported in his dissertation, *The Negro Miner in West Virginia*, "the Negroes took fully as large a part in the building of [the N&W] as they did in the building of the Chesapeake and Ohio" (Laing 1933, 65). How many African Americans were employed is uncertain but, given its length and the challenges associated with its construction, it seems logical to suppose that several thousand were involved, and like that of the C&O, the workforce that completed the Norfolk & Western remained in the state either to work for the railroad or to dig the coal that the railroad would ship out of state.

Construction of the third railroad to serve the southern coalfields was begun in 1902, underwritten by the wealth of Henry Huttleston Rogers, whose fortune came from Standard Oil. The Virginian opened up coalfields lying between those served by the C&O and N&W operations and linked those fields to Sewalls Point on Chesapeake Bay just east of Norfolk. Its several branches snaked up narrow valleys within the Winding Gulf field in Raleigh and Wyoming counties, eventually serving more than fifty mines. Frederick Kimball initially conceived the N&W exclusively as a coal hauler, only to have it diversify once it reached into the middle west; Henry Rogers's vision was more narrow: the Virginian's sole purpose was to transport coal (Lambie 1954, 264–66).

Laing drew attention to the impact of the Virginian Railway on mining operations in the Winding Gulf field, noting the growth of the population of miners in Raleigh County, part of which lies in that field. He observed: "When operators in other fields were prospecting in the Winding Gulf coal area they took their trusted negroes. Many of these negroes who helped open up the mines in this newest field are still working at these same places" (Laing 1933, 69). Laing quantified the effect of the railway's arrival on the population of Raleigh County by comparing the populations of black and native white residents in 1908, just before it went into operation, and two years later, at which point the white population had grown by 178 percent and the black population by 186 percent. He went on to state that "The growth of Negro population in Raleigh county has been steady until today it is the second county in the number of Negro miners" (Laing 1933, 70). McDowell County, served by the N&W, was first.

The forty-year period of railroad construction and mining development created an industrial economy in the West Virginia coal fields that continued to attract large numbers of blacks from Virginia, the Carolinas, and Ohio, as well as from other more distant states with the promise of work that paid better than sharecropping or other unskilled or semi-skilled agricultural occupations back home. By fulfilling that promise, this economy also provided the foundation for the musical culture of big band jazz and dance music that flourished during the 1930s.

Black Mountaineers' Musical Culture before the Big Bands

West Virginia's black immigrants brought a lively and diverse musical culture with them that would continue to be cultivated both in the numerous coal company towns as well as within the middle class residing in larger communities. The company towns, for which the vernacular term was "coal camps," and the county seats constituted separate though related musical scenes, defined as "cultural space[s] in which a variety of musical practices coexist, interacting with each other within a variety of processes of differentiation, and according to widely varying trajectories of change and cross-fertilization" (Straw 1991, 373).

The repertories created by residents of the coal camps, largely fall under the heading of black "roots music," comprised of a mix of several of the United States' many oral musical traditions. While most of this repertory had been handed down through the generations, some of it no doubt began life in published form (early examples being songs by Stephen Foster) but had become so totally absorbed by one folk tradition or another that it came to be preserved in the collective memory of performers and audience alike rather than in print. Performers were either self-taught or part of a master-apprentice relationship with an admired musician of the previous generation, such as the area's best fiddle player or banjo picker.

In addition to those musicians, gifted singers within each community could be counted on to improvise four-part harmony in the service of a gospel hymn on Sundays, and in some instances to create spontaneously individual calls during the week to synchronize the work of railroad trackliners. Recall that Jedidiah Hotchkiss had noted in 1873 that as "is usual with the negroes, they were musical . . ." (Hotchkiss 1873, 289). Until track maintenance became mechanized, thus eliminating the need for gangs of laborers to align the rails, replace and tamp crossties, and tend to other tasks requiring concerted physical effort, many continued to express their musicality in a variety of work songs. The father of John M. Watson of Beckley, one of the informants for this study, worked for the Norfolk & Western in various capacities, most related to track construction and maintenance. Watson's memories of the singing by trackliners and the coordination of various physically demanding tasks thereby, remained quite vivid even after the passage of more than sixty years (Cranford et al. 2008).

One important genre of folk music was surely the blues, a tradition many would associate first with the Mississippi Delta and later with Chicago's South Side but which is known to have flourished widely among southern blacks, including those residing on the eastern side of the central Appalachians in the Piedmont of Virginia and the Carolinas, the ancestral home of many black Mountaineers. A lifelong African American resident of Bluefield at the eastern edge of the Pocahontas coal field, Sam Bundy reported that while blacks living in his town gravitated to big band jazz and dance music, those living west of Bluefield in McDowell County favored the blues. He attributed this to the fact that many had migrated from further south where the blues was an indigenous music (*BO* 2.15.89, 8).

Not only were there blues musicians among the residents of the Mountain State, they were to be found within the casts of minstrel, medicine, and vaudeville tent shows that regularly toured the coalfields. A "route book" maintained by a bass player named Mose McQuitty, a native of North Carolina, documents much of his career extending from 1896 to 1937. He came to West Virginia on several occasions with two circus companies, Forepaugh & Sells Circus and Sparks Circus; with the Miller Brothers 101 Wild West & Far East Show; and with two minstrel shows, Voelkel & Nolan's Dandy Dixie Minstrels and Silas Green from New Orleans (Albright 2009). Nat Reece, born in Salem, Virginia, in 1924, but whose family moved to Itmann, West Virginia, four years later, told Barry Lee Pearson in 1990 that the Silas Green show "used to come to Mullins [seat of Wyoming County in the Winding Gulf coalfield and ten miles from Itmann] all the time. They came down for ten years straight.... They had blues musicians, guitar pickers" (Pearson 2000, 39). Employed by Silas Green between 1928 and 1931, Mose McQuitty recorded engagements by Silas Green in Mullins every summer in that period.

Nat Reece's recollection of blues singers and guitar pickers among the entertainers in the Silas Green shows draws attention to one important contribution these touring shows made to the musical life of black Mountaineers: the introduction of the latest commercial musical styles to black West Virginians in the course of numerous performances. During a tour in late July and early August 1929, the Silas Green show traveled between Huntington and Bluefield playing twelve engagements in fourteen days (resting on Sundays). Except for Williamson and Bluefield, both large towns, every stop was at a coal camp or was situated close to several along the main line of the Norfolk & Western or on one of its branches. Departing Huntington, the tour went to Williamson, Iaeger, War, Kimball, Keystone, Gary, Vivian, Pocahontas (a coal camp just across the Virginia line), Maybeury, Bramwell, and Bluefield before departing the state (McQuitty n.d.). The following year the company returned to the southern coalfields with a new show, *Funny Money*, which it performed in the McDowell County town of Keystone on August 11, 1930. According to the *Pittsburgh Courier*, those in attendance were treated to "a scintillating musical comedy with mercurial situations, funny and laughable speeches and actions, tuneful music in two acts and seven scenes." In addition, the show's "costumes, electrical effects, etc. are new and of modern detail" (*PC* 8.16.30, 2/6).

During the 1920s a number of tent shows included or indeed were presided over by women blues singers, whose performances introduced the latest examples of formally composed blues to audiences throughout African America. Best known of these was "the Empress of the Blues," Bessie Smith, who toured with a tent show during the summers of the 1920s and continued to do so early in the next decade. Among her West Virginia engagements were three in Wheeling on May 14, 15, and 16, 1931. Her presence provides further evidence that the culture of black West Virginia included the influence of commercially produced music, a fact notable for several reasons.

Unlike folk music, commercial music was not a music of place (except in "places" imagined by a lyricist), nor was it explicitly rooted in the histories and collective experiences of the residents of the West Virginia communities where it was performed. This repertory had not been imported from Virginia, the Carolinas, nor any other southern state by black migrants, unlike the folk styles previously discussed. It came primarily from New York City, a place distant in miles and culture from the rural setting of the coalfields. When performed by elegantly costumed performers—Bessie Smith was well known for her attire—it acquired at least a veneer of sophistication associated with an urban life with which few black Mountaineers had much, if any, direct experience.

Just as they led the way in introducing products of New York and other northern cities' music industries to the central Appalachians, the tent shows may have provided the business model for big bands on the road. The advance men promoting a forthcoming performance by a circus or vaudeville troupe would have learned which local communities would turn out in large numbers for a show and what days were paydays—on which a show could expect greater attendance, particularly if it pitched its tent close to several company towns. Of great importance both to the tent shows and subsequently to the bands were the names of people in those towns who would welcome a placard in the window of their business or on the side of their building, would sell tickets in advance, and could be counted on to deal honestly with the shows' representatives when they came to collect the proceeds from those sales.

The song-and-dance acts of a vaudeville tent show included music that would later become part of the jazz repertories of dance bands. Regardless of any differences, in both instances the music was being performed by strangers, not by banjo-picking and fiddle-playing neighbors who, during the week or even earlier on the same day, might have dug one or more tons of coal in the same mine alongside the owner of the house in which they were performing. Like the tent shows, the touring dance bands may have contributed to a sense of community among audience members during a performance, but they were not part of that community; indeed, they moved on as soon as the engagement was finished.

After the early 1920s, the blues also came to the Mountain State on records. Wind-up Victrolas appeared throughout the coalfields, and race records could be purchased by mail order. In August 1973 Tom Brown, a member of the faculty of West Virginia University, interviewed Charles Walker, then residing in the McDowell County town of Jenkinjones, a former coal camp near the border with Virginia. Born on the banks of the New River in predominately white Summers County in 1914, beginning at age seventeen Walker had played the banjo as a member of a string band whose other members were two whites playing mandolin and guitar respectively. The trio primarily played for white square dances. Walker also picked up the guitar and began to acquire a repertory of blues and other vernacular songs, some undoubtedly originating as recordings but coming to him through oral transmission.

During the interview he performed "My Baby's Gone Blues," which he said he learned from a black miner in Coalwood, McDowell County, sometime in the mid- to late 1930s. The performance consisted of five twelve-bar choruses and a bit more: a short guitar introduction, three vocal choruses, an instrumental chorus, another vocal chorus, and a partial repeat of the instrumental chorus, at which point he stopped. The fact that the song was limited to five choruses suggests that Walker had learned it from a recording, since blues recordings on ten-inch 78 r.p.m. discs typically accommodated only this much music. In addition, the instrumental chorus seemed formulaic, further evidence that he appropriated it from a recorded performance. Nothing about this performance suggests it was either spontaneously improvised or had originated in live performance where no time constraints would have limited the number of verses. In essence, Walker "covered" a recording, evidence that black Mountaineers could actively participate in a national musical culture that came to them through recordings, radio, as well as by means of performances by traveling musicians. (Walker 1973).

Other varieties of secular music were also part of African American life of the company towns. String-band music,—primarily to accompany dancing, with prominent roles for fiddles, banjos, and guitars—was one such variety, as Charles Walker's testimony confirms (Walker 1973). In Gary, located in McDowell County and the site of a mine owned by U.S. Steel, a black five-piece string band played regularly during the 1930s (Cranford et al. 2008). Black parade bands presented another musical repertory and sound on patriotic and other celebratory occasions, and their older musicians taught the rising generation to play the brass and woodwind instruments that would later anchor the dance bands.

While the preceding genres were appropriate for Saturday night, Sunday morning's music included gospel and other types of black sacred musical expression cultivated within black Baptist and Methodist churches, as well as those of other denominations. As with the blues, the Piedmont region east of the central Appalachians was no doubt one source of this music. In Itmann, a coal company town, six young men, two of them brothers, formed the Starlight Gospel Singers in the late 1920s or early 1930s to perform at various black churches in the southern coalfields. Similar ensembles could be found within many black congregations in the

Mountain State at that time (Kline 1987, 10). Among more socially conservative congregants dancing and the music with which it was associated was frowned upon, and gospel and other sacred music constituted one of the few acceptable repertories (Cranford et al. 2008).

Quartets performed on secular occasions as well. At a Republican party rally on July 20, 1934, in the Logan County community of Holden, a company town of the Island Creek Coal Company, Rector Charles McIver, in his "Local Colored News" column for the *Logan Banner*, reported that "the Carey Jug band and several quartets are to alternate with patriotic selections . . ." (*LB* 7.20.34, 2). One wonders if in Logan County political differences were accompanied by aesthetic differences when it came to music. On the following evening, the Southern West Virginia Negro Democrats held a dance in the Logan armory for which Speed Webb's dance band from Indianapolis provided the music (*PC* 7.14.34, 1/5).

While these musical styles and genres defined much of the black musical culture in the coalfields, the influence of other musical traditions and collaborations among musicians both black and white were also part of these scenes. Studies of West Virginia's mining industry in the period have often drawn attention to the fact that most mine owners created segregated communities within their company towns, establishing distinct neighborhoods for blacks, for European immigrants, and for native whites. In terms of the musical life of company towns, racial and ethnic segregation meant little. Sounds traveled, and musically talented neighbors of varied ancestries and ethnicities could have easily heard something they liked of a tradition other than their own. Shared interests in making music undoubtedly brought diverse people together on one another's front porches or in other social settings to exchange elements of their respective musical styles and practices. Folklorist Alan Lomax's broad observation about cultural exchanges between diverse people certainly applied to residents of company towns: "Blacks and whites lived [as] neighbors, swapped favors, and stole each others' music" (Lomax 1990). The results of such "theft" were surely to be heard in the types of music community-based musicians performed, reflecting in part the settings in which they played.[5]

In *Virginia Piedmont Blues: The Lives and Art of Two Virginia Bluesmen*, Barry Lee Pearson enumerated the variety of "community-based social events" that were major occasions in the lives of African Americans in the rural agricultural communities of the Piedmont in Virginia and the Carolinas, the "home places" of many black Mountaineers. These included "frolics, suppers, selling parties, hoedowns, breakdowns, and seasonal collective work parties all [of which] served as homegrown recreation." Central to these occasions was the music made by local musicians, most of whom "played for fun, recognition, and a chance to test their skills against [those of] other performers" (Pearson 1990, 14).

The one occasion shared by residents of the Piedmont and those of West Virginia coal camps would have been parties held at the end of the work week. Nat Reece recalled that in Itmann where he had lived from the age of four:

> On Friday nights one house would have beer, home brew, and whiskey, and they would hire someone to play, or two people to play guitar. And they'd have one of the biggest house dances ever was, boy! People'd be dancing everywhere. A man'd knock the paneling out between two rooms [of a company house] and make one great big space. People would get in there and dance just the same as they was in a ballroom, boy, at the Holiday Inn! Yes sir. And they would dance all night long, as long as the music was there. Of course, when you seen one house party you seen them all. They were no different, wasn't nothing but a couple of walls knocked out, where you'd have enough room to jitterbug. (Kline 1987, 15)

Not only guitarists were involved. E. Ray Williams of Welch recalled traveling "professors" who played the piano here and there in McDowell County and found plenty of work in homes where an upright piano and partygoers ready to dance might be found (Cranford et al. 2008).

That the hoedown did not endure in the Mountain State is suggested by a brief article in the *Williamson* [West Virginia] *Daily News* for January 26, 1938 (see Fig. I.2). It announced: "Gingham dresses and overalls will dominate at an old-fashioned 'Barn Dance' to be sponsored by the elementary department in Liberty high school gymnasium Monday night [February 1].... Grownups will be given an opportunity to show the youngsters a thing or two about the Virginia Reel, Georgia Stomp, and other dance floor capers.... Square dancing will be the main diversion of the evening..." (*WillDN* 1.26.38, 7). Liberty was Williamson's and Mingo County's sole school for African Americans, and despite its name it included both primary and secondary grades.

That the barn dance was characterized as "old-fashioned," and that the "grownups" had to "show" young people how to perform various dances, such as the Virginia Reel, implies that these had become passé, presumably

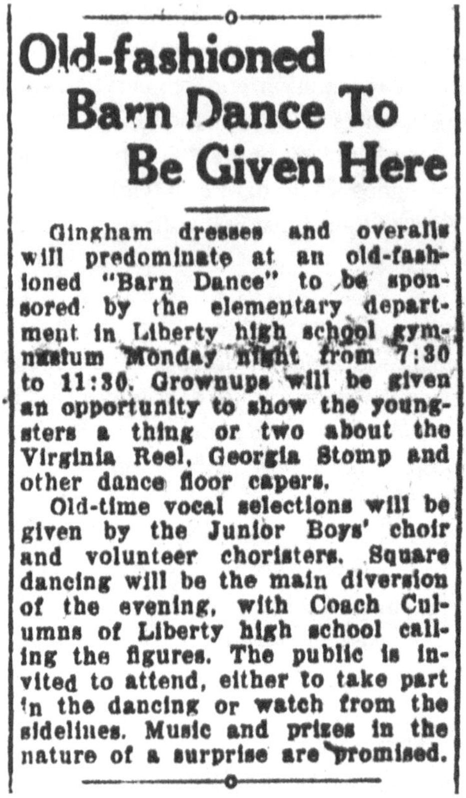

> # Old-fashioned Barn Dance To Be Given Here
>
> Gingham dresses and overalls will predominate at an old-fashioned "Barn Dance" to be sponsored by the elementary department in Liberty high school gymnasium Monday night from 7:30 to 11:30. Grownups will be given an opportunity to show the youngsters a thing or two about the Virginia Reel, Georgia Stomp and other dance floor capers.
>
> Old-time vocal selections will be given by the Junior Boys' choir and volunteer choristers. Square dancing will be the main diversion of the evening, with Coach Culumns of Liberty high school calling the figures. The public is invited to attend, either to take part in the dancing or watch from the sidelines. Music and prizes in the nature of a surprise are promised.

Fig. I.2. "Old-fashioned Barn Dance To Be Given Here," article in the *Williamson Daily News*, January 26, 1938. Liberty High School served the black students of Williamson (seat of Mingo County) and vicinity. (*Williamson Daily News*)

along with the music to accompany them. It would seem that only by deliberately creating an occasion for their performance might devotees of these older musical traditions attract the attention (and perhaps the interest) of those otherwise entranced by the fox-trot and the Lindy and by the big bands that played the music appropriate for those dances.

By contrast, in the northern coalfield, where there were comparatively few blacks in any one company town, the situation was very different. Square dances and polkas, the latter possibly introduced by immigrant Slavic miner/musicians, were the principal dances in Cassville, Monongalia County. For this reason, Marcus Cranford, a member of one of only three black families residing in that community, learned these dances long

Coal, Railroads, and African American Life   23

before he encountered the fox trot, the Lindy, or any other dances associated with the black big band jazz of the period before World War II (Cranford et al. 2008).⁶

❖ ❖ ❖

Little is known for certain about the diversity of musical genres cultivated within the small middle-class African American communities of Beckley, Bluefield, Charleston, and other county seats, but it is hard to imagine that it would have been significantly different from that of middle-class neighborhoods in other parts of the nation. Popular songs, hymns, and dance music—whether syncopated in the tradition of ragtime and jazz or more stylistically conservative as in the case of the waltz—would have constituted the repertory played primarily by the women of the house on the parlor piano to entertain family and friends. In addition to, or in place of, the piano might be a radio, a phonograph, or both, intended for the family's entertainment and for private social gatherings during which the carpet might be rolled up for dancing. One such dance occurred in Fairmont in the northern coalfield on August 27, 1934, when "a radio party was staged at 218 Jefferson Street on Monday evening by Ernest Owens. Noble Sissle, Wayne King, and Claude Hopkins entertained. Sissle was heard from the French Casino in Chicago, and Hopkins was playing a dance in Charlotte, N.C." (*PC* 9.1.34, 2/6). Whatever else he did in life, Mr. Owens was known in the community for his tap dancing (Nallen, 2001). While his may have been a special interest in dancing, this event was surely not the only occasion when black Mountaineers danced in their homes to music broadcast on the radio. From the perspective of the music involved, the only differences between the Friday night parties in coal camps as described by Nat Reece and Ernest Owen's radio party would have been the style of the music performed and the medium through which it was presented to the partygoers.

Commercially published repertories, found on the rack of a piano or in its bench, and broadcast performances that provided music for "radio parties" turn our attention from the homemade folk musical styles of the mountains toward the commercial music imported into West Virginia, repertories making little use of banjos, fiddles, guitars, and other "folk" instruments, instead favoring the brass, reed, and percussion instruments of the band tradition, and above all the piano. Dependent on musical notation, this music required performers who could not only play their instruments with technical facility but also read music and play parts that became more and more demanding as arrangements grew more sophisticated, expectations also to be met by the members of a dance band at that time.

The Social and Political World of Black Mountaineers

The migration of large numbers of African Americans to West Virginia was prompted in part by the promise of economic prosperity. Working on a railroad paid better than working as sharecropper or farm laborer. Those building the C&O, for instance, earned an average of $1.75 per day and were paid in cash once or twice a month (Taylor 1926, 114). In the same period, black farm workers in Virginia and elsewhere might earn between nine and fifteen dollars a month; a sharecropper might get between a quarter and half of the crop, but what that was worth depended upon the price paid for the commodities grown in a given year (Franklin and Moss, 212).[7]

Miners' wages were comparable to those of railroad workers, which motivated Thomas Cannady, a former sharecropper, to move to McDowell County to mine coal simply because he "could see [the money] better. The miner got paid once or twice a month. On the farm you had to wait till the fall of the year when you gathered your crops, and then the other fellows, the landowner, merchants, etc., got it all and that way we didn't make nothing." This sentiment was echoed by Bill Deering, another black miner: "On the farm I was no[t] making anything; in West Virginia I made a dollar on my first day, and I thought I was rich!" (Corbin 1981, 63, based on interviews conducted by the author in 1975).

Beyond the opportunity to receive hard cash on a regular basis, a second benefit of mining in West Virginia was comparative job security. The rapidly expanding industry experienced a chronic shortage of miners until the 1920s, so blacks and whites were not competing for jobs. Consequently, there was little or no racial conflict over employment in the coalfields—a very different situation from northern cities, where the fact that there were fewer jobs than available workers at times caused racial tension, if not outright violence. Most trade unions denied African Americans membership in an effort to reduce the competition for employment; a conspicuous exception was the United Mine Workers of America, a fact having major implications for black miners in West Virginia during the 1930s.

There were political benefits to living in the Mountain State unknown to African Americans both in adjacent states and in Alabama, site of another major coalfield from which there was considerable migration to the Mountain State between 1910 and 1930 (Trotter 1990, 78–79). Drafted in 1872, West Virginia's constitution followed by only a few years the ratification of the U.S. Constitution's Fifteenth Amendment guaranteeing the right to vote to all adult males. The state's constitution adopted similar language, and by implication, "all adult males" included African American men, who could also testify in court, hold political office, and (after 1881) serve on juries, though schools were racially segregated and interracial marriages were outlawed by the same document (Ambler and Summers, 270–73).[8] Because white Republicans and Democrats were more or less evenly divided in the Mountain State, the black vote was often crucial to a party's electoral fortunes, and African Americans' interests were taken seriously by the political establishment, as shown by several developments.

Most impressive perhaps was that West Virginia never passed a law requiring racially segregated seating of passengers on trains traveling through the state, something many southern states quickly did following the U.S. Supreme Court's decision in 1896 in the case known as *Plessy v. Ferguson*. The railroads found the preservation of the rights of black passengers inconvenient, since it meant that trains originating in or passing through Virginia or Kentucky had to include a "Jim Crow" car (usually an old, substandard piece of equipment always located immediately behind the coal tender and locomotive, all the better to have coal dust and fly ash blow in through the open windows in warm weather), which would be empty during passage through the Mountain State. State Democrats proposed outlawing integrated seating in 1908, but no such legislation was ever enacted. June Glover of Williamson in Mingo County recalled in an interview that whenever she boarded a Norfolk & Western train eastbound for Bluefield, the conductor would routinely ask if she wanted to go forward to "the car." She always declined, indicating that her destination was the last stop before the train entered Virginia (Glover 2005). A member of Lionel Hampton's band, trumpeter Joe Wilder, remembered traveling on a train in 1942 that had originated in New York and passed through Virginia. At its first stop in West Virginia, he was amazed to see all of the occupants of the Jim Crow car immediately stand up, pick up their luggage, and move to other locations on the train. One white passenger, upon seeing the African Americans seated among whites, was heard to ask, "What are all these niggers doing here?" Someone responded that they would leave once the train got to Kentucky (Wilder 2008).

Two actions by the state legislature provide further testimony of the political clout of black Mountaineers in the first decades of the twentieth century. In 1919, a law declared it illegal "to advertise, exhibit, display, or show any picture or theatrical act in any theater or other place of public amusement or entertainment within this state which shall in any manner injuriously reflect upon the proper and rightful progress, status, attainment or endeavor of any race or class of citizens against any other race or class of people." The immediate target of this law was D. W. Griffith's 1915 film *The Birth of a Nation*. Challenged by the manager of the Rialto Theatre in Charleston who had attempted to show the movie, the law was upheld by the State Supreme Court of Appeals (Posey 1934, 70–71). Two years later at the behest of two black legislators, McDowell County delegate Hugh J. Capehart and Kanawha County delegate T. G. Nutter, Governor William Conley signed what came to be known as the Capehart Anti-Lynch law. It held that if someone charged with a crime and in legal custody was lynched, the county in which this occurred was required to pay five thousand dollars to the family or the deceased's estate. Moreover, action to compel payment could be brought in any state court, not necessarily in the county where the crime had occurred. This would be tested in 1931 following the lynching of two blacks in Greenbrier County and was also upheld by the State Supreme Court of Appeals (Posey 1934, 78–79). In sum, beyond its obvious economic advantages, West Virginia provided a relatively welcoming social and political environment for its African American citizens.

West Virginia's Black Middle Class:
Key to the Culture of Big Band Jazz in the Mountain State

As coal miners and railroad workers, the vast majority of African American males in the Mountain State were part of its working class, but there was also a small but important black middle class. Owners of small businesses, doctors, lawyers, and clergymen resided in Beckley, Bluefield, Charleston, Fairmont, Logan, Welch, and Williamson (all but Bluefield the seats of their respective counties). One member of this group was Hugh J. Capehart, the driving force behind the state's anti-lynching bill, a leader in Democratic politics in McDowell County, and owner of several businesses in Welch, the county seat, including a hotel catering to black travelers among whom were members of touring dance bands.

Undoubtedly the largest cohort of black middle-class Mountaineers were the teachers employed in the black primary and secondary schools of the state, one of whom was Edward LeRoy Morton. Beyond his own accomplishments, he merits attention as the father of a key figure in the business of big band jazz in the Mountain State, George E. Morton, who arranged engagements for many of the black name bands during the second half of the 1930s. Edward Morton, one of seven children born to former slaves Calvin and Harriet Scott Morton, completed his high school education in 1895 and a year later began a teaching career in Buckhannon, West Virginia. Later, as a principal he presided over black high schools in various parts of the state and organized the black Teachers Association of Northern West Virginia. His final appointment, in 1916, was as principal of Stratton High School in Beckley, Raleigh County, which during his tenure grew from two teachers and 57 students to seven teachers and 262 students by the early 1920s. In addition to his work as an educator, Morton owned and operated a drug store in Beckley's black community for many years. He and his wife Mary Jordon Morton, an alumna of Fisk University, had three children, all of whom would graduate from West Virginia State College (Flippen 2005). Taken together, Morton's profession along with his social and political activities—he was an active Republican—place him squarely within the black middle class of the early twentieth century.

Morton's career as a public educator draws attention to another incentive for black immigration to West Virginia: the availability of both primary and secondary education. Ray E. Williams, a longtime resident of Welch, recalled that his father left the sharecropper's life in Newberry, South Carolina, in the early 1920s and moved to the coal town of Wilder in southwestern Virginia to work in a mine. When it shut down, he chose to take his family to Gary, West Virginia, because "he heard there were five high schools for black children in McDowell County" (Cranford 2008).[9]

As will be demonstrated in subsequent chapters, middle-class black Mountaineers played an essential role in promoting big band jazz and dance music in the state. While many resided in the county seats and other larger towns where dances usually took place, others who lived in smaller communities, among them teachers, knew which high school gymnasia could accommodate large crowds and, equally important, which principals would allow this use of their facilities. Also important were the professional contacts among educators, members of the business community, and alumni of the same college that fostered networks of men interested in booking bands, in part for the entertainment they would provide and in part for the additional income the local booker might earn. Beginning in the mid-1930s, such networks repeatedly organized sequences of one-night engagements that took black bands of national reputation across the state within a matter of a few days during the course of tours of far larger geographical range. At each venue waited a member of one of these state-wide groups who was responsible for promoting the dance as well as staging it.

Simply put, members of the black middle class in West Virginia brought the bands to the state's dance venues while the working class of miners, railroad workers, and others constituted the majority of those in attendance, thus providing the revenue to underwrite those engagements. None of this would have been possible but for economic policies that the Roosevelt administration initiated in its first one hundred days in office in 1933, policies that led to a rising level of prosperity for many black Mountaineers.

The Impact of the National Industrial Recovery Act upon the West Virginia Coal Industry

A brief history of West Virginia's mining industry, from 1910 up to passage of the National Industrial Recovery Act in the first one hundred days of the New Deal, will explain its significance. In that period, West Virginia's coal industry was subject to a range of extraordinary social and economic forces. What had been forecast to be an ever-expanding market in the late nineteenth century proved otherwise when various forces capped its growth, ranging from the introduction of more fuel-efficient boilers and steam engines to campaigns against air pollution and the end of railroad expansion. Despite these inescapable realities, more coal was mined than could be profitably sold. Historian John Alexander Williams summarized the consequences: "Producers sought to offset lower profits with lower wages; the fledgling United Mine Workers of America sought to defend wage levels while working politically for federal intervention into the industry's stormy relations. The result was an almost continuous crisis in the coalfields after 1910, interrupted only by booms during and following World Wars I and II" (Williams 2002, 253).

The most dramatic evidence of those "stormy relations" were four "mine wars" between 1912 and 1927 in West Virginia that pitted members of the United Mine Workers of America against mine owners unanimous in their resistance to the labor union. The term "war" is only a slightly exaggerated characterization of the bloody conflicts that on different occasions pitted miners and their allies against company mine guards, private detectives from the (in)famous Baldwin-Felts agency based in Bluefield, local police, the state police, the National Guard, and even the United States Army. Companies not only refused to recognize the union as their workers' bargaining agent but obtained injunctions prohibiting union organizers from seeking members. Where possible, they imported strikebreakers, evicted families of striking miners from company houses, and in several instances fired on tent communities set up by the UMWA for those evicted from nearby coal camps. African American miners were in the thick of the conflicts, for they too were members of the UMWA and sided with their white co-workers against black strikebreakers. (Williams 2002, 266–72; Lewis 1987, 140).

If the 1910s and 1920s were a time of gradual deterioration of the industry's fortunes and those of its employees, the onset of the Great Depression in the fall of 1929 represented the nadir. The contraction of the nation's industrial output shrank the market for coal. After 1929 the number of active mines dropped by 10 percent, and production fell 42 percent. Unemployment rose by 19 percent. By 1932, in-state coal production had dropped to 83.3 million tons from a high of 147 million in 1927. In that same year, of 1,900 mining operations filing returns with the Internal Revenue Service, only 16 percent reported a net income (Baratz 1955, 48). Coal operators cut production, prices, wages, and the size of their workforces in an effort to stay in business. Thirty-three thousand mine industry jobs vanished. While some mines in West Virginia's southern coalfields paid $4.80 for an eight-hour shift, others cut wages to $2.80 for a ten-hour shift (Tams 1963, 70). Black miners suffered especially, and many appear to have been the first let go. The state's Bureau of Negro Welfare and Statistics made the extraordinary claim that black miners could tolerate unemployment more easily than their white counterparts because they had known hard times in the past (Bureau of Negro Welfare and Statistics 1933, 5). The core problem was summarized by Jerry Bruce Thomas: "Despite the Depression's persistence in the face of the painful readjustments, businessmen and government officials tended to insist on unrealistic policies. The prime example was the nearly universal adherence to the idea of the balanced budget and strict economy in expenditures" (Thomas 1998, 28).

Clearly, another strategy had to be devised to extricate the coal industry from the boom-and-bust cycles of strong and weak markets accompanied by virtually no job security for miners. A solution would not present itself until the summer of 1933 when passage of the National Industrial Recovery Act established the National Recovery Administration (NRA), suspended antitrust agreements for those businesses willing to abide by policies intended to govern the industries of which they were a part, established minimum wages and maximum work hours, guaranteed collective bargaining for workers, and initiated the Public Works Administration and the associated creation of publicly funded jobs for the unemployed. Policies to govern the coal industry were contained within the Bituminous Coal Code, for which agreement was hammered out in September 1933 between the UMWA and the coal operators.

As soon as the NIRA legislation was signed by President Roosevelt on June 16, 1933, and before the Coal Code had been approved, the union acted with dispatch to organize West Virginia's miners. On June 23, Van Amberg Bittner, president of Local 17 in Charleston, reported to John L. Lewis, the president of the UMWA, that "The entire Northern Field as well as the New River, Kanawha field, Mingo, and Logan are all completely organized. We will finish up McDowell, Mercer, and Wyoming counties this week" (Dubovsky and Van Tine 1977, 185). When those three counties were "finished up," the state's entire coal industry was unionized.

The advantage of union representation for miners was demonstrated by the fact that the Code stipulated that, though it had established minimum wages for "inside work" and a maximum number of work hours by day, week, and month, where any union-negotiated contract resulted in wages higher than those minimums, "the contract rates shall govern" (Bituminous Coal Code 1933, Article 4). The Code's advantages for the mine owners lay in the fact that it provided the means to establish a fair-market price for various grades of coal based on a consensus of two-thirds of the coal producers in each of fifteen districts. Anyone selling coal at less than the fair-market price would be confronted with "*prima facie* presumption that such person is engaged in destructive price cutting and unfair competition" (Bituminous Coal Code 1933, Article 6, sec. 1). This dramatically reduced the threat to mine owners of being undersold by a competitor, a chronic problem in the past, though what the Code did not address was the fundamental overcapacity of the industry. When small operations started up after the price of coal had been set at a higher level than in the past, they increased employment but also added to the already unwanted surplus of coal (Thomas 1999, 99).

With the Code in place, the union and the coal operators quickly negotiated a contract known as the Appalachian Agreement that governed approximately 70 percent of the industry spread over all or parts of six eastern states (the Alabama field was excluded). It provided for an eight-hour day, a forty-hour week, and gave the miners the right to select the "checkweighman": the person who weighed each mine car and credited the individual who had mined the coal. It freed miners from the requirement that they live in company towns, trade at company stores, or receive their wages in scrip as opposed to cash. Finally, it set a minimum age of seventeen for any mine employee. As evidence of the fact that the UMWA neither excluded nor discriminated against black miners, one of the contract's terms guaranteed equal pay for equal work, thus preventing discriminatory wage scales. As they too were union members, the checkweighmen also had an interest in preserving this standard for both their white and black co-workers (Thomas 1999, 98).

The impact of the Bituminous Coal Code and the resulting Appalachian Agreement was dramatic. Comparing employment, wages, and production in 1932, the last year of Herbert Hoover's Presidency, with those of 1935, the year in which the U.S. Supreme Court declared the NRA unconstitutional, one notes significant improvements. By 1935, mining jobs in the nation increased by 85,000, of which 24,000 (28 percent) were created in the Mountain State. Wages in the same period jumped by 75 percent from $677 per year to $1,096. Tons of coal mined rose from 86.1 million to 99.8 million. Not surprisingly, as a consequence retail sales in 1935 were 35 percent higher, including a 41 percent increase in groceries purchased (Thomas 1998, 99).

In the short term, the NRA and the Coal Code were welcomed by both labor and management. The most compelling evidence of this is the federal legislative record following the Supreme Court's verdict in 1935 that the NRA was unconstitutional. Whereas other industrial leaders welcomed the end of government regulation, the mine owners sought to preserve many of the features of the Coal Code through new legislation, particularly in the area of price regulation and production quotas. In exchange, they were willing to continue to negotiate with the union, accept standards regarding the workplace, and even provide assistance to unemployed miners. The first such legislation was known as the Guffey-Snyder Act of 1936. When declared unconstitutional, the next year it was followed by a revised version known as the Guffey-Vinson Act, which established the National

Bituminous Coal Commission to regulate the industry. When in 1937 it established what major consumers regarded as unacceptably high minimum prices for coal, the industry took the initiative to set prices regionally (Thomas 1998, 106–8).

Whatever its limitations nationally, the NRA was welcomed in the Mountain State. By stabilizing and regulating the industry, it resulted in higher incomes for miners. Higher incomes increased the workers' discretion concerning how to spend their money. The growth in retail sales cited earlier is one piece of evidence of their increased spending; their support of a culture of big band jazz and dance music was another.

Taken together, the combination of economic and political conditions established within the Mountain State was unique in the mid-Atlantic region. It also explains how the state could become an inviting destination for touring black dance bands in the 1930s and early 1940s. The link between the miners' labor and their support of big bands is the topic of the next chapter.

PART ONE

The Economic Foundation of Big Band Dance Music in the Mountain State

CHAPTER ONE

From the Coal Face to the Dance Floor: Black Miners as Patrons of Big Bands

Understanding the connections between the work of coal miners, the major audience for jazz and dance music, and the big bands that played the music that meant so much to them during the 1930s and early 1940s is key to understanding the economic foundation of this musical culture. This chapter follows the money from the coal seam to the dance venue and from there to the band providing the music—and then, in many instances, to the New York–based corporation that managed that band, paid it a part of the proceeds of each engagement, but kept the majority of the earnings.

The black population of the coalfields was not concentrated in any one place. Mining operations depended on the creation at each mine of communities in which miners and their families resided. The reason for this was succinctly explained by William Purvience Tams Jr., (1883–1977), one of the pioneering mine owners in the state and a major force in the coal industry in southern West Virginia during the first half of the twentieth century—a coal baron, in other words. In the early 1960s Tams published a memoir entitled *The Smokeless Coal Fields of West Virginia: A Brief History* (Tams 1963), a no-nonsense, businesslike discussion of coal mining from the perspective of an owner that explained the necessity of constructing coal company towns: "The mining of coal requires miners; miners require houses. Since most mines were opened in virtually unsettled areas, there was no existing housing. Thus new houses had to be built, and the operators were the only ones with the capital and organization to do the job. Since the almost complete absence of all-weather roads made it necessary for the miner to live close to his work, small villages (often called [coal] 'camps') were built close to each mine" (Tams 1963, 51).

As there were hundreds of mines, so too there were hundreds of coal camps. Thus there was a multitude of small communities of black miners and their families scattered throughout the coal fields. So numerous were the mines and the "small villages" erected nearby that in certain areas only property lines separated one company town from the next—not unlike major urban regions today where one suburban community is separated from the next only by a major thoroughfare.[1]

Creating an Image of Black Miners in West Virginia

In order to study the audience for big band jazz and dance music, it is desirable to form a visual impression of the African American miners of the period who constituted the majority of that audience. Fortunately, several photographers who resided in the Mountain State took pictures of mining operations, the company towns associated with them, and the miners themselves.

Sometime during the course of 1931, one of these photographers, Ruffus E. "Red" Ribble, drove not quite two miles from his home in Mount Hope, West Virginia, to take pictures at the Price Hill Colliery Company's mine located just south of Mount Hope in the New River coalfield. His camera was a distinctive Kodak #8 Cirkut Outfit. "Cirkut Outfit" was the manufacturer's term for a camera that could take two kinds of pictures: conventional photos and panoramic ones. Ribble gained a reputation in the state for his panoramic photos of various locations in the region, groups of high school graduates, church congregations, family reunions, and, with some regularity, coal miners (Mark Crabtree. Cirkut Panoramic Photos by Ruffus E. "Red" Ribble. homepage.mac.com/crabtree/ribble.htm [accessed January 6, 2011]).

At different times in the 1930s, 1940s, and 1950s, dozens of miners posed while Ribble's camera swept from left to right as much as 180 degrees. The resulting pictures are quite impressive: a #8 Cirkut Outfit routinely created images eight inches wide and up to four feet long. One such photo was taken at the Price Hill operation, located at the end of the Loup Creek branch line of the C&O Railway built to serve several mines south of the New River. The miners arranged themselves in two long rows, forty men sitting in front, fifty-eight standing behind them (see detail, Fig. 1.1). Joining the miners was A. P. Burdiss, the mine superintendent and foreman at the time (*Annual Report of the Department of Mines, 1931*, 45). A second man, probably his assistant, was more casually dressed. All of the rest were wearing heavy dark coveralls, hard hats equipped with battery-powered

Fig. 1.1. *The Afternoon Shift at the Price Hill Colliery Company Mine, Price Hill, W.Va. 1931* (detail). Six of the shift's thirteen black miners stand in the back row to the right. (West Virginia and Regional History Collection)

electric lamps, and heavy boots. Each of the miners in the front sat next to his shiny metal lunch bucket.

Ribble's photograph is labeled simply *Price Hill, W.Va. 1931*. The names of the individuals in the image are nowhere to be found nor is the specific date on which the photo was shot. It was taken in full daylight, making it probable that these men made up the second or afternoon shift that would have begun work around 3:00 p.m. and returned to the surface around 11:00 p.m. Further evidence that the photograph was taken before the men went underground is that their faces and hands were clean.

Of the total of thirteen African Americans who appear in the complete picture, six stand together in the back row to the right in the portion shown in Figure 1.1. That one can distinguish them from their white co-workers is further evidence that this image was taken before the shift entered the mine. At the end of the work day, it would have been virtually impossible to identify any of the men by race; coal dust would have turned everyone's face black.

Knowing nothing of the identities of these black miners is unfortunate, because it would have been desirable to profile one or another of them as representatives of the black communities of West Virginia's coalfields: to learn where he was born, when he entered the mines, the nature of his work, and how he spent his leisure time. Did he go to dances? Did he like big band jazz? Despite the absence of such information, any one of these individuals can serve as the prototypical African American Mountaineer who mined coal for a living and entertained himself and members of his family by attending dances for which some of the leading black dance bands of the 1930s and early 1940s provided the music.

The Work of a Miner

What was the nature of the work done by the men at the Price Hill mine and at the hundreds of similar operations in West Virginia's coalfields? Here again, William Tams's personal history of coal mining is informative for its discussion of the work of a typical miner ("the loader"), beginning with a description of the job as performed early in the twentieth century and followed by a discussion of its subsequent evolution with the gradual arrival of mechanization. The following excerpt focuses attention on the loader's job in the early 1930s:

> The loader carried into the mine his picks, shovels, auger, tamping bar, fuse and a can of black powder. He was charged fifty cents per month for the services of the company blacksmith in re-sharpening and tempering the pick.... There were two men in each room face and one man at the narrower entry faces. The man's partner was called his "buddy."... After taking two-and-a-half to three hours to make an undercut, the miners drilled, loaded, and fired the holes, bringing down the undercut coal. They then pushed up empty mine cars from the room mouth, loaded them, and returned them to the entry. They set the necessary safety props, extended the room track as needed, ate their mid-day meal, and continued to the end of the shift. The miner put his brass check near the bottom of each car he loaded. The check was removed after the car was dumped at the tipple and the load credited to the proper man. (Tams 1963, 35–36)

Tams's use of his industry's terminology calls for some explanation. "To make an undercut" required the miner either to get down on his knees or to lie prone in order to create, using his pick axe, an opening at the

Fig. 1.2. A pile of coal just blown down from the coal face. Now the hand loading begins. (West Virginia and Regional History Collection)

bottom of the coal face that was as wide as the "room": the area he was assigned to mine. Rooms extended at right angles to the "haulage road" that connected them to the mine's entrance. "Haulage" was facilitated by narrow-gauge railroad tracks on which rolled the cars of mined coal, initially pulled by mules or ponies, later by electric engines termed "motors." A room might be as wide as twenty-four feet. As Tams put it, "forearms and wrists furnished the power" to make that undercut, typically five feet into the coal seam (Tams 1963, 39).

The auger and tamping bar enabled the miner first to drill several holes into the coal seam above the undercut and then to tamp tightly into each hole paper cartridges of dynamite followed by clay and dirt, along with a fuse. Once the charges were in place, the fuses were lit, and the miner warned those within earshot of the impending blast by shouting "Fire in the hole!" The dynamite exploded, bringing down the coal that the undercut had undermined, so to speak. Only at that point did the term "loader" take on its full meaning: the miner put a round metal tag, the "brass check" on which was stamped his payroll number, on a hook near the bottom of the interior of a mine car and then loaded that car with the loosened coal (see Fig. 1.2). Once it was filled, he and his assistant would push the car toward the haulage road for others to take to the surface. Then the entire process was repeated. The miner would be credited for the tonnage dug when his cars were weighed and unloaded, literally tipped over, in a building appropriately named "the tipple."

Tams subsequently described the impact of the first widely used mechanical equipment: the cutting machine. "In the old days, two miners, working in a room twenty-four feet wide, required two-and-a-half to three hours to complete a cut five feet deep. The electric cutting machine made a cut six feet deep across a thirty-foot room in thirty minutes. These machines were operated on the night shift, and miners working on the day shift had only to shoot down and load coal" (Tams 1963, 40).

Issues of Safety: What Tams Neglected to Discuss

While to some readers discussion of mine safety may appear to represent a significant departure from the culture of big band jazz in black West Virginia, the topic is important to an understanding of the risks to the lives of those who underwrote that culture. Though highly informative, the description of mining provided by Tams is quite selective. Read uncritically, his description of the work involved in mining coal suggests a fairly simple process with few risks, if properly done. In truth, mining was arduous work and very dangerous. He did mention one cause of accidents: improperly tamped explosives that would direct their energy not into the coal that surrounded them but back out the hole drilled by the miner, possibly igniting coal dust and/or methane gas, another by-product of the geological processes that had created the coal in the first place. Such accidents could be disastrous, as Tams noted elsewhere, and, rather conveniently for the mine's owners, their cause could always be attributed to the miner's carelessness since he would not have been alive to defend himself. One instance of such a "blown-out shot" killed fifty miners in 1907 (Tams 1963, 48–49).

He also neglected to mention the principal cause of injury and death: the "roof fall." While the vegetation of the Carboniferous Period of geologic history metamorphosed into coal, the mud that often surrounded it was transformed into shale, erroneously but commonly referred to

Fig. 1.3. A black miner propping up the roof of a haulage way; note portion of track in the lower left hand corner. The props were essential to supporting the roof. At the time of the photo, the beams appear to be sagging in the upper right; the props should secure them. (West Virginia and Regional History Collection)

as "slate" in the industry. A sedimentary rock, shale lacks any internal strength and without support could come crashing down on unsuspecting miners. To prevent such roof falls, as Tams noted, setting "safety props" was an important first step to be taken after coal was blasted from the face and shoveled into the mine cars (see Fig. 1.3). But the period of time between the explosion and the placement of those props was dangerous: the roof could fall before they were in position. In some instances, the props could also prove inadequate to support the weight of the overhanging shale, resulting in injury or death when they gave way. The evidence of the risks of roof falls is unmistakable: from 1883 to 1941, of 14,587 miners killed underground, 8,134 (55.76 percent) died from roof falls (Department of Mines 1941, 174–75).

Moreover, Tams did not address accidents resulting from environmental conditions underground, such as the development of pockets of methane gas or accumulations of coal dust caused by the numerous, otherwise controlled, explosions. Neither of these conditions was within the individual miners' power to prevent, and it was precisely these conditions that led to massive explosions that killed dozens, if not hundreds, of miners. Companies were supposed to provide fire hoses for the purposes of watering down coal dust as early as 1900 but only if a mine had "generated gas in dangerous quantities," an assessment made *not* by the hand loaders exposed to it but by the mine superintendent whose primary responsibility was overseeing maximum productivity, not ensuring safe working conditions.

In this same period, the state's governor, George Atkinson, was heard to say, "It is but the natural course of mining events that men should be injured or killed in accidents," a laissez-faire attitude no doubt welcomed by his political allies in the industry. The few mine inspectors who were hired were almost without exception beholden to the owners for their positions. Any who sought to enforce what safety standards there were discovered that if legal action were initiated, the owners would be granted injunctive relief in local courts, which they also controlled (Corbin 1981, 16–17). Again and again, in reports of accidents causing death published in the *Annual Report of the* [West Virginia] *Department of Mines*, responsibility almost always was placed on the deceased miners.

In his description of the hand loader's work, Tams also failed to address the implications for the ease and extent of production associated with the height of the particular coal seam to which a miner and his buddy were assigned. Figure 1.2 shows what can be recovered from a seam that appears to be as much as five or six feet thick. Working such a seam would be comparatively easy: miners could stand fully erect as they first prepared to blast coal from the face of the seam and then to shovel it into the mine cars. Not all seams were so accommodating. John McPhee described the rock sequences formed in the Carboniferous Period as "often striped like regimental ties" (McPhee 1998, 247) but, unlike the equal width of the stripes on a regimental tie, coal seams were not. A miner could find himself saddled with one as thin as two or three feet. Depending upon his size and strength, he might set about to get the coal out of the seam by working on his hands and knees, crawling through a narrow tunnel of his own creation.

Logically, one might imagine a miner blasting away not only the coal but the shale or sandstone above it in order to create a "room" big enough to permit him to work in greater comfort. But the solidity of the roof itself was uncertain, and anyway he was not being paid to mine shale or sandstone; he was paid to mine coal. Nat Reese, whose recollections of musical life in the coal camps was discussed in the introduction, said when referring to the expectations of the superintendent of one of the several mines in the southern coalfields in which he worked during the 1930s: "And he didn't pay for no rock. The time that you took to load that rock and carry it outside and dump it, you didn't get anything. You just got paid for the coal" (Kline 1987, 11).

The physical wear and tear of working in such confined spaces took a toll over months and years of work underground, along with the damage brought about by inhaling coal dust and other airborne pollutants common to underground mines. The miner's job was not the neat and tidy occupation that William Purviance Tams led one to believe.

Economic and Other Benefits of Mining: The Black Miners' Perspective

The work of the hand loaders was carried out within the evolving economic conditions of the industry and of the nation in general. As discussed in the introduction, the NRA's Bituminous Coal Code stabilized the industry, established minimum wages, and empowered the United Mine Workers of America to organize miners and engage in collective bargaining with the mine owners on their behalf. African American miners and their families enjoyed a share of this comparative prosperity thanks to the principle of equal work for equal pay that governed contacts between mine operators and the UMWA. White or black, a miner who hooked his brass check to the side of a mine car before loading it with the coal he and his buddy had just "shot" from the coal face was paid the same for his labor as any other miner employed in the same operation. Non-mechanized mining constituted piecework labor: one was paid by the tonnage dug out of the mine. Under such circumstances there was every incentive to be as productive as one was able. Indeed, one of the perceived merits of coal mining was the sense of control that such piecework labor afforded individual miners (Lewis 1989, 90–91).

David Corbin noted that, given the "physical structure of the coal mine—a honeycombed tunnel extending in all directions for miles under the earth," the coal miner was "an isolated piece-worker" who saw his boss no more than once a day (Corbin 1981, 38). Absent direct supervision, hand loaders enjoyed a degree of freedom that was, in the words of

Carter Goodrich writing in 1925, "unique in American industrial life" and "so utterly unlike the order and regimentation of a plant like [auto maker Henry] Ford's that it is hard to believe the two are continuing to exist side by side" (Goodrich 1925, 92).

While this level of autonomy may have been enjoyed by black miners in the states adjacent to West Virginia—Kentucky, Tennessee, and Virginia—during the 1930s, an equal degree of prosperity was not. Unlike coal operators in the Mountain State, those elsewhere strenuously resisted any role for the UMWA as soon as they saw an advantage in doing so following the demise of the NRA. In eastern Kentucky not only coal operators but local government officials actively (and, in a number of instances, violently) opposed collective bargaining. When compared to West Virginia, the consequences were lower wages and poorer working conditions for *all* miners regardless of race in that area (Thomas 1998, 93).

The Coal Field County Seats: The Sites of Engagements and the Residences of Those Who Booked Them

To move from the mines where their money was earned to the venues of dances at which miners and their families spent a portion of those earnings, we are in effect moving from hundreds of company towns (almost as many as the number of mines in operation) to the county seats in the coalfields. These communities in West Virginia, like their counterparts throughout the nation, were more than just the location of the courthouse; they were centers of commerce as well. Long before supermarkets and shopping malls dotted the landscape, these towns were magnets for the rural population of the vicinity. Welch, seat of McDowell County, was characterized by an anonymous contributor to *West Virginia: A Guide to the Mountain State* as "the trade center of the surrounding coalfields" (West Virginia Writers Project 1941, 476).

The description of Beckley, the seat of Raleigh County (which straddled both the New River and Winding Gulf coalfields), is revealing of the number of rural communities economically joined to those county seats: "Beckley . . . is the hub around which revolves the life of more than 200 small mining communities, farming communities, and railroad junctions. Called the 'smokeless coal capital of the world,' Beckley is the center of a large area, which annually produces 50 million tons of the finest steam and domestic coals" (West Virginia Writers Project 1941, 458).[2]

Beckley and its counterparts elsewhere in the coalfields were also sites of National Guard armories, which more than any other location served as venues for dances organized for black Mountaineers. They were large enough to accommodate several hundred people and were regularly rented for such events. The gymnasia of black high schools were also used for dances, though not as frequently. The Alhambra Night Club, founded only in the late 1930s and located in the Ferguson Hotel in Charleston, a black-owned establishment catering to African American travelers, and the Elks Rest, headquarters of the Monongahela Elks Club, a black fraternal organization, were the only nightspots catering exclusively to African Americans in the Mountain State. On certain occasions nightclubs normally patronized by whites could be rented for a dance, one being the Vanity Fair in Huntington, the seat of Cabell County on the Ohio River.

Those responsible for organizing dances for black Mountaineers and engaging bands to play for them may be divided into two groups: social organizations and entrepreneurial individuals residing in the county seats. Both groups were dominated by members of the black middle class. Among the social organizations that booked bands for their own dances were the West Virginia State College Club, which held a dance at Huntington's Vanity Fair for which Noble Sissle was engaged in December 1930 (*PC* 12.27.30, 1/8). Another was the Bears, a men's club in Fairmont that booked two Chicago bands, Walter Barnes's Royal Creolians and Erskine Tate's Orchestra, to play at the local armory on separate occasions in 1931 (*PC* 2.21.31, 2/31; 5.23.31, 2/6). The Parent-Teacher and Alumni Associations of Dubois High School co-sponsored a Colonial Ball on February 19, 1932, at the armory in Mount Hope, northwest of Beckley (and, as noted above, less than two miles from the Price Hill mine) for which a band called the Campus Nighthawks provided music (*PC* 2.20.32, 2/3). On July 21, 1934, the Southern West Virginia Negro Democratic Convention ended with a dance at the armory in Logan at which Speed Webb's band from Indianapolis performed (*PC* 7.14.34, 1/5).

The newspaper record of the period demonstrates that individuals took far more responsibility for booking bands and holding dances than did social organizations. Such work constituted a second source of income for most of these local bookers, but one that entailed a certain amount of financial risk, because only a large turnout could make these entrepreneurs a profit. Samuel Carpenter and his partner James Jackson (then bellhops at the Fairmont Hotel) lost money when they booked Blanche Calloway's band to play at the Fairmont armory on June 26, 1931, because too few people attended the dance (*PC* 6.27.31, 2/8). Others fared better. James A. West, butler for a white Fairmont family and sometime local correspondent for the *Pittsburgh Courier*; Vernon Morrow, a "driver" according to the 1934 Fairmont City Directory; and Quenton Dalton, occupation unknown but allegedly a numbers runner, profitably booked the Sunset Royal Serenaders from Miami, Florida, into the Fairmont armory in July and again in October 1934 (*PC* 7.28.43, 2/6; *WV* 10.5.34, 2). In Huntington, Sylvester Massey, owner of a hotel and restaurant catering to African Americans, went beyond booking isolated engagements by acting as regional booker for Alphonso Trent's band in August and September 1930, when it was touring the West Virginia-Ohio-Kentucky region. In 1935 Massey booked Ruth Ellington and Her Orchestra for a dance at Huntington's Vanity Fair (*PC* 8.30.30, 2/7; 12.28.35, 2/7).

The most prominent booker of the period from 1935 until 1940 appears to have been George Edward Morton (1909–1940), a resident of Beckley. An alumnus of West Virginia State College, Class of 1935, he began booking bands that same year, starting with a dance at the armory in Beckley for which Earl "Fatha" Hines provided music (Flippen 2005; *PC* 3.30.35, 2/9). So central is Morton to the big band scene in the Mountain State between 1935 and the year of his untimely death that he will be the focus of attention in chapter 8 of this study, where his activities and their significance will be examined in detail. At this point, it will suffice to note that he worked as a regional booking agent for Joe Glaser, initially during Glaser's association with the Rockwell-O'Keefe agency in New York and later when he headed Associated Booking Artists as manager of numerous bands. Collaborating with associates throughout the southern coalfields and at least one residing in Fairmont in the northern field, Morton repeatedly engaged virtually all of the leading black bands of the swing era for multiple performances in West Virginia.

The promotional activities of Morton and his counterparts throughout the coalfield counties drew miners from the company towns to the county seats and other larger communities where dances were held. The frequency of engagements by national bands and the sizes of the crowds attending most of those dances give reason for taking seriously Herbert Hall's recollection that all the bands went to the Mountain State because of the high levels of employment in the mines. What is to be demonstrated is that, thanks to the Bituminous Coal Code, West Virginia's comparatively prosperous mining industry enabled black miners in the Mountain State to pay touring dance bands more per engagement than did African

American dancers (and European American ones, for that matter) elsewhere in the region. Recall that Hall's testimony set West Virginia apart from other states by virtue of its mining industry and the consequent high levels of employment and wages. The next chapter will discuss in detail the compelling evidence in support of Hall's contention.

CHAPTER TWO

Validating Herbert Hall's Contention: Paul Barnes's Gig Book

Herbert Hall's recollection that "all the bands were goin' through West Virginia in the 1930s *because* [emphasis added] the mines were in operation . . . and everyone was employed" is supported by evidence found in a rarely encountered document: a record kept by the saxophonist/clarinetist Paul D. Barnes (1901–1981) documenting various details of his performances. The term used by certain jazz musicians for such a volume is "gig book."

A native of New Orleans and known there by his nickname "Polo," Barnes's musical career was largely played out in the Crescent City and elsewhere in Louisiana, first as co-leader of the Original Diamond Band with Lawrence Marrero beginning in 1919, later as sideman in bands led respectively by Henry "Kid" Rena, Oscar "Papa" Celestin, and Ferdinand "Jelly Roll" Morton. During three separate periods—1927, 1931, and 1934–35—he played for Joe Oliver. In 1932, in between the latter stints with Oliver, he led his own band, the Paul D. Barnes Orchestra. After he left Oliver in 1935, he returned to New Orleans for the next fifteen years or so. After that he divided his time between California and his home town, ultimately playing at Preservation Hall. He retired in 1977. In sum, "Polo" Barnes was one of the legion of highly capable sidemen to come out of New Orleans—"full of elegance and impeccable taste," was how Marcel Joly characterized his playing in *The New Grove Dictionary of Jazz*—but an individual whose career does not loom large in jazz history. Perhaps more so than for the legacy of his recordings, Barnes merits attention for what his gig book tells us about daily life in one black band in the mid-1930s (Joly 1988, 73).

Barnes's diary would ultimately fill most of two ledger books covering the period from 1933 to 1952. Each was twelve inches high and seven and a half inches wide, a size that meant each could have traveled in one of his instrument cases. The first covers the period from 1933 to early October 1935. The second embraces a much longer time span, though in less detail: from October 10, 1935, to August 2, 1952.[1]

What motivated Barnes to maintain such a document may in part be inferred from the fact that the initial entries were made during the period when he led his own band. Having kept records of his own operation during 1933 and 1934, he simply maintained the habit when he joined Oliver. While entries varied in length, almost without exception all provided the following information: the name of the town in which the band played, the race of the audience (either "colored" or white), as well as the amount of money paid to each member of the band. Accompanying many entries were annotations describing various incidents that occurred during the band's tour, from quarrels among musicians to breakdowns of the band's bus. What follows is a transcription of entries for December 25 to 28, 1934, reproduced in Figure 2.1:

Dec 25th Orchestra leaves Huntington and Play dance
at Ashland, Ky colored @ $5.00 William Purnell
joins Orchestra—Orch returns to Huntington W.Va.

Wed. Dec 26th Orchestra Plays Welch West Va
white world war Veterans' Hall—@ $4.00
reside overnight.

Thursday Dec 27th Orchestra plays Williamson W. Va.
(Col) @$4.00 on this trip (to Williamson) from Welch
The left front wheel of the buss [sic] was coming off.
Eldridge who was riding on the outside saw it in time
to prevent an injury—Orch hires truck and taxi to town
about 8 miles.

Friday Dec 28th Orchestra hires taxie [sic] to Kermit
W. Va.—White—@ $4.71—tips included—Lionel Bob goes on
train—Buck brings the Buss afterward and get it stalled
near dance Place. Bob gets truck to Push Buss [sic]
which got it started.

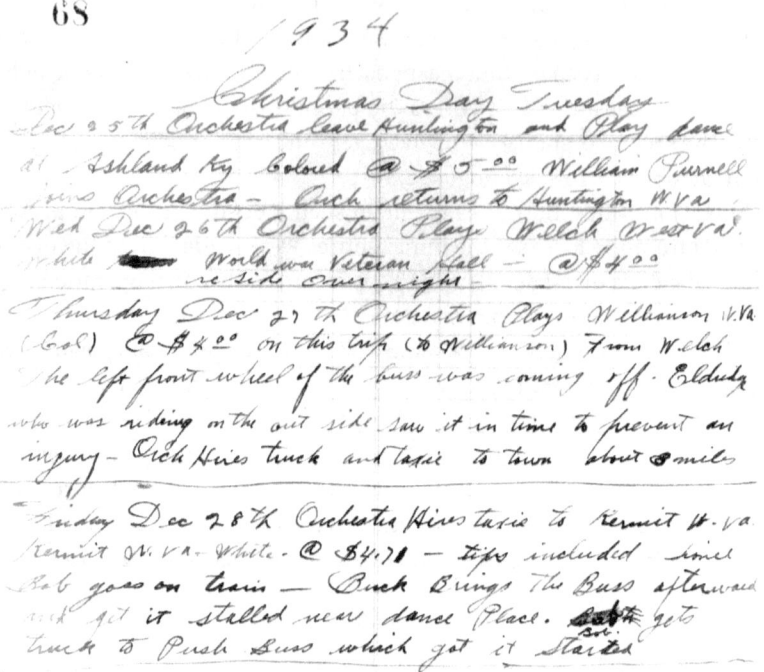

Fig. 2.1. The upper portion of page 68 of Paul Barnes's "Gig Book," showing citations for December 25–28, 1934, concerning engagements in Ashland, KY, as well as in Welch, Williamson, and Kermit, WV. (Hogan Jazz Archive, Tulane University)

One piece of information that Barnes provided, though not consistently, was the gross amount paid to the band's manager, Ross McConnell, by the organizers of the dances for which the band performed. McConnell had joined the band as booking agent in Hopkinsville, Kentucky, on April 2, 1934, perhaps not coincidentally the first date on which Barnes recorded his affiliation with Oliver. McConnell's presence may have aroused Barnes's attention, since having managed a band himself he may have been curious to learn how another manager might operate.

From early April until the end of September of that year, the band played mostly in Illinois, Indiana, and Michigan. It appeared on two occasions in Williamson, West Virginia, and also played in Virginia. On the last day of September, it arrived in Huntington, West Virginia, and Oliver and/or McConnell apparently decided soon thereafter that the band would use that city as its base of operations for an indefinite period. There are several reasons, some logistical, others economic, that may have accounted for this.

Table 2.1. Engagements Played by King Oliver's Brunswick Recording Orchestra during the period of the Huntington, West Virginia, "residency," October 1934 to February 1935.

By state	October	November	December	January	February	Totals
WV	2	8	6	1	5	22
IN				1		1
KY	2		2	2	2	8
NC	3					3
OH	2			1		3
SC	5					5
TN		4				4
VA	2	2	1		2	7
By month	16	14	9	5	9 =	53

With a population of 75,572 in 1930, Huntington was the largest city in the state and the largest city in the Ohio Valley between Cincinnati and Pittsburgh. Its size alone may have been attractive: where there are a lot of people, there may be gigs. It also had a small black community that could provide accommodations for the band. Among its residents was Sylvester Massey, owner of a hotel and restaurant catering to African Americans, whose activities were occasionally reported on in the *Pittsburgh Courier*, including his work as regional booking agent for Alphonso Trent's band during what turned out to be an ill-fated tour of the upper Midwest (*PC* 9.6.30, 2/6). Presumably, either McConnell or Oliver might have known of Massey and may have hoped that, given his prior experience, he could assist in setting up engagements in West Virginia and adjacent states.

From a logistical standpoint, Huntington had other attractions. West of the highest ridges of the mountains and lying on the south side of the Ohio River, it was the junction of three major east-west highways through the Appalachians. Perhaps the most important was U.S. Highway 52 that paralleled the route of the Norfolk & Western Railway through the heart of the southern coalfields where potentially large African American audiences might be found. Highways running west, north, and south from Huntington provided equally easy access to Kentucky and Ohio as well.

By the end of the summer of 1934, evidence was mounting of the improved economy of West Virginia, thanks to the positive impact of the Bituminous Coal Code. From the perspective of Oliver's musicians, who had played their way from New Orleans north to the Midwest that

Table 2.2. Financial data and analysis of 21 West Virginia dances (10/1/34-2/25/35) for which Joe Oliver's Band provided music.

	Month/Date	City	Race of audience	Amount paid to each player
1.	Oct. 1	Montgomery	Colored	$5.17
2.	Oct. 6	Charleston	Colored	$5.00
3.	Nov. 3	Bluefield	Colored	$4.45
4.	Nov. 6	Huntington	Colored	$1.00
5.	Nov. 21	Huntington	White	$0.00
6.	Nov. 22	Montgomery	Colored	$0.25
7.	Nov. 23	Welch	Colored	$6.00
8.	Nov. 28	Bluefield	White	$3.00
9.	Nov. 29	Bluefield	Colored	$4.00
10.	Dec. 7	Huntington	White	$4.70
11.	Dec. 24	Charleston	Colored	$0.00
12.	Dec. 26	Welch	White	$4.00
13.	Dec. 27	Williamson	Colored	$4.00
14.	Dec. 28	Kermit	White	$4.71[1]
15.	Dec. 31	Huntington	White (Jews)[2]	$5.90
16.	Jan. 31	Huntington	Colored	$2.08
17.	Feb. 4	Parkersburg	Colored	$0.36
18.	Feb. 8	Williamson	Colored	$0.36
19.	Feb. 13	Huntington	Colored	$1.50
20.	Feb. 15	Williamson	Colored	$2.28
21.	Feb. 25	Beckley	Colored	$3.00

Summary:

	Number of dances	Total earnings per player	Average per player
Colored	15	$39.44	$2.63
White	6	$22.31	$3.72

Notes
1. Barnes noted that the earnings per musician at the end of the engagement in Kermit included tips.
2. Barnes's reference to "Jews" was explained by a report in the *Huntington Advertiser*, December 31, 1934, that the Oliver Band was performing for a dance sponsored by the local chapter of B'nai B'rith held at the Spring Valley Country Club just outside of Huntington.

summer, such news might well have provided sufficient incentive to take up residence in the Mountain State, at least for a time.

In the five-month period from the beginning of October 1934 to the end of February, Oliver's band played a total of fifty-three engagements: twenty-two in West Virginia, the remainder in seven other states. Table 2.1 arranges these figures by month (reading from left to right) and by state (reading from top to bottom). This table reveals that the most extensive touring by the band during this period occurred in October before winter would hamper travel through the central Appalachians even with the best of vehicles at one's disposal. The most frequently visited state outside West Virginia throughout this period was Kentucky, in which the band performed eight times: once each in Harlan, Jenkins, and Lexington, twice in Maysville, and three times in Ashland. With the sole exception of the Harlan engagement, the audiences for the band's Kentucky appearances were African American, and apart from the Lexington and Maysville gigs, all of the engagements were in or very close to the eastern Kentucky coalfields.

The Oliver Band's Earnings in West Virginia

Knowing where the band played facilitates a comparative study of the wages it earned in West Virginia and those earned elsewhere. Drawing on Barnes's record of wages paid to each musician, I will begin with the band's earnings for the twenty-one engagements it played in the Mountain State (see Table 2.2).

The wide variation in income per dance shown in this table, as well as in the next one, serves as a reminder that not all bands were paid the fixed fee that Joe Glaser demanded for the New York–based bands he managed. The vast majority of black dance bands in the 1930s did not have national managers. Instead, they either relied on the services of a regional booker or upon their own ingenuity to find engagements. Rather than being paid by the week, they were paid by the gig, and the amount each player received was a reflection of the total number of tickets sold for the dance.

Bands operating in this context played what were called "percentage dates." The organizer of the dance agreed to pay the band a certain percentage of the gate, one standard being 70 percent. In turn, musicians were compensated according to the "commonwealth" principle, meaning that the total amount paid to the band was divided into equal shares among the musicians. In some instances, the leader might take two shares, and it was also the case among the more fiscally prudent bands that a certain percentage be held out to cover travel costs to the next engagement. Such expenses could include those attendant with maintaining and fueling the band's bus or its several automobiles, depending on the preferred mode of transportation.[2] An open question was how much did the organizer of the dance take in? Sensing that bands all too often were shortchanged, many band leaders made it a point to count the number of attendees in an effort to ensure they were not cheated out of some portion of their earnings by the local booker.[3]

The Oliver Band's Income from Dances in States Adjacent to West Virginia and in the Deep South

With the data from West Virginia engagements providing a basis for comparison, attention now turns to the earnings of King Oliver's band from twenty-nine engagements played in neighboring states during the same five-month period, shown in Table 2.3. The band played three additional dances as well; however, Paul Barnes neglected to indicate the race of the audience for these three engagements, so their data are not included here.

The contrast is dramatic between income earned in West Virginia and in the other states it visited during its Huntington residency. This is most obvious when comparing the total earnings of the band in each category. For twenty-one dances in-state, it must have received at least $741.00 in order that each player receive the wages Barnes recorded in his gig book, whereas for the twenty-nine dances played elsewhere in the region, it received a total of only $399.76. The difference of $342.24 means that those twenty-nine engagements earned just 54 percent of what the band was paid for playing twenty-one engagements in the Mountain State. Comparing individual earnings shows similar gaps. Black dances in West Virginia paid slightly more than 62 percent of all income from black audiences, while white dances in-state paid 73 percent of all income from white patrons.

My earlier assertion that black miners' wages were superior to those of African Americans living both in the industrial North and in the agricultural and even urban South is corroborated by Paul Barnes's continued documentation of income from King Oliver's engagements following the band's departure from West Virginia on March 31, 1935, until he quit the band in Biloxi, Mississippi, at the end of June. During that three-month

Table 2.3. Financial data and analysis of 29 dances outside of West Virginia (10/1/34–2/25/35) for which Joe Oliver's Band provided music.

	Month/Date	City, State	Race of audience	Amount paid to each player
1.	Oct. 3	Portsmouth, OH	Colored	$0.50
2.	Oct. 5	Middleport, OH	White	$0.75
3.	Oct. 12	Jenkins, KY	Colored	$1.00
4.	Oct. 13	Harlan, KY	White	$1.60
5.	Oct. 15	Greenville, SC	Colored	$0.50
6.	Oct. 16	Greenville, SC	White	$1.60
7.	Oct. 19	Charlotte, NC[1]	Colored	$0.00
8.	Oct. 21	Greenville, SC	Colored	$0.25
9.	Oct. 22	Flat Rock, NC	Colored	$0.25
10.	Oct. 25	High Point, NC	Colored	$0.25
11.	Oct. 28	Greenville, SC	Colored	$0.15
12.	Oct. 29	Lexington, VA	Colored	$2.00
13.	Oct. 30	Staunton, VA	Colored	$2.00
14.	Nov. 8	Kingsport, TN	White	$0.60
15.	Nov. 9	Knoxville, TN	Colored	$0.00
16.	Nov. 10	Knoxville, TN	White	$1.00
17.	Nov. 12	Kingsport, TN	Colored	$3.00
18.	Nov. 16	Big Stone Gap, VA	White	$1.00
19.	Nov. 30	Big Stone Gap, VA	White	$0.00
20.	Dec. 1	Big Stone Gap, VA	White	$0.80
21.	Dec. 25	Ashland, KY	Colored	$5.00
22.	Jan. 16	Portsmouth, OH	Colored	$0.00
23.	Jan. 20	Indianapolis, IN	Colored	$1.65
24.	Jan. 25	Lexington, KY	Colored	$0.75
25.	Jan. 28	Mayfield, KY	Colored	$1.00
26.	Feb. 12	Ashland, KY	Colored	$1.89
27.	Feb. 14	Mayfield, KY	Colored	$0.62
28.	Feb. 22	Big Stone Gap, VA	Colored	$3.36
29.	Feb. 23	Big Stone Gap, VA	White	$0.76

Summary:

	Number of dances	Total earnings per player	Average per player
Colored	20	$24.17	$1.20
White	9	$8.11	$0.90

Note

1. Entry in Barnes's diary for October 19, 1934, includes the following: "School dance played by [Jimmie] Gunn's Orch. Killed our dance." Jimmie Gunn led a very popular black dance band based in Charlotte, North Carolina, in this period.

period, the band worked the southeastern states, playing for forty-four dances in Florida, fifteen in Georgia, and a dozen in North Carolina, in addition to engagements in Mississippi and South Carolina (ten each), Alabama (five), and Louisiana and Virginia (one apiece): in all, ninety-eight engagements. Of these, Barnes noted that eighty-eight were for black audiences and four (all in Florida) were for white dancers. In six instances, he neglected to indicate the race entertained.

Barnes's entries document the fact that the average payment for the ninety-two black dances in the southeast was $1.71, or just 65 percent of wages in West Virginia. Average earnings from the six white dances in the Mountain State were more than a third higher than the average for those four white dances in Florida. Disregarding the issue of race, the average pay for each musician in this region was $1.73, whereas in West Virginia, it was $2.94. Undeniably, the band did better in the southeast than it had in the states contiguous with the Mountain State in which, as documented in Table 2.3, each player $1.11 per engagement, which was just 37.5 percent of the wage for a dance in West Virginia. By all available measures, the best money was to be found in the Mountain State.

As dramatic as these data are, one must bear in mind that they concern a band flirting with both financial and artistic disaster due to the indifferent leadership of Joe Oliver. A second factor to consider is the season: the milder weather in March through June in the southeastern states would probably have tempted more people to go out to a dance than would the winter months in which the band was located in Huntington.

The difference between the total number of dances played by the band in the southeast and that of engagements in West Virginia and surrounding states is also noteworthy. The band had lots of engagements in the eight southeastern states: ninety-eight dances spread over 120 days between March 1 and June 28, 1935. By comparison, from October 1, 1934, when it took up residence in West Virginia until it played its last engagement on February 25, 1935, in Beckley (148 days in all), the band played only fifty-three dances. More engagements might presumably mean greater popularity with audiences, but, if so, it did not mean greater income for the players.

A fourth consideration that may account for the drastically different earnings by Oliver's musicians in the Mountain State as compared with those in the rest of the territory in which the band played might be the varied income levels of black and white audiences in West Virginia compared to those in the eight southeastern states. As noted earlier, evidence from other studies suggests that the incomes of southern blacks were considerably smaller than the wages of those at work in the mines of West Virginia. Barnes's data provides further confirmation of the economic advantages of working in the coal industry compared to sharecropping, domestic service, or unskilled industrial labor in the South.

It must be conceded that much of this argument on behalf of Herbert Hall's contention hinges upon a single source. One may presume, however, that Paul Barnes's document is an accurate accounting of his income as well as of the relevant data concerning the places Oliver's band performed and the race of audience entertained. Hardly anticipating this use of his gig books, Barnes would have had little reason to misrepresent his professional activities. Nevertheless, comparable documents from other musicians would have been most welcome. For example, were one available, it would be interesting to examine the gig book of a member of one of the leading bands, such as those led by Duke Ellington, Count Basie, or Jimmie Lunceford. So far, none has come to light. Yet, even if one would appear, it is uncertain that it could tell us everything we would like to know. Since those bands were under New York–based management demanding guaranteed engagements, the night-to-night earnings of the band would probably not have been available to a sideman. Moreover, since the cut taken by the managers of the name bands was not always known (though it appears to have been significant), it is impossible to determine a name band's net earnings from individual engagements.

What does reinforce the implications of the figures in Barnes's diary regarding the advantages of performing in the Mountain State is the regularity with which the name bands returned to play there, suggesting that local dance entrepreneurs were confident of attracting large crowds of dancers to successive engagements. Within the period of this study, the Lunceford band played a total of nineteen engagements in West Virginia. Andy Kirk played ten. Chick Webb played five dances in the state before his untimely death in 1938, and Ella Fitzgerald, who kept the band going for a while, brought it back to West Virginia four more times. Erskine Hawkins played nine times in the Mountain State. Combined with the engagements by a number of other touring black dance bands, it has been possible to document 137 appearances by name bands in the state between 1931 and 1942.

The data from Paul Barnes's gig book combined with the evidence of frequent visits from nationally managed bands appears to validate Herbert Hall's recollection of the economic benefits of booking engagements in the

Mountain State. Its distinctive economic conditions provided the foundation for an extraordinary musical culture. At the core of that culture were the bands that played for black West Virginians. In the second part of this study, attention will be turned first to the role of radio and newspapers in disseminating this musical culture in West Virginia and then to the history of the culture of big band jazz and dance music. Central to that discussion will be consideration of the bands that provided this music, the styles in which they played, the place of their engagements in West Virginia within their larger performance histories, and their contemporary and historical reputations.

PART TWO

Big Bands in Black West Virginia:
1929–1935

CHAPTER THREE

Newspapers and Radio Bring the World of the Big Bands to Black West Virginia

The establishment of big band music as a vital part of the musical culture of black West Virginia reflected the impact of multiple forces of which the two most powerful were newspapers and radio. African Americans in West Virginia were avid readers of the *Pittsburgh Courier*, "*the* newspaper for people of color" as Francis Flippen recalled (Flippen 2005). The *Courier* appeared every Saturday and almost always devoted at least two full pages to news of the world of black entertainment, including the activities of leading dance bands. Some of this reportage took the form of short articles summarizing the future destinations of a band on tour, often accompanied by a photo of that band or of its leader. Publicity photos accompanied by a brief caption announcing one or two of a band's next engagements could also be quite informative.

Late in the 1930s the destinations of touring bands were listed without comment. Readers, knowing the bands' reputations, presumably made plans to attend upcoming dances in their community on the basis of these brief notices. Occasionally there were announcements as to when a particular black band might be heard on the radio. In September 1932 the unidentified reporter of news of the black community in Fairmont drew attention to the fact that "Local well wishers of Bennie Moten's Kansas City Orchestra may tune in on WLW every Saturday and Sunday evening at 10 o'clock" (*PC* 9.17.32, 1/7).

Like the *Courier*, some of the Mountain State's newspapers included news of upcoming dances within their local communities. This information was often found in a column entitled "Local Colored News" that regularly appeared in several of the dailies published in the southern coalfields, Whether the dance was to take place in the town where the paper was published or elsewhere in the region, local black readers were kept informed.

For the historian, this documentation of the musical culture of black Mountaineers is invaluable. It provides evidence of the activities of bands that never recorded, that may have had only local or, at best, regional reputations, and that as a consequence have had little or no place in the larger historical narrative of this music. Despite this, their existence is important to an understanding of the impact of big band jazz and dance music on black West Virginia, because they played a key role in implanting this musical culture within the state's African American communities. Unlike Lunceford's, Basie's, Kirk's, or Ellington's bands, the local bands, as long as they performed regularly, served as a constant reminder of the existence and appeal of the music for which the touring name bands justifiably earned both national and enduring reputations, though their presence in the Mountain State was of very short duration on any given occasion.

The Importance of Radio in the Mountain State

The impact of radio on the evolving musical tastes and sophistication of black Mountaineers was profound. Its influence on American society as a whole was enormous, for it was the first electronic medium to reach the entire nation. This resulted in the gradual creation of a national musical culture and simultaneously an accelerating transformation of local musical scenes by its introduction of music from other regions. As a consequence, regional styles attracted new fans and gradually the multiple regional styles within a certain tradition were in a sense homogenized into what could be termed a national style (Schuller 1968, 242).[1]

To argue for radio's influence on the musical life of black West Virginians living in the coalfields requires answers to three questions. In this rural and mountainous state, was electricity widely available to power radios, particularly those in the company houses where miners resided? Even if it were available, what is the evidence that miners had radios that could pick up the signals transmitted by the stations then in existence? Finally, what is the evidence that radio stations broadcast performances of jazz and other dance music by big bands, especially black ones, in this period?

Electricity was widely available in the coalfields for one reason: it was essential to operate the mines. As Figure 3.1 shows, the state's electrical grid overlapped the boundaries of both the northern and southern

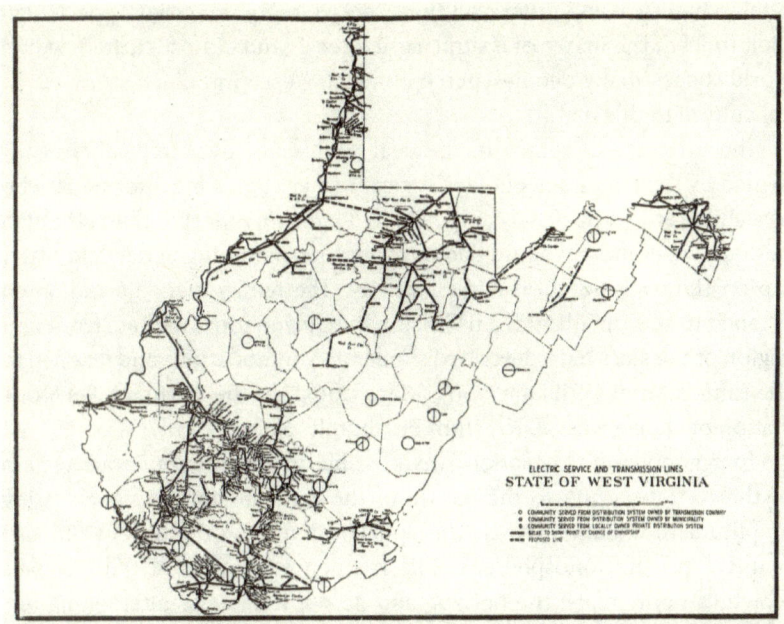

West Virginia service and transmission lines reach rural communities as well as urban industrial centers

Fig. 3.1. Electronic Service and Transmission Lines, State of West Virginia [1927]. *West Virginia: One of America's Most Astounding Concentrations of Power-Wealth-Opportunity* (1929), 12. (West Virginia and Regional History Collection)

coalfields. Thus, 70 percent of houses in company towns had electricity by 1927. In sharp contrast to the coalfields, in much of the rest of West Virginia electrification was rare or entirely nonexistent (*Report of the Coal Commission* 1925, III, 1473, Table 19). In 1934, only 3.3 percent of West Virginia's farms had electricity. As a consequence, the state was ranked thirty-fifth out of the forty eight states in rural electrification (Rural Electrification Administration 1940, 332).

One implication of this sharp discrepancy between the coalfields and the rest of West Virginia was the apparent coexistence of two distinct cultural spheres. Coalfield areas were linked by radio to the larger national culture and thus, comparatively speaking, were more cosmopolitan. This stands in dramatic contrast to many of the central counties of the state that lacked rural electrification and consequently remained largely cut off from the national musical culture (and therefore, to a far greater extent, retained musical and other traditions rooted in preindustrial Appalachian life). Indeed, the image of a rural, agricultural (and almost entirely white) world shapes many peoples' perceptions of West Virginia's historic musical culture to this day.

The presence of radios in the coal camps has been repeatedly confirmed by the testimony of older African Americans. One informant, who as a child resided in a coal camp near Williamson, reported that, although her family's company house had only outdoor plumbing and a cold water tap on the back porch, it had electricity. The family owned a radio and listened to station WLW from Cincinnati (Glover 2005). Others from that region of the state have described similar accommodations and listened to the same station (Williams 2005; Mack 2005). In the northern field, one station of choice was KDKA from Pittsburgh (Nallen 2001).

That good radio reception was possible in the mountainous terrain of the state was due to the nature of the transmission of signals using amplitude modulation (AM). The signal both follows the terrain and also bounces off the ionosphere, unlike frequency modulated (FM) signals which can only reach the horizon and do not follow the intervening terrain. From late fall through early spring, the absence of foliage further aids transmission as do cold dry winter nights when AM signals skipping off the ionosphere can travel as much as a thousand miles or more from the transmitter's antenna. Even now, with the atmosphere filled with all sorts of electronic "clutter," it is possible to pull in distant AM stations late at night during the winter. By 1930 Charleston's WOBU, for instance, transmitting with just 250 watts of power, was heard as far away as Chula Vista, California, Halifax, Nova Scotia, and Havana, Cuba, as documented by correspondence received from listeners in those cities (Owston 1989).

Beyond the environmental benefits of AM radio, a station like Cincinnati's WLW had definite advantages over much of its competition, including WOBU. It broadcast with 50,000 watts of power and was a clear-channel radio station, meaning no other station occupied the same frequency, 700, on the AM dial. Thus, particularly at night, virtually nothing would interfere with its signal. This was particularly helpful to listeners in Logan, McDowell, and Mingo Counties in the southern coalfields, for not before 1939 were stations established in their respective county seats: WLOG in Logan, WBRW in Welch, and WBTH in Williamson.

That WLW dominated the radio waves did not mean other stations had no role in disseminating the national culture of swing to the state's residents. Located in Pittsburgh, the first commercial radio station in the

United States, and another clear-channel, 50,000-watt station, KDKA also broadcast big band jazz and other dance musics and was heard in the Mountain State (Cranford 2008).

The Columbia Broadcasting System had in its network five stations in West Virginia as of 1940: WWVA in Wheeling, WMMN in Fairmont, WCHS in Charleston (which had begun as WOBU), WSAZ in Huntington, and WPAR in Parkersburg. Of these, WPAR was the decided latecomer, having gone on the air only in 1935, while the rest had been founded between 1926 and 1929 (Tribe 1984, 76–78). Like WLW and KDKA, the CBS network featured a succession of big bands performing in various locations around the country on Friday and Saturday nights. Those able to tune in WLW as well as the nearest CBS station could hear a great variety of big band music. Consider the programming on Saturday, November 20, 1937. An evening of live music could begin as early as 7:00 p.m. with the program *Swing Session* on CBS. After a miscellany of other programs, at 10:00 p.m. WLW broadcast the dance band led by the African American composer and arranger Noble Sissle, a program opposite *Your Hit Parade* on CBS. At 11:00, one could choose among several minor dance bands; at 11:30 Benny Goodman, the "King of Swing," began a half-hour program on CBS, after which one could "swing and sway with Sammy Kaye," the leader of a "sweet" society dance orchestra and a marked contrast to Goodman's hot jazz sound (*CE* 11.20.37, 16). Evidence of the stations' interest in building audiences in the coalfields appeared in the *Logan Banner* in the form of advertisements for specific programs broadcast on WOBU, KDKA, and WLW as early as 1932 (*LB* 9.27.32, 7; 12.2.32, 7).

The Synergy of Radio and Newspapers: The Impact of the *Pittsburgh Courier*

The importance of newspapers and radio to the reconstruction of the history of big band jazz within the musical culture of the Mountain State is in large part due to their interdependence. Newspapers documented the importance of radio by printing program schedules, something now associated only with television. The popularity of the bands heard over the radio explains in part the papers' attention to them. The *Pittsburgh Courier* during the early 1930s regularly listed the broadcasts of nationally prominent black bands in a column called "Radio Highlights," compiled by the paper's radio editor, Allen E. Eckstein, who also wrote a companion column entitled "Wave Lengths." In his column of February 20, 1932, Eckstein confirmed the reach of radio stations located at great distances from Pittsburgh and, by extension, the central Appalachians, noting that, while a particular program had not been broadcast on a Pittsburgh station, most local listeners "find in Cleveland or New York itself convenient kilocycles to Smoketown" (*PC* 2.20.32, 2/1).

Broadcasts of more local interest were documented in the *Yellow Jacket*, the newspaper published six or eight times a years by students at West Virginia State College located in Institute near Charleston and one of the state's three black colleges. In March, 1931, it reported that three students, "Aggie" Riley, "Red" Payne, and Charles Cheatham, who called themselves "Riley's Night Hawks" were to be heard on four successive Thursday evenings over WOBU (*YJ* 3.27.31, 1). The *Yellow Jacket* also proved to be an invaluable source of information about dance music in the Mountain State for it documented numerous dances, both on and off campus, and the bands that provided the music for them.

That black West Virginians did in fact listen to broadcasts by big bands is also documented by newspaper coverage. Already mentioned was the notice in the *Pittsburgh Courier* of the fact that Bennie Moten's band could be heard on WLW by listeners in Fairmont in the northern coalfield. During the *Courier's* "Most Popular Band" contest conducted in the Fall of 1932, Mrs. Talitha G. Saunders of Winding Gulf, West Virginia, a company town located south of Beckley in the southern coalfields, wrote to say that "Noble Sissle and his international orchestra are to my way of thinking superior to all the rest. He is my ideal and is appreciated most because of his ultra rhythmic syncopation that is so sweet and hot" (*PC* 10.15.32, 2/1). Her opinion could only have been formed by listening to the radio; Noble Sissle did not perform anywhere in southern West Virginia until February, 1934 (*PC* 2.17.34, 2/8).

In the same "Wave Lengths" column in which he noted that New York and Cleveland radio stations could be heard in Pittsburgh, Allen Eckstein published portions of a letter from a West Virginian identified only as "Mr. Redd" who described himself as a "regular radio maniac" always happy to hear the bands led by "Fatha" Hines, Don Redman, Cab Calloway, and Noble Sissle, but "if you want to give me an idea of Paradise kindly let me have an occasional idea of the whereabouts of the incomparable Duke Ellington, the renowned Fletcher Henderson, and the one and only McKinney's Cotton Pickers ... these three constitute the radio world's idea of heaven"(*PC* 2.20.32, 2/1).

It is thanks to such testimony as well as more conventional newspaper coverage that we can recover both the history of and enthusiasm for big band jazz and dance music among black Mountaineers during the 1930s and early 1940s. This reportage, along with the evidence within Paul Barnes's gig book, previously discussed, further corroborates Herbert Hall's testimony concerning the state's exceptional support for dance music of the period.

If the evidence in that gig book constitutes only a snap shot of the importance of this music to black West Virginians in one short period, newspapers provided a panoramic view of the popularity of big band jazz in the Mountain State throughout the remainder of the 1930s and the early years of the following decade. The fact that this reportage grew in frequency and extent points to growing interest in this music on the part of the African American population in the period. At the same time, it would suggest that those folks were able and willing to underwrite engagements with some of the wages that had been secured by various labor agreements between the coal industry and the United Mine Workers of America beginning with the Bituminous Coal Code of 1933.

CHAPTER FOUR

Local and Territory Bands in the Emerging Culture of Big Band Jazz and Dance Music in the Mountain State

The early 1930s were a time of near economic chaos in the coalfields. The newspaper record shows that in the Mountain State the vast majority of live dance music was provided by local bands and by touring "territory bands," mostly based in the southeast and south-central part of the country as well as in the Midwest. These ensembles would be either partially or totally eclipsed when New York–based name bands began to arrive in the state with increasing regularity after the NRA stabilized the mining industry and wages increased beginning late in 1933.

Given the prominence of the name bands, why should the mere existence of such seemingly lesser groups detain us? The territory bands recorded rarely, if at all; the local ensembles never, making judgments of their quality virtually impossible. That fact alone would imply that they hardly merit attention. Like many such bands performing today in any style of American vernacular music, both categories of dance bands presumably depended on the name bands to determine the repertory and style to be played for the local audiences. If the audience heard a song over the radio performed by Andy Kirk's or Cab Calloway's band, we may assume that song earned a live performance by the local talent.

The local bands' job was, therefore, to "cover" such hits with performances of their own, many of which would probably have been based upon commercial "stock" arrangements. Such arrangements were quickly produced by music publishers for any song that proved popular by adhering to simple arranging formulas. Jeffrey Magee summarized their usual characteristics in the course of discussing innovations made by Don Redman (1900–1964) when he was a member of Fletcher Henderson's

Orchestra in the early 1920s. Redman is widely regarded as perhaps the first great arranger of music for jazz band.

> Stock arrangements of popular songs in the early 1920s usually had a four- to eight-bar introduction, followed by the song's verse and two or three statements of the song's [thirty-two measure] refrain, also known as "the chorus." Each section featured one predominant texture and timbre—whether played by the full ensemble, a section of the band, or, more rarely, a soloist—from beginning to end. Most stocks offered a choice of instrumentation by aligning two staves on each part. An occasional duet or trio break might be inserted for color. Largely, however, instrumentation on stocks tended to change more *between* chorus statements than *within* them. Although stocks would become more intricate through the 1920s, the publishers' in-house arrangers of stocks generally aimed more for maximum accessibility than for ingenuity.... (Magee 2005, 41)

"Maximum accessibility" implies that the purpose of such arrangements was to satisfy a market for dance music that could be played at sight by reasonably competent musicians (and, after a few performances, in their sleep).

Discerning listeners almost instantly can distinguish Basie's band from Lunceford's or Ellington's by the manner in which their arrangers exploited the distinctive instrumental colors and styles of the individual performers regardless of the song being played. In contrast, it did not matter which group of musicians played a stock arrangement; one band's performance would sound pretty much like another's, because the arrangement lacked any personality.

Yet before writing off West Virginia's local black dance bands, it would be well to consider several facts. The first concerns the stock arrangements themselves: they did not have to constrain imaginative musicians regardless of where they played. Don Albert founded a band in October 1929 in New Orleans, for the purpose of fulfilling engagements in Dallas during the Texas State Fair, and was given a large quantity of "stocks" by another bandleader who had no use for them. While getting started, Don Albert and His Ten Pals played them as written, but after a while they began to alter those charts in the course of rehearsals by figuring out how to interpolate solos and other new material within them to allow individual musicians to stand out (Wilkinson 2001, 71). Indeed, Don Redman's first innovations as an arranger had been prompted by a desire to "doctor" the commercial arrangements that in its earliest years Henderson's band relied on for its repertory (Magee 2005, 41).

Another important point regarding West Virginia's bands is evidence of the presence of one or more arrangers within at least two of those ensembles, which suggests the possibility that still other local bands also had their own arrangers. Chappie Willet's Campus Revelers of West Virginia State College included at least two arrangers. There is more to Willet's story than the fact that he led a band of fellow college students, but for now it is sufficient to draw attention to the fact that in a five-paragraph story in his "Wave Length" column of January 16, 1932, Allen Eckstein noted that, as a result of the band's broadcasts over WOBU, they were earning the praise of both black and white listeners, "with their extended repertoire of music which includes some special arrangements by Richard Poore and Chappie" (*PC* 1.16.32, 2/1). Poore was a saxophonist; Willet played piano. Willet is known to have studied composition with Joseph Grider, a member of State's faculty; presumably, Poore also received some formal education in the same subject from the same instructor (Wriggle 2007, 4).

The band director at Garnett High School in Charleston also provided instruction in arranging for interested students. She was reportedly formidable both in name and appearance. Dr. Maude Wanzer Lanes was, according to an alumnus of the high school, both a large individual and highly dedicated to her subject: "220 pounds and all music," in the words of Hughie Mills. She encouraged Mills, his sister, and his brothers to learn the dances associated with big band jazz and taught William "Keg" Purnell, among others, how to arrange music for dance band (Cranford et al. 2008).

Purnell studied at State from 1932 to 1934, and in that period reportedly created arrangements for Cal Grear's Sweet Swing Orchestra, which was based in Huntington but played frequently both in Charleston and at West Virginia State (Cranford et al. 2008). For nine or ten months beginning on December 25, 1934, he was the drummer in King Oliver's band; his arrival was noted in the entry for Christmas Day in Paul Barnes's gig book (see Fig. 3.1). After quitting the Oliver band in the fall of 1935, he returned home but subsequently departed for New York, played with Benny Carter and Claude Hopkins's bands between 1939 and 1942, and remained in the city until his death in 1965 (Vollmer Grove Music Online).

The newspaper record in the Mountain State provides limited information about local bands, but it does confirm that they performed with some regularity. Table 4.1 lists a number of local bands and the cities in which

Table 4.1. West Virginia's black dance bands

Name	City where based	Period of documented activity
Bands serving the northern coalfields:		
The Mountain State Orchestra	Clarksburg	August 1930
Virginia "Peppy" Parker's Orchestra	Fairmont	September 1932–
Gilmore's Midnighters	Piedmont	1920s–1940s
Louis Redman's Bellhops	Cumberland, MD	September 1934–February 1935
Bands serving the southern coalfields:		
Elmer Anderson and His Rhythm Kings	Charleston	December 1935
Dixie Blue Devils	Huntington	May 1934
Cal Grear's Sweet Swing Orchestra	Huntington/Charleston	1932–December 1938
Charles "Inky" Preston and His Harlem Knights	Charleston	May 1933
Ed Watkins and His Harlem Hotshots	Bluefield	May, December 1937
College bands:		
Edwards' Collegians	Bluefield	1925–1934
The Campus Nighthawks	Institute	1932–1935
The West Virginia State Collegians	Institute	1937–
Eddie Billups and His Campus Revelers	Institute[?]	December 1930
Chappie Willet and His Campus Revelers,	Institute	1932–1933

they were based, as well as their respective periods of existence as documented either by newspaper coverage or other sources. Most are grouped by the region of the state they served: the northern or southern coalfields. There were also several bands affiliated with two of the state's black colleges that for various reasons deserve special attention.

Newspapers usually documented little apart from the date, place, and start time of engagements by these bands. Taken at face value, the limited coverage suggests that most existed for only brief periods. What must be borne in mind, however, is that black bands did not rely primarily on newspaper coverage to draw crowds. Publicity usually took the form of handbills circulated within black communities and word-of-mouth advertising.

This is not to argue that some bands did not have short lives, but rather to assert that their absence from the newspaper record is not in itself evidence of this. The following pair of items in a single story of news from Fairmont that appeared in the *Pittsburgh Courier* suggests that more was going on than made the paper. Fairmont's correspondent informed readers that "[Virginia] Peppy Parker's orchestra clicked favorably last Monday night [September 12, 1932] in the Elks Rest, where a dance was in progress" (*PC* 9.17.32, 1/7). The Elks Rest was the lodge of the Monongahela Elks Club, a black social organization. That Parker's band was a hit was confirmed by a notice in the same column that it would be providing the music for "the regular weekly dances to be staged in the Elks Rest in Cleveland Avenue" (*PC* 9.17.32, 1/7). While it is regrettable that we learn nothing of the size, personnel, or repertory of her "orchestra," that it was for a time the house band of the Elks Rest suggests two conclusions: first, that it provided music for dancing of a standard that satisfied the members; second, that as a house band it would not elicit continuing attention from the press. It is not the routine that is newsworthy; it is the exceptional.

Another of the bands of interest is Louis Redman's Bellhops, known to some as the Cumberland Bellhops, led by the younger brother of Don Redman, the innovative arranger for Fletcher Henderson's band in the early 1920s. Though based in Cumberland, Maryland, the Bellhops played in West Virginia's northern coalfield communities from time to time and even played an engagement at the Rose Garden Inn in Beckley in February 1935. By August of that year the band had relocated to Utica in central New York State. The *Courier* article conveying that information also described it as "one of the best swing bands of the up-State [*sic*]. They feature 12 all finished musicians," meaning musicians who could read music and presumably were well trained on their instruments; who those players were remains a mystery (*PC* 8.3.35, 2/6).

At least one of the bands based in the southern coalfields was led by a second-generation dance bandleader: Edward Watkins of Bluefield. His father, Harry Watkins, had formed Watkins' Orchestra right after World War I, a six-piece band that would break up in 1925. Wherever else it played, it was to be found at the white Bluefield Country Club on Saturday nights. Sometime in the early 1930s Edward started his own small band, known variously as the Harlem Hotshots and Watkins Serenaders, made up of players from Bluefield and vicinity. Among its steadier though probably uncompensated engagements was to broadcast over Bluefield's radio station, WHIS, on Sunday afternoons (*TSNO* clipping 9.1992).

Notice was taken of Edward Watkins's band twice in the *Courier*. The issue of May 15, 1937, reported that it furnished music for "the most glamorous event of the season" in the McDowell County town of Keystone: "a Colonial Garden party given by the Les Precieuses Club at the American

Legion building on May 7" (*PC* 5.15.37, 21). The Hotshots were joined by singer Viola Clark, whose home at that time was in Elkhorn, a few miles east of Keystone, and whose brother Walter was the band's pianist (Meador 1987, 29). Just before Christmas of that same year, the *Courier* carried a report of the "annual Snow Ball given by the Beta Lambda Omega Chapter of the Alpha Kappa Alpha Sorority . . . the leading event of the social season" to benefit the scholarship fund for Bluefield State College. "The music and dancing was furnished by the much improved augmented Watkins Serenaders" (*PC* 1.1.38, 2/9). One wonders at the reference to the band being "much improved." Had the reporter been previously unimpressed by its collective musicianship or did the fact that it was now larger constitute improvement, bigger presumably being better?

The circumstances surrounding these two engagements cast light on another dimension of African American life in the coalfields: the array of social activities that linked women of like values, interests, and social standing from across the region. There were several social organizations such as the Les Precieuses Club in the coalfield counties, both north and south. Local newspapers reported frequently on their many activities. Such groups were a secular counterpart to the numerous and busy church-based social circles organized by black Mountaineer women, which also were extensively covered.[1]

Both types of organizations were not limited in their membership to the residents of a single company town. Rather, they drew their numbers from the many coal camps located in close proximity to one another in the numerous valleys that defined the terrain of the coalfields, as well as from the larger towns nearby. If organizations such as Les Precieuses appear to suggest (if only by its French name) the aspirations of some for what might be termed a middle-class way of life, the Snow Ball sponsored by the local chapter of Alpha Kappa Alpha is unmistakably emblematic of middle-class black America. It was and remains one of the two oldest and most elite black sororities in the country, the other being Delta Sigma Theta. There were chapters of A.K.A. not only at Bluefield State but also at West Virginia State. Each organized frequent social events on campus and off. Like those of the closely affiliated fraternity, Alpha Phi Alpha, its members could be seen as part of W. E. B. DuBois's Talented Tenth of African America: well-educated, ambitious, and prepared to lift up the race through their accomplishments. This chapter's efforts to support the educational mission at the local black college, from which presumably many of its members had graduated, were entirely congruent with that larger purpose.

Gilmore's Midnighters:
A Local Black Dance Band of the Period

Before turning to the subject of bands made up of students at West Virginia State, we should consider what may be learned of the local bands that played in the coalfields during the 1930s beyond the limited evidence provided by the press. Though we do not know who the members of these bands were, they were no doubt on a first-name basis with their neighbors in the black communities in which they were based. From the testimony provided years later by Edward Watkins, Nat Reece, and others mentioned in this discussion so far, the local bands did not serve as major sources of income for their members. Some, like Thomas Clark of the Harlem Hotshots, were miners (Meador 1987, 29). Others worked for one of the railroads or were schoolteachers.

Thanks to two lengthy conversations with a former sideman, I have discovered a great deal of information about one of these local bands that enlarges our understanding of the contributions made by all of these groups to the culture of big band dance music in the Mountain State. My informant, Lester Clifford, during the 1930s played saxophone in Gilmore's Midnighters, a band based in the town of Piedmont.[2]

There are two towns named Piedmont in the Mountain State. One is in McDowell County in the southern coalfields; the other is in Mineral County, at the southern edge of the Cumberland-Piedmont Field, just to the east of the northern West Virginia field. This second Piedmont was home to Lester Clifford, James Gilmore, and to most of the members of Gilmore's band. The community was, and remains, a small one. It lies on the west branch of the Potomac River which forms the boundary separating eastern West Virginia from Maryland. Along the river and through the town runs one of the two major routes of the Baltimore & Ohio Railroad, the one that ran across the northern counties of western Virginia before the Civil War and that because of its strategic importance led to those counties being incorporated into the new state in 1863.

Though in a coalfield, Piedmont was not a coal company town. Rather, it was (and remains) one of three communities wherein have resided much of the work force for a paper mill owned by what was originally the West Virginia Pulp and Paper Company, subsequently became Westvaco, and today is part of Meade-Westvaco. The other communities (constituting what are known locally as the Tri-Towns) are Westernport and Luke, Maryland. Less than a mile separates the towns from one another, and the

Fig. 4.1. Piedmont, WV, City Band, c. 1910. Front row from left: Wesley Streets, Ed Bursh, Hennis "Henny" Taylor, Don Redman, "Shavey" Scott, Richard Gilmore (not a member), Melvin Washington, Eulis Kent, Pete James. Back row from left: James Gilmore, Clarence Martin, Mack Clifford, Harry Stewart, "Happy" Washington. (Author's collection)

Potomac, which at that point is very small, is bridged in two places to connect them.

Westvaco did not operate company towns in the manner of the coal companies. The black workers in many cases rented their homes from white landlords, but the company was not directly involved either in their construction or ownership. If strictly speaking they were not company towns, Piedmont, Luke, and Westernport were nonetheless virtually one-industry towns.

Residential segregation separated Piedmont's blacks, Irish, Italians, and Anglo-Saxons, but such divisions were not quite so obvious as in many coalfield communities. Different streets were home to different ethnic groups. While a number of black families lived on a single street, their European-American neighbors lived just above or below them. At the same time, schools and businesses were segregated, and blacks were reportedly denied the right to buy property until the 1970s (Gates 1994, 5–12).

According to one of its two most famous sons, Henry Louis Gates Jr., Piedmont's black men mostly worked on the loading dock of the paper mill or for the B&O. A few might commute northeast to Cumberland,

Maryland, to work in one of its factories. Though the black community was small—only 350 or so in the middle of the last century—not surprisingly it included a number of musicians, and if more were needed they could be found in Luke, Westernport, or elsewhere in the vicinity. Early evidence of the presence of active black musicians is found in a photograph taken around 1910 of the Piedmont City Band (see Fig. 4.1).

Of the fourteen men and boys included in this photograph, four merit special attention. The first of these is Piedmont's *other* famous native son: Don Redman, arranger for Fletcher Henderson, subsequently leader of William McKinney's Cotton Pickers and later his own band, and finally music director for Pearl Bailey. Born in 1900, he would have been around ten years old at the time this picture was taken on Main Street in Luke, Maryland. He stands in the front row fourth from the left holding a trumpet in his left hand, the smallest member of the group.

Mack Clifford, third from the left in the back row, was the principal music teacher in Piedmont and, according to his nephew Lester, was director of the town band. He could play a number of instruments, though which one he was holding during the taking of the photo cannot be determined for it was hidden behind Redman and "Shavey" Scott, the band's drum major.

The other two individuals of importance to this study are James Gilmore, the future leader of the Midnighters, standing at the left end of the back row, and Hennis "Henny" Taylor, third from the left in the front row, who played saxophone and clarinet in that dance band. In the photo he holds an alto horn. Henny, who taught Lester Clifford the sax, was, like Mack Clifford, a multi-instrumentalist who also played and taught the violin. Clifford recalled Taylor playing square dances for white folk. Unknown is if he did so for blacks.

Gilmore's Midnighters was a nine-piece ensemble, typical of a dance band at the beginning of the 1930s but smaller than average by the middle of the decade, when most bands included between twelve and fifteen musicians. Another increasingly anachronistic fact was the use of a tuba or baritone horn, a "brass bass" in the terminology of the time. Such instruments had become obsolete in most dance bands very early in the 1930s, replaced by the upright or string bass. The personnel of the band and their instruments appear below.

Lester Clifford	Alto Saxophone
Hennis "Henny" Taylor	Alto Saxophone

Clarence Walters	Tenor Saxophone
Lee Edmundson	Trumpet
Earl Allen	Trumpet
Charles Penn	Piano
Gene Balmer	Guitar
? Snowden	Brass Bass
James Gilmore	Drums and Leader

While most of the players lived in Piedmont, Lee Edmundson lived in Cumberland, Maryland, twenty miles northeast down the Potomac, and Gene Balmer lived and worked in Davis, West Virginia, almost fifty miles to the southwest. As was true of the musicians in the southern part of the state, none of the Midnighters depended on engagements for the major part of his income; all had day jobs, most on the loading dock of the Westvaco mill. Charles Penn, the pianist, taught at Howard High School, which served the black students of Mineral County. Gene Balmer's occupation is unknown.

The band usually performed only on weekends and, moreover, did no touring but rather limited itself to "run-outs," single gigs after which it returned home. The players traveled in Gilmore's nine-passenger Buick, which seated three in front, three on the back seat, and three on folding seats that faced the back, which Lester Clifford referred to as "monkey seats." To transport the band's instruments, in addition to trunk space, Gilmore installed racks on both the roof and the top of the trunk.

As noted previously, as a rule black bands did not rely on newspaper advertisements to promote dances. They used more dependable and less expensive strategies: the handbill and word of mouth. James Gilmore patronized a printer in Westernport, Maryland, named Rip Lanniger, who regularly turned out dozens of handbills for each upcoming Midnighters dance. Gilmore would mail these to the promoter in the town where an engagement was scheduled, who could be relied upon to circulate them widely. After all, the promoter had a financial interest in a good turnout (Clifford 2001). Since most black communities were close both socially and physically, it would take little time, once someone had seen one of these advertisements in, say, a barbershop, tacked to a utility pole, or stuffed into a mailbox or under a windshield wiper blade, for word to get around that the band would be in town in the near future (Cranford et al. 2008).

Clifford recalled that the Midnighters played for black dances in the county seats of the northern coalfield: Clarksburg, Fairmont, and Morgantown. Of

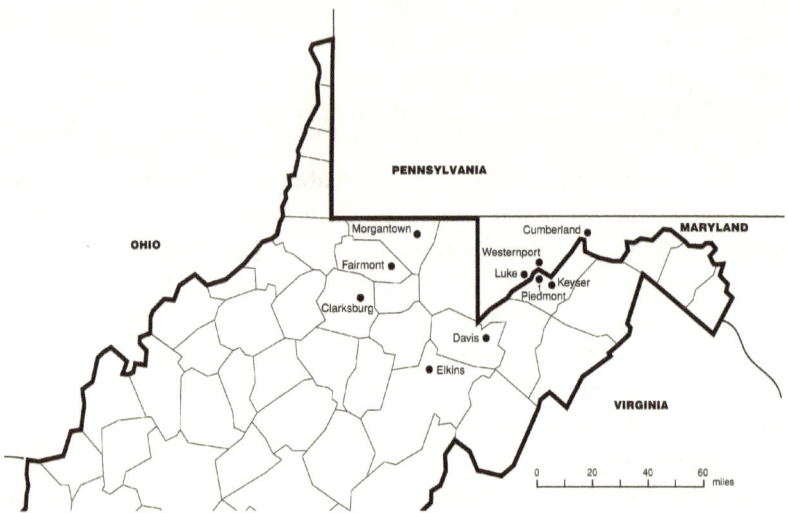

Fig. 4.2. West Virginia territory in which Gilmore's Midnighters performed. (West Virginia University–University Relations–Design)

these, Fairmont was their most frequent destination; its central location drew dancers from the neighboring counties. In addition to playing at the Elks Rest in Fairmont, they also played at the black Dunbar High School. The black high schools in Clarksburg and Morgantown provided the venues for dances in those communities, along with black American Legion halls. The Midnighters also played for blacks closer to home, in Keyser, West Virginia, just five miles from Piedmont, as well as in Cumberland, Maryland. On one occasion, they traveled down south to Wyoming County in the southern coalfields to play in Mullins, the home town of their pianist.

The Midnighters frequently played for whites in northern West Virginia as well as in Maryland, mostly in high school gymnasia. Their destinations included Moorefield and Petersburg to the east and Davis, Thomas, and Elkins, West Virginia, to the south, the latter being the site of the annual Forest Festival to celebrate the timber industry that defined the economy of that region of the state. In essence, they worked a territory that extended little more than a hundred miles from Piedmont in any direction (see Fig. 4.2).

The band also performed in a different manner depending on the race of the dancers. As Clifford put it, for African Americans it played more "jump" music; whites reportedly wanted "smoother," "softer" music. This introduces a topic to be discussed at greater length in chapter 9: the apparent dichotomy between music that is "hot," i.e. in a jazz style, versus that which is "sweet." In a number of discussions of big band dance music of this period, scholars have suggested that there were two cohorts of bands: jazz bands and sweet, or "commercial," bands. It is true that when considering the entirety of their recorded repertories, many bands fall into one of these two categories: Duke Ellington was hot; Guy Lombardo, sweet (indeed, he claimed to play "the sweetest music this side of Heaven"). However, put those bands before a live audience, and one soon learns they could play at a variety of "temperatures," depending upon the crowd's disposition. Rather than dichotomous, "hot" and "sweet" represent the extremes of a stylistic continuum, with each band moving back and forth along that continuum in response to its customers' preferences.

From Clifford's description it seems clear that Gilmore's band played "percentage dates," accepting a portion of the admission fee paid by dancers to the venue. Typical of most black bands not under New York–based management, it operated on the same commonwealth principle that determined the pay of King Oliver's musicians, as described in chapter 3. Clifford recalled that he earned six dollars for the first dance he played as one of the Midnighters and ten for the second.

When asked what the band played, Lester Clifford recalled that James Gilmore provided a large stack of commercial stock arrangements. In an effort to determine at least some of the repertory, I asked if he could recall any of the numbers they played. While he claimed the band did not have a theme song, he said that Gilmore liked to open and close a dance with Hoagy Carmichael's 1929 hit "Stardust," a practice that would imply that, for all practical purposes, this *was* the band's theme song. I read off a list of songs regarded as the jazz standards of the time, and the numbers he indicated were in the band's "book" are listed in Table 4.2.[3]

Knowledgeable readers can undoubtedly call to mind recordings of many of these numbers that each would regard as definitive. Among the more obvious associations would be Duke Ellington's Orchestra and his three compositions: "Mood Indigo," "Solitude," "Caravan." Is the *ur*-rendition of "I Got Rhythm" Ethel Merman's performance with all those high C's toward the end when she introduced the song in the Gershwins' *Girl Crazy* in 1930 or the highly energized performance by the Benny Goodman

Table 4.2. Popular Songs played by Gilmore's Midnighters as recollected by Lester Clifford, July 11, 2001

Title	Year of Publication
Dinah	1925
Sweet Georgia Brown	1925
I Never Knew	1925
I Found a New Baby	1926
I Can't Believe that You're in Love with Me	1926
Blue Skies	1927
Ain't She Sweet	1927
I Can't Give You Anything but Love	1928
Sweet Sue	1928
Nagasaki	1928
Ain't Misbehavin'	1929
Liza	1929
Honeysuckle Rose	1929
On the Sunny Side of the Street	1930
St. James Infirmary	1930
Body and Soul	1930
Rockin' Chair	1930
I Got Rhythm	1930
Three Little Words	1930
Mood Indigo	1931
You Rascal You	1931
Basin Street Blues	1933
Moon Glow	1934
Solitude	1934
Caravan	1937
Tuxedo Junction	1938

Quartet on the stage of Carnegie Hall in January 1938? Whose performance of "Stardust" set the standard? Harry James's or Louis Armstrong's?

The purpose for posing these questions is to draw attention to the fact that in all instances they refer to soloists and bands whose reputations (and recordings) were first made in big cities, principally in the Big Apple. The composers of these great songs were also part of New York's music industry. The performances cited above occurred either there or in a recording studio elsewhere as a result of a contract signed New York. Envision a jazz performance of any of these standards, and where would it likely have taken place? In a nightclub. Where would many people imagine that club was located? New York? Chicago? San Francisco? Los Angeles?

In sum, this music was (and remains) emblematic of urban life, urban tastes, urban sophistication. However, Gilmore's Midnighters were never a part of that world; they brought the music of Hoagy Carmichael, Duke Ellington, George and Ira Gershwin, among others to life in West Virginia. They played these standards in ways that got black people out of their seats and onto the dance floor, people whose livelihoods came from, among other jobs, coal mining and lining track. They played it for whites the diversity of whose occupations were surely the equal of those of their African American neighbors. In doing so, they made this seemingly urban music part of the soundscape of the Mountain State. Neither banjos nor fiddles were involved; this was big band, not string-band, repertory. Its presence transformed the musical culture of black (and white) West Virginia.

Dance Bands at West Virginia's Black Colleges

The discussion of the college dance bands is last because in one sense it provides a transition to the discussion in the following chapters of black big bands that came to West Virginia from out of state, those for whom the comparative prosperity of its mining industry was so attractive. Whereas one might imagine that students attending a college located in West Virginia would have been primarily Mountaineers, that was not the case with the state's black colleges. West Virginia State in particular attracted a considerable number from elsewhere in the country, and Bluefield State did so as well, though apparently to a lesser extent. One consequence was that the college bands included students from both in and out of state; in a manner of speaking, these bands were not completely indigenous to West Virginia.

Dance bands at black colleges were a logical outgrowth of a longstanding tradition of academic musical ensembles intended not simply to provide an aesthetic experience for their members and to entertain the college community but also to promote their institution's interests more broadly. Black collegiate dance bands contributed to the social life of a campus by playing for dances sponsored by fraternities and sororities as well as other campus organizations, and in their own way brought heightened visibility to their institutions when they accompanied the college's football team to an away game or when hired by a chapter of their college's alumni association to play for a dance. At least in the instance of West Virginia State, membership in the band was a form of work-study: the musicians may not have been paid directly, but their collective service to the college helped to lower their educational expenses.

These players embodied what it meant to be a collegian in a time when few blacks were able to obtain a higher education. Indeed, at that time, particularly in the segregated South, education beyond the eighth grade was unavailable to most African Americans. Thus, as a consequence of their pursuit of a bachelor's degree, the musicians in these college bands might be said to have constituted yet another manifestation of W. E. B. DuBois's vision of a Talented Tenth of the African American population; for by their collective artistry and formal appearance, they presented themselves as sophisticated, modern, ambitious young men. The term "collegian" appears in the names of two of the bands to be discussed: Edwards' Collegians and the West Virginia State Collegians.[4] Other bands were named the Campus Nighthawks and the Campus Revelers.

Among the bands with the most continuous histories was the Campus Nighthawks, which apparently merged with the other band on West Virginia State's campus, the Revelers, to form the West Virginia State Collegians early in 1935. Made up of students at State, the Nighthawks' leader changed more or less annually, suggesting that the senior having either the best leadership qualities, musicianship, or both held this position. Riley's Nighthawks, led by "Aggie" Riley, broadcast over Charleston's WOBU in March 1931 (YJ 3.27.31, 1). On February 19, 1932, the band, now led by "Red" Payne, who had been a sideman when Aggie Riley led the group, played in Mount Hope, near Beckley, for the Colonial Ball sponsored by the Mount Hope P.T.A. This dance coincided with a basketball game between DuBois High School and State's high school team (PC 2.20.32, 2/3). That the college had a high school division reflected its intention to compensate for the absence of opportunities for secondary education for African Americans elsewhere. On March 25 the band played for a dance sponsored by the college's faculty club (YJ 4.15.32, 3).

The other dance band located at State, the Campus Revelers, had been led early in the 1930s by Eddie Billups. Subsequently, it was taken over by Francis "Chappie" Willet, mentioned previously, a Philadelphia native and pianist who studied composition at the college with Joseph W. Grider, which no doubt prepared him well for a much later career as an arranger for big bands, Lucky Millinder's among them. In June 1932 Willet secured an engagement for the Campus Revelers in Clarksburg in the northern part of the state, and at that time the *Courier* reported that it was "the official orchestra for dances at West Virginia State College" (*PC* 6.18.32, 2/6). That fall it played engagements at a Charleston country club and during the winter broadcast regularly over WOBU. No doubt Willet's accomplishments caught the attention of Edwards for, shortly after graduation in 1933, Willet joined Edwards' Collegians and by 1934 had become its leader (Wriggle 2007, 2–5).

By the end of 1934 the names Nighthawks and Campus Revelers ceased to appear in either the *Pittsburgh Courier* or the *Yellow Jacket*, the student newspaper of West Virginia State; Collegians took their place. On February 1, 1935, Bobby Smith and His Collegians played for a prom sponsored by the West Virginia State Scrollers, a social organization made up of the freshman pledge class of Kappa Kappa Psi (*YJ* 2.25.35, 3). On March 2 the band played for the Rhythm Club Ball, sponsored by another social organization with the obscure name P.O.N. (*YJ* 3.15.35, 3); on April 4 for the West Virginia State College Chamber of Commerce Dance; and on April 12 for the Omega Psi Phi fraternity's annual dance (*YJ* 4.29.35, 3). The band continued to be active, off and on, during the second half of the 1930s and into the early 1940s, led at different times by Herman "Tubby" McCoy (*YJ* 6.4.37, 3) and Gloster Current (*YJ* 2.25.41, 7). At the same time, the student newspaper documented increasing reliance on "adult" bands from the region by various social organizations that sponsored dances. This may reflect the comparative prosperity of the Mountain State (or, it must be conceded, the possible mediocrity of the college band).

The decision to adopt the name West Virginia State Collegians surely reflected not only the status that "collegian" presumably conferred upon the band, but perhaps as well the regional reputation of Phil Edwards' Collegians, formed sometime in 1928 in Bluefield. This band was formed by pianist Phillip H. Edwards, a native of Ohio, who it is believed had enrolled in the secondary studies division of Bluefield State College during two terms in 1914 and 1915. Whether he completed the high school curriculum is unknown. The band included former members of Harry Watkins's Serenaders (Edwards among them), which had broken up prior to 1925, other musicians from the vicinity of Bluefield, and others from West Virginia State College and Wilberforce College in Ohio (Wriggle 2007, 5–6). As of July 1929, the band consisted of ten musicians:

Leon Jackson	Saxophone/Director
Howard Abbott	Saxophone/Manager
Charles Moore	Saxophone
Joseph Branch	Cornet
Hugh Taylor	Cornet
Frank Fairfax	Trombone
Phil Edwards	Piano/Leader
Phillip Jefferson	Banjo
Douglas Anderson	Bass
Eugene Scott	Drums

According to one report, in 1928 it toured the South with the *Stepin Fetchit Review* (*NO* 2.15.89, 8). For a time it was managed by Sylvester Massey of Huntington, who, as noted earlier, was briefly the regional booker for Alfonso Trent's Texas-based dance band. At some point in the first half of 1930, thanks in part to Massey's promotion, Edwards' Collegians landed a job as the house band for Cincinnati's Greystone Ballroom, from whence it regularly broadcast over WLW for at least eighteen months (*PC* 10.31.31, 2/7).

Such was its reputation that in 1931 it earned eighth place in the *Pittsburgh Courier*'s Most Popular Band Contest, a consequence, at least in part, of its continuing presence on the airwaves. In 1932 and 1933, still led by Edwards but managed by Frank Fairfax, another West Virginia State alumnus, the Collegians made an extensive tour of the southeastern United States (see Fig. 4.3). By September of that year Chappie Willet assumed leadership and subsequently the band left what had become its home base in Cincinnati and relocated to Philadelphia, Willet's hometown. Regrettably, by 1934 the band broke up. Whether this was a consequence of too much competition from resident bands, an uncertain economy in the black community of Philadelphia, or because its members developed new professional agendas is unclear (Wriggle 2007, 13).

What this evidence confirms is that black Mountaineers were closely connected to the larger musical culture of the nation. As shown in the introduction, they brought a great deal of that world with them when they migrated to the state, and they imported much of the rest by means of radio, recordings, and the printed page, the latter including commercial arrangements of popular songs to be played by local bands.

Gilmore's Midnighters, Chappie Willet's Campus Revelers, and Cal Grear's Sweet Swing Orchestra played the music of Berlin, Ellington,

Fig. 4.3. Phil Edwards' Collegians somewhere on the road, perhaps during their tour of the southeast during 1932 and 1933. (Eastern Regional Coal Archives, Craft Memorial Library, Bluefield, WV)

Gershwin, Waller, and others from New York for dancers residing in African American communities throughout the Mountain State. And thanks to the availability of electricity, if one could not attend a public dance to hear this repertory performed live, there was always the radio, which blanketed the coalfields with music of all kinds, not the least of which would be the reigning popular style of the nation after 1935: big band jazz.

Given this cultural environment, as well as economic conditions after 1933, it seems natural that West Virginia would be an attractive destination for touring dance bands, as Herbert Hall later recalled. In the chapters to follow, the identities of those bands and their places of origins, the routes that led them to the Mountain State, as well as the music they played for black (and white) Mountaineers will be examined.

CHAPTER FIVE

Big Band Jazz Comes to the Mountain State: 1929–1933

The complexities of the musical culture of black West Virginians before World War II should by now be obvious. Sacred and secular, oral and notated, indigenous and imported, the styles and genres of African American music found in the Mountain State during the 1930s were every bit as diverse as those found elsewhere in the nation. Situated between urban northern and rural southern black culture, the Mountain State accommodated the musics of both domains with equal ease. Black music had arrived from further south and east with the miners, railroad workers, and their families, while newer styles cultivated further north, among them being hot and sweet styles of big band dance music, were introduced over the air and in the grooves of recordings as much as by appearances by the dance bands both local and touring. Concurrent with the formation of dance bands in Fairmont, Charleston, Huntington, and Piedmont, black Mountaineers had opportunities to hear and dance to bands from elsewhere in the nation. Until the fall of 1934 most of the visitors were territory bands; in the remainder of the decade and in the early 1940s name bands based in New York City became the dominant force.

Gunther Schuller associated the term "territory band" exclusively with black dance bands—based not in New York but elsewhere in African America—that toured extensively because that was the only way their members could make ends meet, contrasting their experience with that of white bands which "tended to have the more lucrative and permanent jobs and therefore were not required to travel as much as the black bands" (Schuller 1989, 770, n1).

In the 1930s, when the term apparently became commonplace, there were in effect only two categories of dance bands: those based in or near New York and all the rest. The number of territories and the states found in each one reflect well-established assumptions about the regions into which the United States may be divided: Northeast, Midwest, Southeast, West Coast (i.e., California), and the Northwest. The one exception concerns the designation of those states in what might conventionally be termed the south-central part of the country: Arkansas, Kansas, Louisiana, Missouri, Oklahoma, and Texas. In jazz history, this territory was known as the Southwest for reasons having to do with the approximate boundaries of the Confederacy during the first half of the 1860s, these states making up the southwestern portion of that region, and among African Americans the term "Southwest" apparently stuck.

In the years of the Great Depression, the vast majority of African Americans resided in the Southeast and Southwest, even as many were participating in the Great Migration either to midwestern cities of which Chicago, Cleveland, Detroit, Indianapolis, and Toledo represented the principal destinations, to the northeastern cities of which New York was the most attractive, or to the West Coast.

Where one situates West Virginia within these geographical subdivisions is problematic. Its early history and name would connect it to Virginia, a southeastern state, and thus by implication with that territory. The history of West Virginia following the Civil War does provide some support for this. The constitutional ban on interracial marriage and the requirement of racially segregated schools would appear to be emblematic of a southern orientation. But that same history also rejects affiliation with the Southeast as demonstrated by black voting rights and consequent political power, non-segregated public transportation, the state's anti-lynching law, and the principle of equal pay for equal work in the mines during the 1930s.

Until this study there has been no systematic consideration of the big band jazz culture in the state, and therefore, not surprisingly, almost no one has considered where to locate the Mountain State within the territories. The exception appears to have been Thomas Hennessey, who placed West Virginia among the midwestern states (Hennessey 1994, 54). Hennessey's rationale for the territorial boundaries he drew stated that his choices reflected "musical styles, geographic contact between bands and musicians, similarities in social and racial structures including racial segregation, and the size of the black population" (183, n1).

In *From Jazz to Swing: African-American Jazz Musicians and Their Music, 1890–1935* (1994), Hennessey also observes that at the beginning of the 1930s, the music industry had "adopted an informal structure resembling professional baseball with major leagues and various grades of minor leagues from AAA down to A" (135). Thus, there were four tiers of bands. At the bottom were the local bands, of which the reader has already been introduced to four: those led by James Gilmore, Virginia "Peppy" Parker, Charles "Inky" Russell, and Cal Greer. Above them were bands originally associated with a particular city which subsequently cultivated a regional reputation extending beyond a state's boundaries thanks to run-out engagements, regular broadcasts on the local radio station, or both. Phil Edwards' Collegians surely attained this status during its residence as the house band at the Greystone Ballroom in Cincinnati in 1930 and 1931. On the third tier were bands that enjoyed a widespread following in a particular region of the country. The Collegians were undoubtedly aiming for that status when they toured the southeastern part of the country in 1932 and 1933. Bands that had clearly attained this standing (Hennessey's equivalent of the Triple-A minor leagues in baseball) were the territory bands, including Don Albert and his Ten Pals from San Antonio, and thus the Southwest; Bennie Moten's Kansas City Orchestra, also a Southwest territory band; and King Oliver's Victor Recording Orchestra from New Orleans, and thus to be associated with the Southeast. At the top (playing in the major leagues, to continue Hennessey's metaphor) were bands enjoying national reputations, including those led by Duke Ellington, Cab Calloway, and Louis Armstrong (Hennessey 1994, 135).

The introduction of big band jazz in West Virginia began with local and territory bands. Only when the economic benefits became obvious did name bands regularly come to the Mountain State. By that time any association of the state with a particular territory would seem to have been irrelevant: name bands played their way through the state heading either east or west, north or south, as they were doing with every other state to which they traveled.

The available evidence argues for a division into three periods of the history of big band jazz and dance music in West Virginia during the 1930s and early 1940s. The first began in the fall of 1929 and ended with the adoption of the Bituminous Coal Code in September 1933, which mitigated the impact of the Crash of October 24, 1929, on the coalfields by changing the economic landscape for the coal industry, for the railroads that served it, and for the local economy of the coalfield counties. The resulting significant financial gains by miners and railroad workers proved more than sufficient to create a market for the music of touring bands.

The middle period, during which New York–based bands began playing multiple engagements within the state, continued through the spring of 1935, when the *Pittsburgh Courier* first documents the activities of George Morton of Beckley. As a regional booker for Joe Glaser of the New York booking company Rockwell-O'Keefe (later General Artists Corporation), Morton's work brought many of the name bands to play in the Mountain State and by doing so linked black West Virginians to the national culture of big band jazz. That they came with such frequency is further testimony to the comparative prosperity of the coalfields. Thus in this final period, from April 1935 until June 1942, a combination of local, regional, and national bands played for African American Mountaineers, thereby linking them with their counterparts elsewhere in the country as active participants in the predominant popular musical style of the second half of the 1930s through World War II. After the spring of 1935, West Virginia came increasingly under the control of the New York–based music industry when it came to participation in the national culture of big band jazz and dance music.

The First Period: Emerging Interest in Big Band Music, October 1929–September 1933

All was not silent in the early years of the Depression, although the effects of the economic collapse included reduced work weeks and closed mines. Newspapers document the fact that black Mountaineers attended dances for which a total of twenty-nine bands provided music. Twenty-one were from out of state, of which one had gotten its start in West Virginia, and seven or eight were local. The home bases of three others could not be determined either from the newspaper record or from previously published histories of the dance bands of this period.

It bears repeating that to expect the newspapers of the time to have documented all dances for one or another black community is unrealistic, since there were more effective and less costly ways to get the word out about an upcoming dance that unfortunately did not appear in the historical record. The same holds true for the number of dances for which these bands provided music, since those data are also a product of newspaper reportage. In 1930 there were eleven documented dances, the next year nineteen, in 1932 seventeen, and in the period from January 1 to September 1, 1933, there

Table 5.1. Bands playing for Black Mountaineers October 1929–September 1933

Territory and name of band	City of origin
Midwest	
Walter Barnes and His Royal Creolians	Chicago, IL
Blanche Calloway and Her Joy Boys	Chicago, IL
Phil Edwards' Collegians	Bluefield, WV ⇒ Cincinnati, OH]
Jordan Embry's "Bluebird Entertainers" (later the "Kentucky Bluebirds")	Madison, WI ⇒ KY(?)]
Earl Hines Victor Recording Orchestra	Chicago, IL
McKinney's Cotton Pickers	Detroit, MI
The New Dardanella Girls Band	Springfield, OH[1]
Erskine Tate and His Chicago Orchestra	Chicago, IL
Speed Webb's "Movie Star Band"	Indianapolis, IN
Southeast	
The 'Bama State Collegians	Montgomery, AL
Belton's Florida Society Syncopators	West Palm Beach, FL
Smiling Billy Stewart and His Floridians	Sanford, FL
Southwest	
Bennie Moten's Band	Kansas City, MO
Alphonso Trent's Orchestra	Dallas, TX
Northeast (including New York)	
Ike Dixon's Orchestra	Baltimore, MD
Reese Dupree's Rhythm Rascals	Philadelphia, PA
Emory Howard's Syncopators	Uniontown, PA[2]
Mills Blue Rhythm Band	New York, NY
Noble Sissle's Orchestra	New York, NY
Chick Webb and His Chicks	New York, NY
In-state bands	
Eddie Billups and His Campus Revelers ⇒ Chappie Willet's Campus Revelers]	WV State
Campus Nighthawks ⇒ Red Payne and his Kampus Nighthawks]	WV State
Campus Syncopators = Campus Revelers or Campus Nighthawks?	WV State[3]
The Nightingales	Parkersburg(?)[4]
Peppy Parker's Orchestra	Fairmont
"Inky" Preston's Harlem Knights	Charleston
Wolfe's Orchestra	Parkersburg(?)[4]

Bands from unknown locations	
Carl [...] Meade and his Midnight Bellhops	
The Royal Ambassadors Orchestra[5]	
Perry Smith and His Broadway Buddies	

Notes

1. Apart from a short notice of undated performances in Clarksburg and Parkersburg during the course of a tour of Kentucky, Tennessee, and West Virginia and the fact that the band consisted of "ten accomplished musicians," nothing is known of what was apparently an early "all-girl" dance band (PC 5.20.33, 2/6).
2. Uniontown, PA, the home of Emory Howard's Syncopators, lies about 50 miles north of Fairmont, where its sole documented engagement in West Virginia took place on May 20, 1930. It was also reported to have played an engagement in Brownsville, PA, about 20 miles west of Uniontown. From the available information, it would appear to be another example of a local band, though not based in the Mountain State. It is grouped with other Northeast bands by virtue of its place of origin.
3. A single article about upcoming dances between Christmas and New Year's Eve 1932 in the West Virginia State College newspaper, the *Yellow Jacket*, makes reference to "The Campus Syncopators." Whether this was the reporter's own term for either the Campus Nighthawks or the Campus Revelers or the name of still another college dance band cannot be determined (YJ 12.21.32, 3).
4. Other than the fact that Wolfe's Orchestra and The Nightingales each played for a single dance in Parkersburg, nothing is known of these bands. It is possible that they were one and the same.
5. The caption of a photograph of the Royal Ambassadors Orchestra printed in the January 24, 1931, issue of the *Pittsburgh Courier* informs readers that the band had performed for two weeks at the Virginia Theater in Wheeling, immediately following "three successful years of playing in Eastern Canada." The band was headed to the Hotel Vendome in Buffalo, New York, for "an indefinite run."

were only five. In this period, then, there was a total of fifty-two dances according to press accounts and advertising. There can be little doubt that flying under the radar of newspaper documentation were additional public dances, to say nothing of those Friday or Saturday night dances in homes in the multitude of company towns as well as in the parlors of families residing in the larger communities of the coalfields.

Since twenty-nine bands played for fifty-two dances, it is obvious that most made only a single appearance in the state, additional evidence of the economic crisis of the period. Only eight bands played more than one engagement, and of these the band with the most gigs was Chappie Willet's Campus Revelers, which played on a number of occasions on the campus of West Virginia State College where most, if not all, its members were students. The only bands from elsewhere in the country that secure multiple engagements were those led by Phil Edwards, Jordan Embry, Earl "Fatha" Hines, Walter Barnes, C. S. Belton, and Blanche Calloway. In all but one case these bands played for two dances; after playing for one dance in Wheeling, Hines returned for a weeklong engagement there after completing a circuit of several Ohio towns. The rest played a single engagement and moved on.

Table 5.1 groups all of the bands that played for black West Virginians between October 1929 and September 1933, by the territories from which they came and indicates, where this can be determined, where they originated. From the data, it seems apparent that while West Virginia might appear, for sociological reasons, to have been part of the Midwest territory, as Thomas Hennessey proposed, nobody informed either those booking touring bands or the bandleaders of this fact. Nine bands from that territory did come to the Mountain State; of these, seven had a major regional following in their time. In contrast to bands led by Walter Barnes, "Fatha" Hines, and Lawrence "Speed" Webb, among others, the New Dardenella Girls and Jordan Embry's Band appear to have had only limited appeal. The New Dardenella Girls do not reappear in the newspaper record following the notice in the *Courier* of their appearances in Clarksburg and Parkersburg sometime in May 1933 (*PC* 5.20.33, 2/6). Embry's reputation would grow at least at West Virginia State College later in the decade, when his band would be booked regularly to play for dances there. Organized in Madison, Wisconsin, and known then as Jordan Embry and His Bluebird Entertainers, according to a report of a dance held at the Fairmont armory on April 25, 1930, the band was later known as the Kentucky Bluebirds, suggesting that it had relocated to the Bluegrass State, perhaps to Ashland, which lies just west of the Big Sandy River separating Kentucky and West Virginia (*PC* 4.12.30, 1/11; *YJ* 5.15.33, 15).

When we include the three bands from the Southeast, the two from the Southwest, along with the five bands from major eastern cities, West Virginia's ties to the Midwest appear to be somewhat more tenuous. Instead, just as it was a border state during the Civil War, these data suggest that it was located along the boundary separating the northeastern, midwestern, and southeastern territories as Hennessey defined these.

Looking at the numbers and locations of performances, we also see that, regardless of their places of origins, for some bands one city in West Virginia, Wheeling, was a brief stop simply because it was on the route to other towns lying west in Ohio or, from the opposite direction, east in Pennsylvania. In other instances, a West Virginia town represented the furthest extent of a tour. A tour by Earl Hines's band based in the Grand Terrace Ballroom in Chicago, and another by C. S. Belton's Society Syncopators from West Palm Beach, Florida, illustrate each of these patterns.

Big Band Jazz Comes to the State: 1929–1933

Fig. 5.1. In and out of the Mountain State: the routes taken by Earl "Fatha" Hines's Grand Terrace Orchestra and C. S. Belton's Society Syncopators in 1930 and 1931 respectively. Neither band played more than a single engagement in West Virginia. (West Virginia University–University Relations–Design)

Solid lines indicate documented routes; dashed lines indicate possible routes between documented performance sites.

Hines's band departed Chicago (1) at some point late in June 1930 for Pittsburgh (2), where it played on June 23. It then played in Wheeling, WV (3), on the 24th; Akron, OH (4), on the 25th; Columbus, OH (5), on the 26th; and Cleveland, OH (6) on the 27th. Subsequently, it returned to Wheeling to play a two-week engagement, after which it made its way back to Chicago.

The extended 1931 tour by Belton's Society Syncopators is less precisely documented. Based in West Palm Beach, FL (a), the band played engagements in close succession in Chattanooga, TN (b), Knoxville, TN (c), and Bristol TN/VA (d), before playing in Beckley, WV (e), on June 19 for the State Medical Association Ball. It immediately left the state to play North Carolina engagements in Asheville (f), Gastonia (g), Salisbury (h), Winston-Salem (i), Charlotte (j), Greensboro (k), and Durham (l). It then headed north to play dates in Danville (m) and Roanoke, VA (n). It would not return home until the middle of November 1931.

Hines's band traveled east from Chicago late in June 1930 to play in Pittsburgh on the 23rd, Wheeling, West Virginia, on the 24th, and then in Akron, Columbus, and Cleveland, Ohio, on the 25th, 26th, and 27th, respectively (*PC* 6.21.30, 1/8). Located on U.S. Route 40—the National Road—a major transcontinental highway (now superseded by Interstate 70), Wheeling is situated in the state's northern panhandle, a little finger-shaped territory not much more than twenty miles at its widest point wedged between Pennsylvania's western border and the Ohio River (see Fig. 5.1). While not on the most direct route from Pittsburgh to Akron, Wheeling could be counted on to produce a crowd of dancers. In addition to members of its own black population, it is easy to imagine a black audience including eastern Ohioans and southwestern Pennsylvanians as well. That there was a substantial audience is confirmed by the fact that following a dance in Cleveland, the band returned to Wheeling for a two-week engagement, filling a vacancy in its schedule created when an engagement of comparable length at the Villa Venice Night Club in Chicago fell through (*PC* 7.12.30, 2/7).

A number of other bands on tour and making use of Route 40 heading either east or west would book gigs in Wheeling if the opportunity presented itself. One was Blanche Calloway (Cab Calloway's sister) and Her Joy Boys on September 21, 1931 (*PC* 9.19.31, 2/9). This band returned a month later, part of a group of four bands that toured together. Between stops in Pittsburgh and Columbus, they put on a "Battle of Music" in Wheeling. The other bands participating in the battle were Chick Webb and His Chicks, which had just finished an engagement at Harlem's Savoy Ballroom, Bennie Moten's Kansas City Orchestra, Zach Whyte and his Chocolate Beau Brummels from Cincinnati, and Roy A. Johnson's Happy Pals, based in Richmond, Virginia (*PC* 10.3.31, 2/9). In December 1931 the Mills Blue Rhythm Band played a one-nighter in Wheeling in between performances in Cleveland and Columbus (*PC* 11.28.31, 2/8).

Little is known of C. S. Belton's Society Syncopators from Florida. The band never recorded and may have fallen victim to the Depression by 1933. We have a hint of its style and reputation from a brief letter by Ruth E. Price of Orlando, Florida, published in the October 10, 1931, issue of the *Pittsburgh Courier* in the course of a contest to select the most popular black dance band of that year (about which more later). According to Ms. Price, "These boys are one hundred per cent musicians and how they can play. Speaking of harmony they have it; jazz, Gee! But they can play it, and when it comes to rhythm they can't be beat at it. Their slogan rings true to all, 'If you can't dance you'll vibrate'" (*PC* 10.10.31, 2/1).

Like many other territory bands, the Society Syncopators toured not only to find engagements outside of its home state and region, which had not been economically prosperous even during the 1920s, but probably also in a quest for a national reputation. Almost a year after Hines's tour discussed above, the ten-piece Society Syncopators were in the midst of an extensive tour that included engagements in Chattanooga, Knoxville, and Bristol, Tennessee/Virginia, before the band made a single appearance in West Virginia at the National Guard armory in Beckley to play for the State Medical Association ball on June 19, 1931. Thereafter, it left the state en route to Asheville, Gastonia, Salisbury, Winston-Salem, Charlotte, Greensboro, and Durham, North Carolina. It then turned north to Danville and Roanoke, Virginia (*PC* 6.20.31, 2/8).

Far removed from towns in Tennessee, North Carolina, and Virginia which were comparatively close to one another and linked by U.S. 11, Beckley represented both the northernmost and most remote destination of that portion of what proved to be a far longer tour reported on in June 1931. The Society Syncopators would not return to their home in West Palm Beach, Florida, until the middle of November, by which time that band had reportedly played in eleven states and traveled 40,000 miles in the course of doing so. Once back home, the musicians settled in to "entertain the aristocrats of the state in their private homes and at the leading hotels, as is their custom each winter" (*PC* 11.28.31, 2/8). Conceivably, as the Depression deepened, those white "aristocrats" who had lost their fortunes may not have traveled south in sufficient numbers to provide the Society Syncopators with the economic foundation they had enjoyed before the Crash and with it the financial backing necessary to stay in business.

What the evidence summarized above indicates is that in the early 1930s, West Virginia was yet to be seen as a particularly desirable place to play. Even Edwards' Collegians, formed in Bluefield but with a growing regional reputation forged from its work as house band for Cincinnati's Greystone Ballroom and regular broadcasts over WLW, played only one engagement apiece in Huntington and Charleston, towns forty miles apart, and comparatively close to Ohio and Kentucky, after which it headed back west. Such in-and-out bookings would change as the decade continued. Beginning in 1934, we see with increasing consistency that name bands under national management played their way through the heart of the Mountain State's coalfields by means of three, four, even five engagements for black audiences on consecutive nights in as many West Virginia towns.

That bands, black or white, toured at all in the early part of the decade was a consequence of a pair of interrelated developments, both of which occurred in the 1920s. The first was the advent of the "talkies" in 1927, which eliminated the need for live musicians to create a soundtrack for movies. The second was the consolidation of ownership of movie theaters into several chains: MGM-Loews, Paramount-Publix, Warner Brothers-First National, and Radio-Keith-Orpheum among a few others. As the Depression tightened its grip, these chains, already heavily invested in sound technology, cut costs by laying off musicians. This was as true of black bands that had played in movie theaters in African American communities as it was for their white counterparts elsewhere (Hennessey 1994, 128).

Although bands were no longer needed to accompany screenings of films, the concept of a theater show that combined movies with live musical entertainment endured (in major cities, well into the 1940s). However, rather than retaining a house band, so to speak, theater owners began booking touring bands for a week or two, thus promising their customers a new band at least twice a month. Erstwhile house bands able to get bookings out of town went on the road. In some instances, they arranged a series of engagements with the manager of a chain of theaters, thus guaranteeing performances spread over several weeks or months in cities that were relatively close to one another (Hennessey 1994, 128).

One former movie house band to come to West Virginia at the beginning of the 1930s was led by Erskine Tate, which had for a number of years performed daily at the Vendome Theater on South State Street in the principal black community of Chicago. A featured attraction of Tate's band during its heyday on the South Side was Louis Armstrong, whose jazz solos galvanized the audience.

Tate's twelve-piece "Hot Band" embarked on what was described as an "extensive tour" on April 20, 1931, including a dance sponsored by a men's social organization in Fairmont known as the Bears Club, on May 15 (*PC* 4.25.31, 2/8; 5.23.31, 2/6). As reported in a dispatch headlined "Fairmont, W. Va," "quite a number of out-of-town people attended the dance," which took place in the National Guard armory. As was the case with the Society Syncopators, once the engagement was completed, Tate left West Virginia for other destinations.

That Tate's and other bands began to plan long tours in the spring of 1931 reflected the belief that the effects of the 1929 Crash were beginning to wane and that there were comparatively prosperous parts of the country that promised profitable engagements even if times elsewhere were still tough. Walter Barnes, another Chicago bandleader and columnist on the entertainment page of the *Defender*, expressed this opinion and in doing so urged bandleaders to make plans to start touring the country:

> Times have changed—and how. Bands, I mean big bands are now taking to the road rather than hold one stand indefinitely. There's more money on the road and in barnstorming, even in one-night jumps. . . . Radio has so popularized good music that the smaller towns want and are willing to pay to hear good bands in person. Big name bands who are barnstorming or will be are . . . Duke Ellington, on a theatrical tour, Noble Sissle, Eubie Blake, Dave Peyton, Andy Kirk, George Lee, Bennie Moten and any number who could get steady stands if they wanted them. But the road calls both with more appreciative audiences and bigger do-re-mi. (*CD* 3.2.31, 9)

It is, of course, impossible to say whether Barnes's announcement prompted the subsequent tours by Tate and the other bandleaders previously discussed. What is revealing is his connecting radio broadcasts to the development of a band's reputation. That black Mountaineers living in the coalfields had radios and listened to bands' broadcasts, as documented in chapter 3, indicates that they were joining people from other parts of rural America to form a national audience for big band jazz and dance music.

It would be a distortion of the historical record to assert that radio begat touring dance bands: Phil Edwards' Collegians, for example, toured prior to extensive radio broadcasting in the late 1920s. That radio was an important element in forging that band's growing reputation was demonstrated by reports of its tours in the fall of 1931 that appeared in the *Pittsburgh Courier* and by its standing in a concurrent popularity contest that the newspaper also conducted. As black bandleader Claude Hopkins stated in an interview with Stanley Dance: "The radio made audiences for you when you went on tour" (Dance 1974, 38).

Under a headline that read "Edwards Collegians Secured for Armistice Night Ball," the report of their impending performance in Pittsburgh on November 11, 1931, at the Grand Military Ball of the Crispus Attucks Post of the American Legion led with the following somewhat voluminous sentence: "Edwards Collegians, toast of the radio world, whose rhythmic tunes have been heard over the air from the Crosley radio station WLW in Cincinnati, who have played for a year and a half at the Greystone Ballroom in Cincinnati, regarded as one of the finest ballrooms in the country, and whose music has hypnotized college youths at big 'proms' in every section of the country, have been secured to appear here for a single engagement" (*PC* 10.24.31, 1/8).

As noted previously, WLW was a powerful, clear-channel AM station most frequently cited by my informants residing in the southern coalfields as the station to which their families listened with greatest regularity. A survey of the broadcast schedule printed in the *Cincinnati Enquirer* in October 1930 revealed that Edwards' Collegians, billed as the "Greystone Orchestra," broadcast for about thirty minutes beginning at either 11:00 or 11:30 p.m., depending on the day of the week (*CE* 10.1.30, 2; 10.18.30, 7). In March 1932 their program began at midnight (*CE* 3.7.31, 11). Theirs was probably a "sustaining" program, meaning that the radio station filled up its air time with the band's music without commercial sponsorship so as to fulfill the Federal Communication Commission's requirement to broadcast for a certain number of hours each day in exchange for the right to the radio frequency assigned to the station. While the musicians were not being paid to perform by WLW, they were being paid by the ballroom from which they broadcast, and, in any case, the publicity from regular broadcasts was itself of enormous benefit in terms of developing a following within the broad reach of the station's signal.

As evidence of that reputation, their standing in the aforementioned popularity contest was clearly as much the result of a fan base of radio listeners as of supporters who heard them live. This is demonstrated in part by correspondence that accompanied individuals' votes for the band they liked most of all. The contest began on August 8, 1931, and concluded on December 5. People voted for their favorite bands by sending in post cards or letters of not more than 200 words; each letter would represent ten votes in favor of a particular band. Letters accompanied by a payment of $2.00 for an annual subscription to the *Pittsburgh Courier* were given 100 votes. The authors of letters chosen for publication would be rewarded with free subscriptions of different lengths depending upon whether theirs was the first, second, or third letter published. The contest was run by Floyd Snelson, editor of the entertainment pages for the *Courier*, who began the contest by listing thirty bands, including the Collegians (*PC* 8.8.31, 2.8).

The third letter that appeared in the issue of November 7, 1931, thus earning its writer a three-month subscription to the newspaper, pointed to the importance of the band's radio broadcasts as a source of what was claimed to be a reputation of national proportions. Written on behalf of a social organization known as the Royal 400, located in the southern coalfield community of Elkhorn in eastern McDowell County, the author at first rebuked Snelson for calling the band the "dark horse" of the contest, arguing that "The Collegians are known from coast to coast as the 'Trail Blazers' of modern jazz music." The concluding paragraph expressed the support of the club for this band and the reasons for it:

> Our whole club is for Edwards; we like him so much until words cannot express our love for him. It was these Collegians who went into the home of the Crossley [sic] Radio Corporation in Cincinnati and created a sensation among radio fans. It was these same Collegians who were invited into the magnificent ballroom in Flint, Michigan, and drove their jazz into the hearts of hundreds of people. Edwards' Orchestra has rhythm and harmony in their music, and these are the two qualities that go to make up a good orchestra. There are 424 members in this organization and all are Edwards voters (*PC* 11.7.31, 2/8).

The Collegians continued to be competitive during the rest of the contest, which was extended more than a month from its announced concluding date, due perhaps to the volume of mail and perhaps as well to the boost it was providing in numbers of paid subscribers. While, not surprisingly, Duke Ellington ultimately won the contest with 50,000 votes, the Collegians came in ninth with 27,000, behind Louis Armstrong (30,000) but ahead of Bennie Moten (25,000). Occupying the eleventh spot was C. S. Belton's Society Syncopators with 16,000 votes. Five bands based in New York were among the top ten bands. Apart from Ellington's, they included those of Fletcher Henderson (#2), Cab Calloway (#4), Noble Sissle (#5), and the Mills Blue Rhythm Band (#6). All of the other bands were from elsewhere in the country. The newspaper associated Blanche Calloway (#7) with Philadelphia, Armstrong with New Orleans (though he was constantly on the move), in addition to the Collegians with Bluefield (though Cincinnati had been home for more than a year), Moten with Kansas City, and the Society Syncopators with West Palm Beach (*PC* 12.12.31, 2/8). This geographical distribution, while admittedly favoring New York as the base of operations of major black dance bands near the beginning of the 1930s, does suggest that some territory bands were still enjoying a rough parity with name bands when it came to their reputations with audiences. The results of this poll (however unscientific) are largely congruent with what the record of performances by touring bands in West Virginia indicates: black Mountaineers, like their contemporaries elsewhere, responded favorably to a band's performance regardless of its home address, and in the first period of the 1930s, those home addresses were widely scattered.

Though inadvertent, developments in the first part of the 1930s were preparatory for the flowering of interest in and support for big band jazz and dance music by black West Virginians later in the decade—inadvertent because African American Mountaineers could hardly have foretold the future place of this music in their lives, preparatory because of the foundation that was laid for the subsequent growth in interest in this music in the Mountain State. The evidence of the growing reputation of Edwards' Collegians based on their radio audience points to both the importance of radio as an audience builder for live performances and to the fact that West Virginians were among those tuning into these broadcasts.

Tours by territory bands from as far south as Florida, as far west as Chicago, and as far east as New York, however brief their stay in the Mountain State, led them to communities large enough to provide both venues for dances and audiences of sufficient size to make their engagements pay off. The towns to which those bands came to play—Beckley, Charleston, Fairmont, Huntington, and Wheeling—were all county seats, had large venues, and attracted not only their own residents to the dances, but also folks from the surrounding region. As the decade unfolded, all of these communities would attract touring bands with greater frequency and would be joined by still other coalfield communities as locations in which dances were held. The annual proms and other formal dances held at West Virginia State College not only attest to students' interest in this music but also introduce us to what would become the future audience for public dances, as those students graduated and began life in the adult world.

At the same time, it must be observed that all of these developments do not set West Virginia apart from neighboring states. Again, reference to the newspaper record of touring bands indicates all the states in which there were audiences for whom to perform. Radios were ubiquitous, and the atmospheric conditions that allowed Mountaineers to tune into WLW in Cincinnati (to say nothing of stations further away) were universal, and thus so was access to the nation's music regardless of the place from which it was broadcast or the location of its listener. In sum, at this point,

West Virginia was no different than any other state with a significant black population, and as a consequence Herbert Hall's recollection that "all the bands were goin' through West Virginia" was not descriptive of developments in the early 1930s.

CHAPTER 6

Comparative Prosperity Arrives: September 1933–April 1935

The fortunes of the Price Hill miners photographed in 1931 changed dramatically after September 18, 1933, as did those of miners throughout the Mountain State. For it was on that day that President Roosevelt signed Executive Order No. 6137, "Code of Fair Competition for the Bituminous Coal Industry." That order ratified labor agreements between the coal operators and the United Mine Workers of America and brought stability to an industry that had been in chaos since October 1929.

As previously noted, the positive effects of the Bituminous Coal Code on the economy of the Mountain State in general and upon its thousands of miners, both black and white, were dramatic. Employment in the mines rose 28 percent by 1935. Job growth led to increased coal production, up by almost 14 percent in the same period. Wages, reflecting standards agreed to by labor and management, began to increase dramatically as well (Thomas 1998, 99).

The last of these developments is most germane to the present discussion. As wages rose above the amount needed simply to feed, clothe, and house their families, miners were in a position to spend a portion of their earnings on entertainment. This occurred after the Bituminous Coal Code was implemented. The improved financial conditions were reflected in a dramatic increase in the number of public dances held and in the number of bands that played for these occasions.

Table 6.1 documents the increase in the number of dances that surely was a consequence of the improving coal economy in the state. It not only shows the upsurge in the number of public dances that occurred beginning in 1934, it also shows that the number of coalfield communities that provided sites for these dances was expanding as well.

Table 6.1. Locations and numbers of public dances in West Virginia September 1933–April 1935

	9–12/1933	1934	1–4/1935
Beckley	---	---	2
Bluefield	---	3	---
Charleston	1	4	2
Clarksburg	---	1	---
Fairmont	---	15	1
Gary	1	---	---
Huntington	---	2	2
Logan	---	1	1
Montgomery	---	2	---
Parkersburg	---	---	1
Welch	1	2	1
Wheeling	1	2	1
Williamson	---	2	2
WV State	2	2	3
Total per year	6	36	16 = 58 dances for the period

As can be seen from the data, it is not until the year 1934 that an unmistakable transformation occurred in the culture of big band jazz and dance music in black West Virginia. One can infer why this might have been the case. If we begin with a consideration of economic conditions in the company towns, the first thing to note is that the miners would have had to adjust to the reality of increased wages. The more fiscally prudent no doubt wanted to make certain that their newfound fortune, such as it was, would not suddenly evaporate, and until they were so assured did not start spending money in ways not previously done. Many may have taken a few paydays to settle longstanding accounts at their company stores, to replace some portion of their families' wardrobe that had been worn thin in the tight times beginning in the fall of 1929, perhaps even to begin to put some money into savings.

From a regional and even national perspective, word had to get out of state to the bandleaders and their managers that the financial situation in West Virginia's coalfields was improving. That may have required several months of word-of-mouth communication of the promising circumstances created by the Bituminous Coal Code as well as whatever reassurance consistent newspaper coverage of its positive economic impact might have provided.

Finally, even if the economics of the band business were improving in the Mountain State, there was the matter of the season: winter weather made it difficult for bands to tour by bus—the most common mode of transportation. While many of the state's highways were paved, where they could not reach their next destination by following a river valley they had to climb out of the state's deep V-shaped valleys, often on steep grades that sometimes included switchbacks as well. These were (and some still are) difficult to negotiate in the summer months when brakes were repeatedly put to a severe test. Add snow and ice to the challenges of the terrain, and many might choose to avoid travel through the central Appalachians altogether until spring.

That something like these multiple developments occurred is reflected in the data presented in Table 6.1. From September through December 1933, only six dances for black Mountaineers took place, one each in Charleston, Gary (located in McDowell County), Welch, and Wheeling, in addition to two at West Virginia State College. Five bands provided the music for these occasions, of which four were territory bands: Jimmie Raschel and his New Orleans Ramblers from the Crescent City, Smiling Billy Stewart's Floridians from Jacksonville, Jordan Embry from eastern Kentucky, and Zach Whyte and his Chocolate Beau Brummels from Cincinnati. Fletcher Henderson's Orchestra from New York played for a Halloween Dance on October 30 in Wheeling as part of a tour of the region.

The presence of these bands shows that the state continued to attract bands from the Midwest and Southeast territories, as well as from New York, during the final third of 1933. The one-nighter in Wheeling played by Henderson's band continued the practice established by earlier New York bands of brief stopovers in the northern panhandle before moving on. The other bands also came and left the state after a single engagement, with the exception of Zach Whyte's band, the Chocolate Beau Brummels, which played on the West Virginia State College campus for a Breakfast Dance in the morning and then for a Victory Ball in the evening of November 4, 1933, the day of the annual football game between Bluefield State and West Virginia State. Thus, in most respects the final four months of 1933 represented an uninterrupted continuation of the pattern established after the start of the Depression.

The next year was a period of enormous growth of interest in dances on the part of black Mountaineers, as well as the year in which name bands

Table 6.2. Territory bands playing for black Mountaineers: 1934–April 1935

Name and number of engagements in West Virginia	City of origin
Midwest bands	
Walter Barnes and His Royal Creolians (3)	Chicago, IL
Jordan Embry (1)	Kentucky/Charleston
Earl Hines Orchestra (4)	Chicago, IL
Speed Webb and His Hollywood Blue Devils (2)	Indianapolis, IN
Southeast bands	
Bill Mears's Sunset Royal Serenaders (4)	West Palm Beach, FL
Joe Oliver's Band (16)	New Orleans, LA
Smiling Billy Stewart's Floridians (2)	Jacksonville, FL
Northeast bands not based in New York	
Olive Douglas and the Savoy Ballroom Orchestra (1)	Pittsburgh, PA
Gertie Long and Her Harlem Nighthawks (1)	Pittsburgh, PA
Lew Redman's Bellhops (2)	Cumberland, MD
Bands of unknown origin	
Russ Crable and His Rhythm Band (1)	
Billy Jones and His Harlemites (1)	

from New York began to take notice of West Virginia's improved economic circumstances. The evidence of the surge of interest in public dances is dramatic. In the four-year period from 1930 to the end of 1933 a total of fifty-six dances were documented in the press: 1.16 per month. In sharp contrast, fifty-two dances took place in the sixteen-month period between January 1934 and April 1935, or 3.25 per month. In 1934 alone there were thirty-six dances, of which fifteen took place in Fairmont in the northern coalfield.

In that sixteen-month period, territory bands played for thirty-six of the dances; New York bands played for eleven. Bobby Smith and His Collegians, the house band for West Virginia State, played for three dances at the college, and two bands of unknown origin played one dance apiece at the Elks Rest in Fairmont. Table 6.2 lists the territory bands, as well as the pair of bands of unknown origin, and the number of engagements each played in West Virginia between January 1934 and April of the following year.

A quick comparison of the number of territory bands that came to West Virginia in this period with the number that played for black Mountaineers between 1930 and the end of 1933 shows a significant reduction. In addition to three bands from New York, which by definition were not

Table 6.3. New York bands playing for black Mountaineers in 1934

Name	Dates of engagements in West Virginia
Cab Calloway	August 24
Claude Hopkins Band	June 5
Jimmie Lunceford Orchestra	September 18
Don Redman	October 10
Noble Sissle Orchestra	February 16, 20, 21, 22

territory bands, nineteen had come prior to 1934 of which eight were from the Midwest, three from the Southeast, two from the Southwest, and three from the Northeast. In the sixteen months considered in Table 6.2, only a dozen territory bands played engagements in the state. This might suggest that the state's economic condition prior to the implementation of the Bituminous Coal Code had discouraged other bands from including West Virginia in their plans. It also suggests that a number of bands may have gone out of business due to the chronically depressed economy elsewhere in the country.

One statistic stands out: King Oliver's Victor Recording Orchestra played sixteen dances in this period for black West Virginians, to which could be added six played for whites. As was discussed at some length in chapter 2, the band's five-month period of residence in Huntington beginning late in September 1934 enabled it to move about the state fairly easily and thus build an audience for repeated engagements in several of the county seats where public dances were held with the greatest frequency. Prior to that residence, the band had played one engagement in Williamson on May 9, 1934, and appeared in Fairmont on September 24, just six days prior to its arrival in Huntington. It is conceivable that those two engagements, along with whatever news of West Virginia's changing fortunes Oliver or his manager Ross McConnell had picked up while on the road, led to the decision to stay in the area for a while. The economic benefits of having done so were documented in Paul Barnes's gig book.

While the engagements of local and territory bands in this second period in some respects represent a continuation of the pattern established at the beginning of the 1930s, the activities of New York–based bands in 1934 foreshadows developments that will shape the second half of the decade and the early 1940s. Without exception, these are name bands, at least within African America. All had established reputations based on regular radio broadcasts. Table 6.3 lists them in alphabetical order along with the dates of their engagements in the Mountain State in 1934.

Cab Calloway's performance in Charleston represented his first appearance in the state. Notice of this dance, in the "Fairmont, W. Va." report of news in that community published in the *Pittsburgh Courier* of September 1, reveals the determination of some fans to see and hear Calloway's band: "Richard Moore, John Miles, and others attended the dance in Charleston Friday night. Music was furnished by Cab Calloway and his band" (*PC* 9.1.34, 2/6). Given the highway system of the state at that time, attending that dance meant a one-way drive of perhaps three to four hours.

Claude Hopkins played an engagement at the Market Auditorium in Wheeling as part of a longer summer tour that included a highly successful engagement at Pittsburgh's Savoy Ballroom on May 25, after which he toured in the Midwest before going to Wheeling (*PC* 6.2.34, 2/8). His had been the house band for three years at the Roseland Ballroom in midtown Manhattan, an engagement enhanced by the fact that it included a nightly broadcast over the fledgling NBC radio network, so his own experience confirmed his statement that "the radio made audiences for you when you went on tour" (Dance 1973, 38). Some in that audience undoubtedly were in the crowd attending the dance at the Market Auditorium.

Don Redman, native son of West Virginia, performed for a dance at the Fairmont armory on October 4. Like Calloway and Hopkins, his reputation preceded him, thanks in part to regular broadcasts over the CBS radio network, so much so that in addition to the African American Mountaineers who were expected to constitute "the biggest crowd of colored terpsichorean experts ever assembled at one time on the local floor . . . because of Redman's local popularity among the white folks, arrangements have been made to seat approximately 100 spectators in the balcony" (*WV* 10.3.34, 5). The spectators would have presumably paid the same admission fee and the dancers, thus adding to the band's income for the engagement.

Taken as a whole, the limited number of engagements by these five bands might appear to contradict the assertion that they represented the wave of the future; but closer examination of the circumstances surrounding engagements by Noble Sissle's and Jimmie Lunceford's orchestras reveals why these were indicative of subsequent developments. Attention will be focused first on Noble Sissle's four performances for black West Virginians (the band also played a separate engagement for whites), because they suggest that some involved in the music industry were discovering that the Mountain State included multiple locations where audiences might now be found. The achievements of Lunceford's band in the months preceding its debut in Fairmont on September 18, 1934, foreshadow other developments in big band jazz and dance music that enlarge our understanding of the role played by radio in building an audience for his music among black Mountaineers.

The succession of gigs played by Noble Sissle's Orchestra constitute the first instance in which, after a name band had played a single engagement in the state, it did not immediately go elsewhere in the country in pursuit of its next one. Moreover, Sissle's engagements show that it was desirable to arrange for a series of dance dates in relatively close succession within West Virginia, thus reducing travel time and costs between them.

The story begins on February 15, 1934, when Sissle's band arrived from Chicago to play an engagement in Wheeling for a white audience. According to a report in the *Pittsburgh Courier*, this dance was "the result of popular demand because when Sissle and his Sizzling Orchestra played in Wheeling several months ago [in October 1933] at a colored dance, more than 500 white people stormed the balcony and raved over his music. At the dance in Wheeling, colored spectators will be given an opportunity to hear Sissle again" (*PC* 2.3.34, 2/6). This reference to the presence in the balcony of a venue of fans of a different race than that for which the band was booked (as was the case in Fairmont at the Redman dance noted above) not only serves as a reminder of practices designed to maintain racial segregation but also provides insight into how elements of the culture of dance music were passed from members of one race to those of the other. No doubt whites had not only enjoyed Sissle's music on that previous occasion but also took in the styles of dancing that it prompted from its black audience. The more adept among the whites surely incorporated some of the moves they observed into their own approach to the dances of the day.

The next night found Sissle in Huntington, down the Ohio River from Wheeling, playing for a black dance at the Vanity Fair Ballroom, rented for the occasion by the local West Virginia State College Club, an alumni organization (*PC* 2.17.34, 2/8). Following an extended engagement in Louisville, Kentucky, it returned to West Virginia to play for three dances on three successive nights (*PC* 3.10.34, 1/8). On March 20 the band played for a black audience in Wheeling, which the dance's promoter anticipated would be larger than the thousand who had turned out the previous fall when there were 500 white observers present. On the 21st it performed at the National Guard armory in Welch for what was described as a dance "for the benefit of the colored youth to start a garment factory in the state" (*WDN* 3.22.34, 1). The dance was to kick off a statewide plan for economic self-help for African Americans conceived by State Supervisor of Negro Education I. J. K. Wells and supported by other black leaders in West Virginia. Known as the Wells Plan, it proposed to raise funds to underwrite new businesses to be owned and operated by graduates of the state's black high schools. According to both the *Welch Daily News* and the *Pittsburgh Courier*, more than a thousand people waited until the band, delayed by bad weather and a wrong turn on the drive, arrived at 11:30 p.m. to perform.

The next day the band traveled through a snowstorm to Charleston for a second benefit dance on behalf of the Wells Plan held in that city's armory, where a crowd comparable in size was in attendance. According to a report by William Nunn, an editor at the *Courier* who attended both dances, "People came to Charleston through that miserable weather from miles and miles around. In fact we met several parties who had motored from distances as far as 100 miles away" (*PC* 3.31.34, 2/3).

Whether the crowds attending the dances in Welch and Charleston turned out in large numbers because of the purpose of the benefit dances to support economic development for black Mountaineers, because they liked Sissle's music, or both, those two dances and the one in Wheeling surely demonstrated both to the bandleader and his manager that the Mountain State had several discrete audiences, each of considerable number, one in each of the three communities in which the band had played.

These towns were all county seats and thus important commercial centers for their regions. Numerous small black communities in coal company towns surrounded Welch and Charleston. As these county seats had venues that would accommodate hundreds of dancers, not only were they promising locations for future engagements, but evidence also suggested that other large towns in the southern coalfields, such as Beckley (Raleigh County), Bluefield (Mercer), and Logan (Logan), might also prove to be profitable sites for future engagements by black dance bands, particularly if dances could be arranged in close succession.

If Sissle's engagements are prophetic of the future patterns for dances by name bands, Jimmie Lunceford's debut performance in Fairmont (seat of Marion County in the northern coalfield) presents an opportunity to see how the influence of radio, recordings, and newspaper publicity worked collectively to build large audiences. More than 700 dancers reportedly crowded into the dance at the Fairmont armory on September 18, 1934, and a number of them had come from some distance to attend. Like Noble

Sissle's earlier engagements, Lunceford's date in Fairmont demonstrated the potential for profitable engagements for black bands in the Mountain State. Also significant for this study is that it is possible to identify at least some of the repertory performed that night, specifically those compositions that the band had already recorded or would record within a few weeks of this performance, music it had previously performed to great acclaim at the Cotton Club in Harlem.

Formed in 1927 at Manassas High School, one of two black high schools in Memphis, Tennessee, and known first as the Chickasaw Syncopators, the Jimmie Lunceford Orchestra would become one of the most popular black dance bands of the 1930s and 1940s (Determeyer 2006, 30). Most bands had distinctive sounds reflecting the aesthetic values of leaders as realized by one or more arrangers. One obvious example was Duke Ellington's band, a creature of his own musical imagination and the talents and timbres of a number of his musicians, supplemented though not fundamentally altered by the presence of Billy Strayhorn beginning in the late 1930s. Another was the Benny Goodman Orchestra, the repertory of which was dominated by Fletcher Henderson's arrangements. Lunceford's band was different. At different times it included as many as four or five arrangers, each projecting a different style. The band both played and recorded a varied repertory that ranged from sweet to hot numbers—in the words of Gunther Schuller: "music for dancing, sentimental ballads, novelty tunes, and virtuoso 'flag wavers'" (Schuller 1989, 202).

By all accounts, the music that it recorded was typical of that which it played for dancers. This fact sets the band apart from most black bands because recording executives usually took great care to limit their range of musical styles. The industry demanded that black bands record jazz and blues ("race" music to be issued on "race" records), even though their collection of arrangements might include dance music in other styles and rhythms that they played during live engagements. Jeffrey Magee observed: "[Fletcher] Henderson's band was admired by some for playing arrangements of the classics and especially for waltzes. But governing racial stereotypes forced Henderson to suppress this repertory when he entered the recording studio" (Magee 2005, 7–8). The same was true for many black bands; Lunceford's appears to have been exceptional in this regard, given the breadth of styles found on its recordings.

The year 1934 was a tumultuous one for Lunceford and his men. After a rocky start in New York's Lafayette Theater the previous September, where its opening night accompaniment to a revue entitled *It's a Knockout* was an unmitigated disaster, the band recovered its form, completed the four-week engagement plus an extension, and then departed for Chicago, where it played at three important venues: the Top, the College Inn, and the Regal Theater. It then returned to New York and the Lafayette Theater for another four-week stint, after which it secured the highly coveted job of house band for the Cotton Club in Harlem, having been preceded in that engagement by Duke Ellington and then Cab Calloway.

That engagement and Lunceford's first recording session in eight months reflected the influence of his manager Irving Mills, though it has been argued that Mills was in reality not merely the manager but the owner of the Lunceford band. In the words of Lunceford biographer Eddy Determeyer:

> Every major black orchestra in New York was owned by music mogul Irving Mills: Duke Ellington, Cab Calloway, Lucky Millinder, Fletcher Henderson, Benny Carter, Willie Lewis, Don Redman. "Owned" is the right expression: they were his, copyrights and all. His artists' songs were exploited by his publishing firm Mills Music, Inc. Mills Artists Bureau had all the right contacts. It had connections with RCA staff and the Cotton Club, and so through Mills's efforts the Lunceford orchestra entered the recording studio on January 26, 1934. (Determeyer 2006, 67)

That January session was the first of eight that year, the others occurring on March 20, September 4 and 5, October 29, November 7, and December 17 and 18. The first two sessions were for the Victor label; the remaining six fulfilled a contract with Decca Records, a British company that had just opened an American branch. Typically, four "sides" were recorded at a session, each rarely longer than three minutes. A pair of sides would be released as a single ten-inch 78 r.p.m. disc, the recording medium for jazz and other American vernacular styles at that time. A total of twenty-nine different compositions were recorded that covered a wide range of styles from hot to sweet, several in two takes, each of which was eventually issued (Lord 1995, L625–L627).

A number of the pieces recorded had all been included in the band's performances at the Cotton Club, some in the floor show called the "Cotton Club Parade," the rest serving as dance numbers for the patrons. In addition to its live performances at one of New York's most popular nightclubs, the Lunceford band broadcast regularly during the same period.

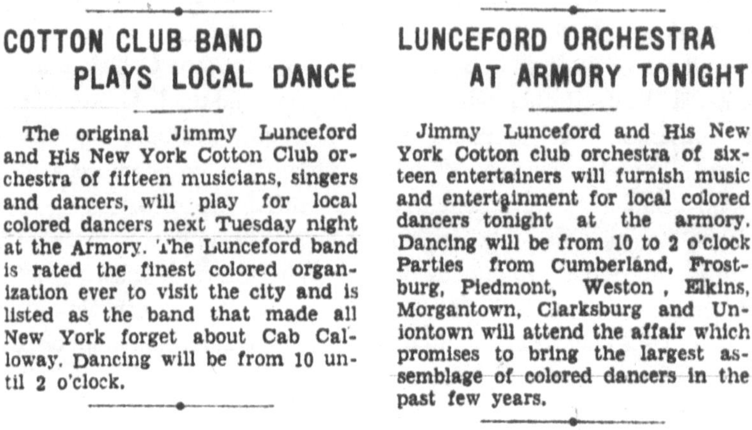

COTTON CLUB BAND PLAYS LOCAL DANCE

The original Jimmy Lunceford and His New York Cotton Club orchestra of fifteen musicians, singers and dancers, will play for local colored dancers next Tuesday night at the Armory. The Lunceford band is rated the finest colored organization ever to visit the city and is listed as the band that made all New York forget about Cab Calloway. Dancing will be from 10 until 2 o'clock.

LUNCEFORD ORCHESTRA AT ARMORY TONIGHT

Jimmy Lunceford and His New York Cotton club orchestra of sixteen entertainers will furnish music and entertainment for local colored dancers tonight at the armory. Dancing will be from 10 to 2 o'clock Parties from Cumberland, Frostburg, Piedmont, Weston, Elkins, Morgantown, Clarksburg and Uniontown will attend the affair which promises to bring the largest assemblage of colored dancers in the past few years.

Fig. 6.1. Two articles from the Fairmont, WV, *West Virginian*. The first appeared on September 11, 1934, announcing the forthcoming engagement by Jimmie Lunceford and His New York Cotton Club Orchestra to perform "for colored dancers." The second, published on the day of the dance, September 18, draws attention to the fact that in attendance will be people residing not only in West Virginia but also in Pennsylvania and Maryland. (*Times West Virginian*)

With all the publicity arising from its success in New York, the band was rapidly establishing its reputation as a name band.

In the course of this mounting success, Lunceford became fed up with Irving Mills's exploitation of the band's talented players, and he and his musicians bought out their contracts with Mills and set out on their own. They would not be alone in making this decision: Fletcher Henderson and Cab Calloway shortly thereafter parted company with Mills as well. The manager retaliated against Lunceford, presumably as the leader of this revolt.

Closely allied with other white managers, including Joe Glaser and William Morris, all of whom were effectively the gatekeepers to well-paying jobs in the dance band business, by the middle of 1934 Mills had ensured that Lunceford was denied access to major hotel ballrooms and theaters that catered to whites. Harold Oxley, who succeeded Mills as Lunceford's manager, was able to secure those six recording dates with Decca between September and December 1934. As a consequence of being blackballed by Mills, missing for a number of years would be access to radio. Thus, Lunceford's reputation would go into eclipse. Cut off from a large segment of his former New York audience, he began to tour the country in search of fans who knew of his music from radio broadcasts, most of whom would be black (Determeyer 2006, 74–75). Among the earliest of what would prove to be almost countless one-night engagements in the course of numerous tours was the Fairmont dance that September.

Newspaper advertising for the Fairmont dance included two short articles in the city's daily newspaper, the *West Virginian* (see Fig. 6.1). Another appeared in the *Pittsburgh Courier*. Word of mouth was also clearly a factor in building the audience, as implied in the concluding sentence of the article that appeared in the *West Virginian* of September 18, 1934: "Parties from Cumberland, Piedmont, Weston, Elkins, Morgantown, Clarksburg, and Uniontown will attend the affair which promises to bring the largest assemblage of colored dancers in the past few years" (*WV* 9.18.34, 10).

Fairmont, seat of Marion County, is centrally located in the northern West Virginia coalfield. About thirty miles southwest lies Clarksburg, seat of Harrison County, the southernmost county in that field, and about the same distance further south and west is Weston. Morgantown, seat of Monongalia County, lies about twenty-five miles north of Fairmont. All four communities are located in the rolling countryside of the Allegheny Plateau and are linked by U.S. Highway 19, making travel among them fairly easy, if slow. Weston might have been as much as an hour away from Fairmont by car.

Located about forty miles northeast of Morgantown in southwestern Pennsylvania is Uniontown; those from that town who attended the Lunceford dance had about seventy miles to drive, which could easily have taken two hours or more. Elkins, southeast of Fairmont in the more mountainous terrain at the eastern edge of the Plateau, was also as much as two hours from Fairmont.

To drive to Fairmont from Cumberland, Maryland, and Piedmont, West Virginia, required crossing the Allegheny Mountains on U.S. 50 with long, and in places steep, grades over the high ridges and down into the river valleys that ran parallel to them. This was the route that Gilmore's Midnighters traveled when they played in Fairmont, and it was not an easy drive. To understand how imposing this terrain was (and remains), it is worth noting that, on the Baltimore & Ohio Railroad's route from Cumberland to Parkersburg that roughly parallels U.S. 50, this stretch routinely required the use of helper locomotives to enable both freight and passenger trains to climb the long, steep grades. Enthusiasts of Jimmie Lunceford's music were obviously prepared to undertake some serious mountain driving to attend this dance.

Lunceford organized his engagements to appeal to audiences having diverse expectations. As a result, according to Albert McCarthy, "To the

Table 6.4. Recordings made by the Jimmie Lunceford Orchestra in 1934 prior to performing in Fairmont, West Virginia, on September 18th

Recording dates	Titles	Arranger
January 26, 1934 (Victor)	White Heat**	Will Hudson
	Jazznocracy**	Will Hudson
	Chillun, Get Up!*	Sy Oliver
	Leaving Me	Edwin Wilcox
March 20, 1934 (Victor)	Swingin' Uptown (2 takes)	Sy Oliver
	Breakfast Ball*	Sy Oliver
	Here Goes a Fool (2 takes)*	Tom Whaley
	Remember When (2 takes)	Edwin Wilcox
September 4, 1934 (Decca)	Sophisticated Lady	Willie Smith
	Mood Indigo (2 takes)	Willie Smith
	Rose Room	Willie Smith
	Black and Tan Fantasy*	Sy Oliver
	Stratosphere	Edwin Wilcox
September 5, 1934 (Decca)	Nana	Sy Oliver
	Miss Otis Regrets	Edwin Wilcox
	Unsophisticated Sue	Sy Oliver
	Star Dust (2 takes)	Edwin Wilcox

* numbers performed as part of the Cotton Club Parade
** numbers known to have been performed by Lunceford's band at the Cotton Club but not as part of this revue

dancers it was a fine dance band; to the people who went to see a show it was a good theatrical spectacle; to the jazz fans it was a good jazz group" (McCarthy 1964, 136). The theatrical spectacle was created in part by the performance practice of the band members themselves as they tossed their instruments into the air, swayed back and forth in time to the music, and performed novelty numbers. Lunceford also brought dancers and other entertainers along on his tours, who were featured at different times during the evening.

As for the repertory that was performed in Fairmont, while not all of it can be determined, it seem probable that many of the numbers recorded during 1934 were, including compositions that had been arranged for the Cotton Club Parade. Table 6.4 lists titles grouped by the dates of their recordings. Where there was more than one take, the total number appears in parentheses following the song title. The arranger of each piece is also identified. The Cotton Club Parade numbers are identified by asterisks (*). Those not part of the floor show but known to have been played by the band at the Cotton Club are identified by double asterisks (**) (Determeyer 2006, 70–70).

Five arrangers, three from within the band, were responsible for the charts recorded in New York and presumably played in Fairmont. Pianist Edwin Wilcox, clarinetist/alto saxophonist Willie Smith, trumpet player and sometime vocalist Sy Oliver were band members; Tom Whaley worked independently, and Will Hudson was employed by Irving Mills to write charts for whichever band in Mills's stable needed them. By a simple count, Sy Oliver was the most prominent of these arrangers in this period: six of the seventeen charts were his. Both their number and quality led Gunther Schuller to argue that "From early 1934 on, for almost two years, Oliver produced a series of arrangements that really set the Lunceford band apart and gave it a sound and performance style that at its best could compete even with Ellington's" (Schuller 1989, 206–7). Of the remaining arrangements, running a close second to Oliver was Edwin Wilcox, who contributed five, Willie Smith three, Will Hudson two, and Tom Whaley one.

The numbers themselves came from a variety of people, including Will Hudson, composer of "White Heat," "Remember When," and "Jazznocracy," which became the Lunceford band's theme song. Harold Arlen and Ted Koehler, who had been hired to write songs for the Cotton Club Parade, composed "Breakfast Ball" and "Here Goes a Fool" for that show. "Black and Tan Fantasy," "Mood Indigo," "Sophisticated Lady," and "Solitude" were, of course, by Duke Ellington and various collaborators among his sidemen. Also recorded in an Edwin Wilcox arrangement was Cole Porter's chilling song about the lynching of a young woman who had killed her lover: "Miss Otis Regrets." Hoagy Carmichael composed "Star Dust," Thomas "Fats" Waller and Andy Razaf collaborated on "Leaving Me," and Mitchel Parrish, Sy Oliver, and Jimmie Lunceford co-composed "Swingin' Uptown."

Just as this band was based in New York, so too were the composers and arrangers of the repertory it recorded and undoubtedly featured in live performances. A common repertory links Lunceford's band with Gilmore's Midnighters. Despite their very different origins and presumed musical qualities, the local band from Piedmont and the national band from the Big Apple presented to their West Virginia audiences a variety of the American popular song repertory of the day, and those audiences were clearly prepared to embrace the musical culture which the big bands represented.

While both bands engaged with the same musical material, that we have the Lunceford band's recordings enables us to consider its audiences' probable musical tastes. Beyond McCarthy's identification of three audiences for this band: one of dancers, a second of those wishing to be entertained, and a third of jazz devotees (and nothing prevented an individual from being part of more than one of these cohorts), we are able to identify arrangements in a hot jazz style, those in a far cooler sweet style, and some that occupy a middle ground, including those that began in a sweet style and gradually "heated up."

From the perspective of the inquiring historian it would have been helpful had someone attending Lunceford's Fairmont dance carefully documented the succession of numbers performed, noting the short breaks between sets and the intermission as well, and then published this information prominently. What we do have is a description by a young New York fan of the band that, though retrospective, appears to focus of the mid-1930s. Ralph J. Gleason, who subsequently would make important contributions to jazz history through his articles in *Down Beat* and elsewhere, offered this description of the Lunceford band in action with particular attention to the centrality of dance music:

> The songs were all played, regardless of their simplicity or complexity, for dancers, basically. And they were programmed in the sets to serve that function. . . . The dance, of course, was the fox trot and its acrobatic extension, the Lindy Hop. Lunceford programmed those sets to take care of the dancers. They began with the slow, dreamy ones, and they ended with the up-tempo stomps, and periodically towards the end of the night the whole house would be rocking and rolling to "Running Wild" or "White Heat" after an interim period of the middle-tempo groovers like "Pigeon Walk."
>
> They would set up the whole evening with swinging versions of "Annie Laurie" or "Four or Five Times" and then cut loose with a screaming version of one of their flag-wavers. Or maybe they would do "For Dancers Only" for half an hour, grinding down the blues-ish sound and feeling in the growls and the riffs and making the whole audience meld together into one homogenous mass extension of the music. (Gleason 1975; 1999, 498)

Of five pieces Gleason cited, only "White Heat" was recorded prior to the engagement in Fairmont; but at least two of the remaining four, "Four or Five Times" and "Running Wild," may have been part of the band's book at that time, given the fact that they were recorded in the same session on May 29, 1935 (Lord 1995, L628).

Gleason referred to three kinds of charts: "slow, dreamy ones," "middle-tempo groovers," and "up-tempo stomps" which could accelerate into "flag-wavers." He noted as well that this dance-oriented repertory was "centered on the fox-trot and its acrobatic extension, the Lindy Hop." Implicit in this description is the idea that a couple would dance in the close position of the fox-trot in response to slow and moderate tempos and then break into the Lindy during fast numbers. Another, and perhaps more conventional, way to think about Lunceford's music is to consider, as Gleason implied, that its styles run from sweet at one end to hot at the other. The faster the tempo, the hotter the style, though Lunceford's arrangers could begin a piece sweetly and then introduce unmistakable jazz elements as the piece went on, almost as if to lure the staid dancers of the fox-trot to try some of faster steps.

In an effort to identify the music that the 700 patrons of the Fairmont dance heard and the styles it encompassed, an analysis of those recordings made in 1934 will confine itself to the seventeen sides made in the four sessions that preceded September 18. Recordings made in January and March for Victor had no doubt been issued during the summer, and fans in West Virginia could have acquired one or more of these, either in local businesses or through the mail. Those made in the back-to-back sessions for Decca on September 4 and 5 were no doubt in the early stages of production but not yet released. Since, as Eddy Determeyer observed, "it was the leader's policy to first test tunes in live situations" before recording them, there is every reason to believe this music was part of the band's growing collection of arrangements and probably near the top of the pile when it came time to put together the program for this dance (Determeyer 2006, 171).

These seventeen numbers present a rough survey of the stylistic range of Lunceford's dance music, providing evidence for the success of the Fairmont engagement and sketching out the range of taste of the audience of black Mountaineers who came from near and far to attend. Table 6.5 suggests where the various pieces would fit along a continuum of style from sweet to hot.

That such a diversity of style may have appealed to black Mountaineers may seem surprising to some, particularly the sweet arrangements

Table 6.5. Styles of the Lunceford Band's repertory recorded between January and September 1934

Sweet numbers
Chillun, Get Up!
Here Goes a Fool
Remember When
Star Dust
Moderate-tempo fox-trots in a jazz style ["middle-tempo groovers"]
Leaving Me
Rose Room
Sophisticated Lady
Mood Indigo
Black and Tan Fantasy
Nana
Miss Otis Regrets
Unsophisticated Sue
Fast tempo Lindy Hop numbers ["up-tempo stomps"⇨ "flag-wavers"]
White Heat
Jazznocracy
Swingin' Uptown
Breakfast Ball
Stratosphere

characterized by the shimmering sound of Lunceford's reed section, square, symmetric rhythms, limited space for improvised solos, generous use of the full ensemble, and sentimental lyrics sung in a crooning style by either the tenor voice of trombonist Henry Wells (as in "Here Goes a Fool") or by a vocal trio made up of Wells, reed man and arranger Willie Smith, and trumpeter Eddie Tompkins (e.g. "Chillun, Get Up"). Recall Lester Clifford's observation noted in the previous chapter that when Gilmore's Midnighters played for white dancers the music was "smoother" than the "jump" style that blacks allegedly preferred; this assumption of style preferences based upon racial identity is overly simple.

Contradicting that assumption are two statements published in the *Pittsburgh Courier* during the paper's 1932 band popularity contest by fans of Noble Sissle. A woman of varied tastes, Mrs. Talitha G. Saunders of Winding Gulf, West Virginia, a company town located south of Beckley in the southern coalfields (see Fig. 6.2), asserted that "Noble Sissle and his international orchestra are to my way of thinking superior to all the

Fig. 6.2. The company town of Winding Gulf, West Virginia, home of Talitha G. Saunders who greatly appreciated the "ultra rhythmic syncopation that is so sweet and hot" performed by the Noble Sissle Orchestra. Note the company houses in the rear to the left and the single-track branch line of the Virginian Railway to the right. That branch terminated in Winding Gulf. (Eastern Regional Coal Archives, Craft Memorial Library, Bluefield, WV)

rest. He is my ideal and is appreciated most because of his ultra rhythmic syncopation that is so sweet and hot" (*PC* 10.15.32, 2/1). Gladys Mike of Wheeling appeared to prefer a sweet style exclusively: "I think that Noble Sissle has the only Negro band on the radio that can compare with my great favorite, Guy Lombardo. His band has tone, harmony, volume, and sweetness; in fact, everything to make an excellent orchestra. He has certainly made a hit with me" (PC 10.29.32, 1/5).

In addition, Geraldine Belmear stated in an interview that the president of West Virginia State College, John W. Davis, was opposed to dancing on campus (Belmear 2000). But judging by reports in the student newspaper, the *Yellow Jacket*, dances did take place there, although the music performed was in a sweet style. On December 7, 1935, the Ivy Leaf Club, the pledge class of the Alpha Kappa Alpha Sorority, and the Scrollers, the counterpart for the Alpha Phi Alpha fraternity, held a Snow Fest for which "Elmer Anderson and his Rhythm Kings played sweet music for the lovely dancers" (*YJ* 12.21.35, 3).

It must be noted that, as varied as their styles may seem, the seventeen recordings made by Lunceford's band around the time of the Fairmont engagement represent neither the manner in which those numbers were performed in live situations nor indeed all of the types of music performed by Lunceford's band. Gleason's recollection of half-hour-long versions of "For Dancers Only" stands in sharp contrast to the recording of June 15, 1937, which lasted just two minutes and thirty-six seconds. In his biography of Lunceford, Eddy Determeyer observed: "Apart from 'For Dancers Only,' selections such as 'Dinah,' 'Strictly Instrumental,' and 'Wham' could, according to the circumstances, be stretched into six- or sixty-minute orgies" (Determeyer 2006, 125). For recordings, arrangements had to be compressed in order to fit the time constraints of a ten-inch disc: entire sections of a number were omitted, and solos were truncated.

In addition to the dance music discussed above, black West Virginians, like the rest of Lunceford's fans, would have been treated to other styles of music. These came to include arrangements of well-known compositions of art music, including works entitled "Chopin's Prelude" and "Beethoven's Pathetique," the latter arranged in 1940 by Chappie Willett, the West Virginia State graduate who had led Edwards' Collegians early in the 1930s (Determeyer 2006, 173–74). Reportedly, there were also charts created in imitation of the styles of other well-known bands of the period. With the exception of the members of the rhythm section, the musicians would, on at least one occasion during a performance, form into a glee club to sing one or more choral works for the audience.

In sum, the Lunceford band presented what was perhaps the most diverse program of music performed by any black dance band during the 1930s—and thereby became one of the most successful. Its tours were highly profitable, attracting hundreds, if not thousands, of dancers to large venues. No longer under Irving Mills's control, the band played percentage dates, as did most black dance bands, and operated on the same commonwealth principle that distributed the proceeds of each engagement more or less equally among the musicians as did Gilmore's Midnighters, King Oliver's band, and numerous other black bands, though Lunceford apparently took a significantly larger chunk for himself. But unlike many other bands, Lunceford's enjoyed tremendous popularity on the road and thus earned higher returns than had it been contracted to play an extended engagement in a nightclub or ballroom at union scale. As Ed Wilcox, pianist and arranger, explained it, "The real reason we did all those one-nighters was that the location jobs didn't pay the same money. It suited Jimmie to do one-nighters because he could make twice as much money that way" (Dance 1973, 117).

There are several reasons why so much attention has been given to Lunceford's debut engagement in Fairmont, West Virginia, in this study. One is that, thanks to Lunceford's numerous recordings around the time of that gig, it is possible to consider specific pieces and the styles associated with them. This permits us to connect audience tastes with those styles and understand the preferences of fans, including those residing in north-central West Virginia and vicinity, for different types of music.

In tandem with its recordings, we also know that Lunceford was known to audiences outside of New York by virtue of broadcasts from the Cotton Club during the early months of 1934. The articles in the *West Virginian* announcing the band's impending visit identified it as "Jimmy [sic] and His New York Cotton Club Orchestra," even though it had not played there since terminating its contract with Irving Mills. The Cotton Club had become an icon of urban sophistication, the venue where Duke Ellington rose to fame to be followed by Cab Calloway. Association with that establishment added to Lunceford's reputation. Thus recordings and radio worked in tandem to create an audience throughout much of the country for his band well before it arrived to perform. To be sure, Lunceford was by no means the only one to benefit from the synergistic effect of these two media. As Benny Goodman would later in the decade, Lunceford, in the words of Jeffrey Magee, "systematically exploited the interdependence of what can be called the three R's: Road, Radio, and Records" (Magee 2005, 7).

The first of those "R's" offers a final justification for the close attention to the Lunceford band, its music, and its debut in Fairmont. The road would lead Lunceford back to the Mountain State eighteen times before World War II severely curtailed, where it did not end altogether, touring by bus for most bands, black or white. The number of his visits far exceeded those of other black bands in the same period. Only Oliver's band came close with a total of fifteen engagements, but of those, fourteen occurred within the six-month period between September 1934 and February 1935. Between 1934 and 1942, with the exception of 1935 and 1938, the Lunceford band played multiple engagements in the Mountain State, usually in the kind of close succession by which the Sissle band had fulfilled three engagements as discussed earlier.

It is for all of these reasons that Sissle's and Lunceford's engagements in West Virginia in 1934 show the way to the future of big band jazz in black West Virginia. They proved that there was a large audience in the

Mountain State for their music—one that could be served profitably by multiple engagements in close succession, that knew their music in advance primarily thanks to radio, and that was prepared to travel great distances for the chance to dance to their music and to that of other leading black bands of the 1930s. A taste for big band jazz was well-established among African American West Virginians by the middle of the decade. At the same time, the New York–based music industry was equally aware of the potential audience in the Mountain State. While local and territory bands would continue to maintain a presence, between 1935 and the start of World War II, black name bands from the Big Apple would soon dominate the scene.

PART THREE

West Virginia in the Swing Era:
1935–1942

CHAPTER SEVEN

The Place of the Mountain State on the Road Traveled by the Big Bands

Conventional wisdom, first expressed in 1956 by Marshall W. Stearns, holds that the Swing Era began on August 21, 1935, at the Palomar Ballroom in Los Angeles (Stearns 1956, 211). On that night, following a decidedly lackluster tour that originated in New York, the Benny Goodman Orchestra appeared suddenly to find its audience for big band jazz. When the band played Fletcher Henderson's arrangement of "King Porter Stomp," half the crowd apparently stopped dancing to listen to the band and was vociferous in expressing its enthusiasm for this number. Goodman later recalled: "That first big roar from the crowd was one of the sweetest sounds I ever heard in my life" (Goodman and Kolodon 1939; 1961, 198–99).

Viewed through the lens of the activities of black dance bands in 1934 in West Virginia, it could be argued that the Swing Era began at least eighteen months before Goodman's engagement at the Palomar Ballroom. A close reading of the *Pittsburgh Courier* as well as eleven newspapers published in the Mountain State reveals evidence of a total of forty dances that took place between February and December 1934.[1]

A variety of bands provided the music for those engagements. King Oliver's Orchestra played fifteen during its stay in Huntington. As noted earlier, Jimmie Lunceford provided music one in Fairmont, and Noble Sissle played four in as many communities as did the Sunset Royal Serenaders. Walter Barnes and Speed Webb's bands played three each, while Cecil Scott performed twice and Don Redman and Cab Calloway performed once each. The remaining six documented dances were played by local dance orchestras.

The large number of dances in 1934 may well have reflected the audience's collective sense of its own economic good times as production and employment picked up in the coalfields. The next year only twenty-eight dances were held, as was the case in 1936; but there was a pronounced shift in the place of origin of many of the touring bands that came to West Virginia in those years and during the rest of the period leading up to World War II.

Unlike the period leading up to 1935, when the Mountain State appeared to be a meeting point for bands from the Northeast, Southeast, and Midwest, New York City would become the primary source of talent. And, as will be discussed in this chapter, the close professional relationship between two men—Joe Glaser and George Morton—would constitute the principal force shaping the culture of big band jazz and dance music in West Virginia. Morton resided in Beckley and worked as Glaser's regional manager for the southern coalfields. The record of their collaboration as well as other evidence provides an opportunity to examine what is usually treated only marginally in discussions of the Swing Era: the characteristics of small-town and rural audiences for this music during the 1930s and early 1940s.

For the big bands of the 1930s, success was defined by prominence in three areas of activity. The first consisted of extended engagements in venues in New York and other major cities from which one could broadcast regularly, so as to build a following beyond the immediate audience. Prominence was also achieved by making recordings to be distributed as widely as possible in order to maintain that larger audience's interest. The third was to travel as frequently and as extensively as possible to play for what had become at least a large regional audience, if not one that was national in scope. Its members included those who had listened to the broadcasts, purchased the recordings, and knew what to expect when the band came to town. As noted in the previous chapter, these three activities made up, as Jeffrey Magee put it, "the three R's" of the big band business: radio, recording, and the road (Magee 2005, 206).

The vast majority of studies of big band jazz, not surprisingly, focus on the bands themselves, their leading musicians, and the recorded repertory that documents their artistic achievement and defines their historical significance. That they broadcast over the radio is of secondary importance unless such programs played a decisive role in creating their reputations. Obvious examples of such programming include Benny Goodman's *Let's Dance* and *Camel Caravan* broadcasts between 1935 and 1939 that, when combined with recordings and tours (including the one that climaxed in Los Angeles in the summer of 1935), established the clarinetist as the "King of Swing" and put his music into every American home in which residents had both a radio and an interest in dance music (Magee 2005, 224–30).

Of the three domains of big band activity, the road is the most difficult to document. That it was essential to a band's fortunes is undeniable, but, barring discussion of an untoward event, consideration of its character has usually been largely limited to musicians' anecdotes about one tour or another. A more discerning view is missing. Often one reads recollections about touring "the South," "the Midwest," or another region and encounters imprecise, broadly drawn memories of a player's experiences in those territories. A case in point is a story told by bass player Arvell Shaw concerning the discovery of the growing popularity of what would turn out to be a hit recording in the early 1960s for Louis Armstrong and his All Stars preserved in the documentary film *Satchmo*. "We were somewhere way out in Ioway [sic], and people kept calling out 'Hello Dolly,' 'Hello Dolly' . . ." (*Satchmo* videorecording 1989). His facial expression and gestures as he told this story strongly suggested that, as far as Shaw was concerned, if "Ioway" was not the end of the earth, one could see it from there.

In view of the evidence in hand, I believe that West Virginia is in many respects an exemplar of "the road," not the sketchy and vague outline that Shaw and other players' memories convey but a comparatively detailed image that includes the work of local promoters, the locations and types of venues, the size, nature, and musical tastes of audiences, and repertories played by the bands that entertained them. Both the artistic and the business sides of the name bands' experience on this particular stretch of the road shed light on the larger subject of the culture of big band jazz and dance music beyond New York and its suburbs.

There can be little doubt that, while big band dance music was new at the start of the Depression, tours of the coalfields by entertainers from elsewhere in the country were not: the evidence of regular visits by tent shows and circuses in the first three decades of the last century makes that clear. As previously noted, because those companies probably discovered the most likely locations for a large audience, the best routes to connect these, and the best means of promoting their performances, by the 1930s such logistical challenges had been largely addressed. Indeed, some of them were further eased as ongoing highway construction facilitated faster and safer travel between engagements.

By the mid-1930s the challenge was how to ensure profitable dances in places close enough together to make a trip through the central Appalachians worth the effort, as opposed to fulfilling a single engagement in West Virginia before heading back to the flatlands, as had been done at the beginning the of the decade. That required people on the ground, so to speak, who knew their own territories and the preferences of a potential audience, who had connections that would ensure adequate publicity, and who had access to venues of sufficient size to accommodate a crowd large enough to guarantee a sufficient return both for the bands (their New York–based managers, in truth) and for the local entrepreneurs themselves.

That an extensive network of such connections existed in the Mountain State as of 1935 (and probably earlier as well) is documented by coverage in the *Pittsburgh Courier* of a series of engagements by Earl Hines in April and Cab Calloway in June of that year. They resulted from the initiative of a man who would prove to be the most important intermediary between the black name bands and fans of dancing in the southern coalfields from the spring of 1935 until early 1940.

George Edward Morton: Black West Virginia's Preeminent Booking Agent, 1935–1940

More than any other individual, George Edward Morton (see Fig. 7.1) appears to have exerted the greatest influence on the growth of African Americans' interest in big band jazz in West Virginia in the period from April 9, 1935, until his untimely death on February 6, 1940. Born in Fairmont in 1909, Morton was the son of Edward L. Morton, an educator and prominent businessman in Beckley's black community whose biography was summarized earlier. Upon completing high school, George Morton attended West Virginia State College, graduating in 1935. He suffered from poor health and found that booking bands was something that his limited physical resources could handle. Even prior to graduation, he booked his first band for a dance at the armory in Beckley, that of Earl "Fatha" Hines (Flippen 2005; *PC* 3.30.35, 2/9). Much about this engagement anticipates his later work.

Perhaps the principal reason so much can be documented about Morton's activities is his family's friendship with the editor of the *Pittsburgh Courier*'s entertainment pages, Chester Washington. "Chet" saw to it that word of Morton's dances appeared regularly in the *Courier*, which was, as Morton's younger sister, Francis Morton Flippen, later recalled, "more or less *the* paper for the people of color" in the Mountain State (Flippen 2005).

Hines's band appeared in Beckley on April 9, 1935, for a dance celebrating what was termed "Emancipation Day," in actuality the seventieth anniversary

Fig. 7.1. George E. Morton, ca. 1938. (J. Bryan Flippen)

of the day Robert E. Lee surrendered to Ulysses S. Grant in 1865. The dance was described in the *Courier* as Morton's "maiden debut in the entertainment field" (*PC* 3.30.35, 2/9). Hines had already appeared in Logan on April 2, in Welch on April 3—where his band reportedly attracted "one of the largest crowds ever seen . . . at a dance," according to Clarence Lilly, reporter of "Local Colored News" for the *Welch Daily News* (*WDN* 4.4.35, 7)—and in Charleston on April 4. After playing in Beckley, it headed north to perform for another record crowd at the armory in Fairmont on April 10, and while doing so broadcast over local radio station WMMN for half an hour, according to James A. West, who had booked the band for that engagement and who filed a story on it for the *Courier* (*PC* 4.27.35, 2/1). Departing Fairmont, Hines headed to Pittsburgh to play the Savoy Ballroom on the 12th. Apart from the Beckley and Fairmont gigs, the dances had been booked by a consortium calling itself the Amusement Kings, "a new powerful organization operating in the mountain state" (PC 3.30.35, 2/9).

In June, Cab Calloway's band toured the southern part of the state, playing for a series of benefit dances presented under the auspices of various posts of the black American Legion to raise money for the Legion and for a scholarship fund. The *Courier*'s coverage of these engagements explains Morton's relationship to the Amusement Kings or, as they were

Table 7.1. George Morton's booking network in West Virginia, 1935–1940

County seats, the sites of dances	Satellite communities
Beckley, Raleigh County (Morton's home)	Hinton
	Mount Hope
Bluefield, Mercer County	Gary
	Kimball
	Keystone
Charleston, Kanawha County	Huntington
	Logan
	Williamson
Welch, McDowell County[1]	Gary
	Kimball
	Keystone
Fairmont, Marion County	Morgantown
	Clarksburg

Note

1. The satellite communities for Bluefield and Welch are identical because they are located between these two cities on U.S. Route 52, making the respective sites of dances equally accessible to their residents.

then identified, "the Kings of Amusement," and also describes the network of associations that Morton would continue to use to build audiences for dances. I suspect that this reportage may also suggest how the traveling tent shows organized engagements prior to the 1930s. It seems logical that they had probably developed similar networks of local entrepreneurs to assure profitable tours.

In stories concerning the Calloway engagements, Morton is described as one of the "Kings." Three men in Charleston were also part of this consortium: Leroy "Tex" Fonteneau, C. W. Hart, and Dr. T. L. Mitchell. Fonteneau's name crops up repeatedly in newspaper reports in the late 1930s and early 1940s as a nightclub operator and occasional booker of touring bands for dances in Charleston. Of the others, the newspaper record says nothing. There were also "Kings" in Bluefield (Dr. J. Ernest Martin) and in Welch (J. A. Shelton). Unknown is whether James A. West, Samuel Carpenter, or others known to book bands in Fairmont were ever members of this group, or whether Morton worked with them simply on an ad hoc basis when he was notified of an open date on a band's tour that might be profitably filled by an engagement in the northern coalfield.

Fig. 7.2. The county seats (in bold) and satellite communities in which resided associates of George Morton who advertised dances and sold tickets for them. (West Virginia University–University Relations–Design)

Coverage of the Calloway benefit dances also reveals a second layer of activity: the sale of tickets for dances in communities surrounding the county seats where the engagements took place. Four businesses in the city sold tickets for the June 8 dance at the Charleston armory, of which two were pharmacies. Unidentified locations in Williamson, Logan, Montgomery, and Huntington also sold tickets. To buy tickets to the dance in Bluefield on June 11 (Calloway had jumped from Charleston to Columbus, Ohio, for another benefit on June 10 before heading to Bluefield), one could go to Kingslow's Drug Store in town; those who resided near the McDowell County communities of Keystone, Kimball, or Gary could get tickets from Sam Wade, C. F. Shelton (possibly the son of J. A. Shelton of Welch), and R. L. Robertson, respectively. For the Beckley dance on June 12, Morton's Drug Store was the place to go, the business owned by George Morton's father, in addition to unidentified locations in Mount Hope and Hinton. That drug stores sold tickets suggests that Morton made use of his father's professional connections to establish this group of local vendors (*PC* 6.1.35,

2/8). Their use also reminds us that in the past many of these businesses served as neighborhood social centers because their soda fountains and associated food service brought members of the community together.

The coverage of the Hines and Calloway engagements of April and June 1935 begins to form a picture of a network of entrepreneurs covering both the southern and northern coalfields, which George Morton would activate upon getting word from New York that a tour was being put together that would come through West Virginia. It is summarized in Table 7.1 below and illustrated by Figure 7.2.

This network clearly served Morton well in his role as middleman booking name bands for multiple engagements in the southern part of the state, usually including one in Beckley, and less regularly facilitating a gig up north in Fairmont, leaving his contacts to make local arrangements in their respective communities. Frances Flippen recalled that her brother worked more or less exclusively with Joe Glaser, one of the principal managers of black bands in the nation in the course of his association first with the Rockwell-O'Keefe agency, later as head of Associated Booking Artists. In that capacity Glaser managed a number of black bands, including those led by Louis Armstrong, Andy Kirk, and Lionel Hampton.

In his study of the music industry during the 1930s, *Swing Changes: Big Band Jazz in New Deal America,* David W. Stowe described Glaser as one of several managers who, in effect, "served as gatekeepers of the venues and media [and] who enabled swing to become a national phenomenon of popular culture" (Stowe 1994, 103). In West Virginia, George Morton effectively unlocked the "gate" to enable black Mountaineers to gain access to swing. As of June 12, 1937, his organization was known as Universal Promoters, consisting undoubtedly of many, if not all, of the Kings of Amusement who, residing in other coalfield communities, handled local arrangements in their own towns (*PC* 6.12.37, 22).

While Glaser was his principal New York contact, when the opportunity presented itself Morton was also prepared to book bands not under Glaser's control. For example, he booked Chick Webb and his Savoy Swing Orchestra with Ella Fitzgerald for a dance in Huntington sponsored by the West Virginia State College Club at the Vanity Fair on June 12, 1937 (*PC* 6.12.37). Webb was managed by Moe Gale, who also owned the Savoy Ballroom in Harlem (Stowe 1994, 103). Morton also arranged engagements for Jimmie Lunceford's Harlem Express (*PC* 3.25.39), Myron "Tiny" Bradshaw's Orchestra (*PC* 9.24.38), and a band based in Miami led by Hartley Toots (*PC* 3.18.39).

Working for Joe Glaser was always something of a gamble, because he demanded a fixed fee for each engagement by one of his bands. No commonwealth principle was in operation as was the case with Joe Oliver's Band or Jimmie Lunceford's, in which each musician got a percentage of the gate regardless of the number of attendees. If for some reason, Morton or one of his associates could not attract a sufficiently large crowd for a dance, that individual was responsible for making up the difference.

Not only did Morton organize successive engagements in the Mountain State, he also oversaw the dances that took place in his hometown. For each of these he had to rent a venue and see to advertising. Such locations in and around Beckley included, in addition to the city's armory, the gymnasium of DuBois High School in nearby Mount Hope as well as the armory located there, and the Rose Garden Inn, a local nightclub that he rented for several dances over the years.

To promote these engagements, while the *Raleigh Register* and the *Beckley Post-Herald* might have seemed logical places to publish notices of upcoming dances, Morton adopted what was apparently more reliable, cost-effective, and informal strategies for spreading the word. His younger sister recalled that he advertised by using "placards in windows of stores and barbershop . . . and handbills, and placards they would nail on telegraph poles." Some of those placards were placed in the windows of businesses that also sold tickets to the dances. Such advertising no doubt led to word-of-mouth communication within and between black communities as well (Flippen 2005). Similar strategies were no doubt employed by his partners in the other towns for which he engaged bands. One consequence is that there was little, if any, notice taken in the local press, despite the fact that hundreds turned out for these events; thus, for the historian the *Pittsburgh Courier* serves as the primary source of information.

Another part of the local arrangements concerned making overnight accommodations for the band members. Hotels owned and operated by black West Virginians included the Travelers' Hotel in Bluefield; the Ferguson Hotel in Charleston; and Capehart's Hotel in Welch, which, incidentally, was owned and operated by Hugh J. Capehart, the same McDowell County member of the House of Delegates of the State of West Virginia who had overseen passage in 1921 of the anti-lynching bill discussed earlier. Fairmont, in the northern coalfield, offered accommodations at Rowles's Restaurant and Hotel (Belmear 2000). In other communities including Beckley, band members had to be lodged with local families. There, the Mortons' home was one of those that accommodated traveling musicians.

Table 7.2. Bands booked by George Morton for engagements in West Virginia between April 9, 1935, and February 6, 1940

Band	City	Date
Earl "Fatha" Hines	Beckley	April 9, 1935
Cab Calloway	Charleston	June 8, 1935
	Bluefield	June 11, 1935
	Beckley	June 12, 1935
Don Albert	Beckley	November 15, 1935
Ruth Ellington	Beckley	January 1, 1936
Thomas "Fats" Waller	Wheeling	February 5, 1936
	Logan	February 6, 1936
	Bluefield	February 7, 1936
	Charleston	February 8, 1936
Earl "Fatha" Hines	Charleston	May 30, 1936
Don Redman	Beckley	June 1, 1936
	Logan	June 2, 1936
	Welch	June 3, 1936
Louis Armstrong with Luis Russell's Orchestra	Charleston	September 19, 1936
[Band unidentified]	Beckley	October 10, 1936
Andy Kirk	Charleston	December 26, 1936
	Beckley	December 28, 1936
	Bluefield	December 29, 1936
Fletcher Henderson	Charleston	February 6, 1937
"Fats" Waller in a battle with Jimmy Raschel	Charleston	April 24, 1937
Jimmy Raschel	Beckley	April 26, 1937
Chick Webb with Ella Fitzgerald	Huntington	June 12, 1937
"Fats" Waller	Beckley	August 28, 1937
Andy Kirk	Charleston	October 16, 1937
Don Redman	Charleston	October 30, 1937
Lil (Harden) Armstrong	Mount Hope	November 29, 1937
Count Basie	Huntington	March 26, 1938
	Mount Hope	March 28, 1938
	Bluefield	March 29, 1938
Chick Webb with Ella Fitzgerald	Bluefield	July 5, 1938
	Beckley	July 6, 1938

Band	City	Date
Hartley Toots in a battle with Lucky Millinder	Charleston	September 3, 1938
Hartley Toots	Mount Hope	September 5, 1938
	Welch	September 7, 1938
"Tiny" Bradshaw	Charleston	September 24, 1938
Jimmie Lunceford	Charleston	March 25, 1939
	Mount Hope	March 27, 1939
	Bluefield	March 28, 1939
	Fairmont	March 29, 1939
Hartley Toots	Charleston	April 8, 1939
	Mount Hope	April 10, 1939
Andy Kirk	Charleston	September 16, 1939
	Mount Hope	September 18, 1939
Roy Eldridge	Charleston	November 4, 1939
Don Redman	Charleston	December 30, 1939

It was essential to the entire enterprise that close attention be paid to the receipts for each dance. The fixed fees had to be paid before Morton could earn any income. Frances Flippen recalled that when she worked for her brother, her job was to sell tickets and track receipts for dances in Beckley because her brother trusted only her with the cash (Flippen 2005).

In the four years and ten months that George Morton booked black bands for engagements in the Mountain State, directly or indirectly, he was responsible for at least forty-six dances as documented in the *Pittsburgh Courier*. Table 7.2 identifies the bands that performed, the towns in which they played, and the dates on which they did so.

This list does not necessarily include all of the occasions for which Morton booked bands, only those in which coverage in the *Courier* cited him as promoter. The newspaper also published reports of engagements of bands that he had often booked that took place in the same communities and in the same venues with which he was associated. In these instances, however, the paper did not identify him as the organizer. Thus these forty-six engagements do not necessarily encompass all of his booking activities. No other individual came close to George Morton in linking black Mountaineers to the music of the national bands that defined the Swing Era of jazz history.

Morton's death was reported in the February 10, 1940, issue of the *Courier* by a captioned photograph as well as a short article that stated that his younger sister would take over the work of Universal Promoters. That turned out to be unfounded speculation; the business died with him (Flippen 2005). The article also listed some of those who had sent floral offerings to his funeral. They included, among others, bandleaders he had booked and their managers: Cab Calloway, Jimmie Lunceford and his manager Harold Oxley, Count Basie, Joe Glaser, Moe Gale, as well as William G. Nunn of the *Courier*, who may well have attended the service and filed the story (*PC* 2.10.40, 20).

Beyond uniting the southern coalfields of the Mountain State with the national African American culture of big band jazz and dance music, Morton's business acumen created a network of venues and the routes that name bands would continue to use after his death. In June 1940 Erskine Hawkins played an engagement in Charleston on the 22nd, followed by another in Mount Hope on the 24th before heading east to play a dance in Richmond, Virginia, on the 25th (*PC* 6.15.40, 21). Departing Charlottesville on July 18, 1940, the International Sweethearts of Rhythm played in White Sulphur Springs, West Virginia, on the 19th, Beckley on the 22nd, Logan on the 25th, Bluefield on the 26th, and Charleston on the 27th (*PC* 7.13.40, 21). In 1941 the bands of Jimmie Lunceford, Tiny Bradshaw, and Ella Fitzgerald would follow through the southern part of the state the well-beaten paths upon which George Morton had relied in organizing engagements (*PC* 1.4.41, 18; 3.22.41, 21; 4.12.41, 21).

No single individual emerged to replace Morton as regional booker for the southern coalfields. Bands continued to come but were apparently engaged by entrepreneurs residing in the towns where the dances were to take place. Perhaps one legacy of his work was that the New York managers who before had worked through him now were content to contact multiple individuals, each in a different coalfield town, who had become well known thanks to George Morton.

Dance Promoters in Fairmont

There were far fewer black Mountaineers living in the northern coalfield during the 1930s than further south. The census of 1940 noted that roughly 85,500 of approximately 114,000 African Americans residing in West Virginia, fully three-quarters of them, resided in Kanawha, McDowell, and

Raleigh counties. In the three counties of the northern field (Harrison, Marion, and Monongalia) lived fewer than ten percent of that number: 8,366 (*Sixteenth Census*, 40–43). Clearly, the black audience for big bands was far more dispersed in the northern part of the state, as evidenced by the distances people traveled to attend dances in Fairmont, seat of Marion County and the most frequent stop for national bands.

Coverage of Fairmont engagements in the *Courier* took two forms: reports written at the newspaper based on promotional materials from New York managers, and references in weekly news columns written by one or another of the residents of the town's black community. Some of these columns provided useful information concerning the numbers who turned out for a dance and from where they had traveled to attend.

There was no single dance promoter in Fairmont, no equivalent to George Morton. Several men tried their hands at booking bands at different times during the 1930s and early 1940s: Samuel Carpenter, Clarence Lee, Vernon Morrow, Charles "Turk" Nelson, Charles Saunders, James W. West, and Yancey Whittaker. Whittaker was the only one reported to have collaborated with Morton's Universal Promoters, bringing Jimmie Lunceford to Fairmont on March 29, 1939, as part of a series of engagements in the Mountain State (*PC* 3.25.39, 21). A group of individuals known only as "the Nighthawks," which may have included one or more of those cited above, was active in for a short time in 1934.

The recollections of Samuel Carpenter's daughter Geraldine Carpenter Belmear provide useful information concerning her father's activities as a sometime booker as well as Fairmont's black community and the audiences that attended dances at that time. Her parents moved to Fairmont from Lynchburg, Virginia, around 1920. Her father worked as a bellhop in the Fairmont Hotel until sometime in 1937, for a time found work in Pittsburgh, and returned to Fairmont in 1940 first to work at a white country club and later as a bailiff in the federal courthouse (Belmear 2000).

Carpenter booked bands in the hope of adding to the family income, reportedly having become aware that elsewhere in the state local entrepreneurs were organizing dances and thereby earning additional money. He was not the first in Fairmont to bring in a national band; the unidentified promoter responsible for the Jimmie Lunceford engagement of September 18, 1934, preceded him. The first name band that Carpenter booked for a dance was Noble Sissle's on July 3, 1935 (*PC* 6.29.35, 2/10).

Belmear recalled that her father had had to persuade the authorities in charge of the armory to allow him to hold a dance for the black community there. Perhaps because of their numbers, the approximately 700 attendees of the Lunceford engagement had disconcerted the white community. Among his arguments may have been the fact that the local black Elks club, the Elks Rest, where several bands had played (including King Oliver's just six nights after the Lunceford dance), was too small to accommodate what would probably be a large crowd, thus perhaps leading to even more problems for Fairmont's white folk than would the black community's use of the armory (Belmear 2000).

Samuel Carpenter's promotional strategies were similar to Morton's. Because he knew his potential audience to be widely dispersed, he began by writing to associates in communities both near and far who could be counted upon to post notices of a dance in barbershops, the meeting places of social organizations such as Elks Lodges, and in Methodist churches. Like Morton, Carpenter distributed posters to businesses in various locations at which tickets could be purchased.

The geographically dispersed audience used various means of transportation, some public, others private, to converge upon Fairmont's armory. About twenty-five miles southeast of the town was Grafton, seat of Taylor County, located on the Baltimore & Ohio Railroad. There were few black miners in Taylor County, but the railroad employed a great many African Americans, mostly as track liners. Dancers from Grafton could take the B&O #35 which departed daily at 7:15 p.m. and arrived in Fairmont at 8:10 p.m. around the time a dance would begin. To return, they would have to leave dances before what was typically a 2:00 a.m. conclusion so as to catch #54/16, which departed for Grafton (and ultimately New York City) at 1:35 a.m. If they missed that train, the next one did not leave until 5:00 a.m. Those coming from Clarksburg to the south or Morgantown to the north could take an inter-urban line. Those from further east, including residents of Piedmont and Keyser, West Virginia, and Cumberland, Maryland, would travel by car; usually a minimum of two vehicles would convoy together over the ridges of the Allegheny Mountains. Given the terrain encountered and the slow speeds that it imposed, these folks probably did not get home until dawn, assuming they did not spend the night in Fairmont before heading back (Belmear 2000).

Opportunities to book touring bands were widely separated because Fairmont was not on one of the well-established routes through the central Appalachians. It was comparatively close to Pittsburgh, and bands that performed in Fairmont usually did so by detouring away from the east-west routes that ran through or at least close to that city. The *Courier*'s coverage confirms Belmear's memory that her father organized just four dances in an eighteen-month period beginning with Sissle's engagement in the summer of 1935. Ruth Ellington's Orchestra performed at the armory on December 26 of that year. Andy Kirk Twelve Clouds of Joy may well have sold out the armory on October 24, 1936.

Disaster struck the night of December 25, 1936, when Zack Whyte and His Chocolate Beau Brummels from Cincinnati failed to appear at the Fairmont armory to play for what was reportedly a crowd of more than 1,000 dancers. Under the headline "Zach Whyte Disappoints W. Va. Crowd," the *Courier* noted: "Carpenter, who had advanced a deposit, had booked the band for the holiday night, following another engagement in Akron, O., on Christmas Eve. Zack and his orchestra disappointed promoters in both spots . . . arriving in Akron, it is alleged, too late for the engagement and then returning to Cincinnati." The story closed by stating that "Just what action Carpenter will take to collect his deposit has not been ascertained" (*PC* 1.2.37, 2/6).

The financial outcome of this disaster is not known, but it marked the end of Samuel Carpenter's activities as a dance promoter. His daughter recalled that Charles Saunders would be the next to take a turn at booking bands for the black community, though it was not until early in the summer of 1941 that Saunders is reported to have booked first Count Basie and then Andy Kirk to play in the armory (Belmear 2000; *PC* 6.28.41).

The work of George Morton, Samuel Carpenter, and other black Mountaineers whose entrepreneurial spirit led them into the booking business was essential to establishing and maintaining the culture of big band jazz and dance music in West Virginia. By linking the big bands of the North to an audience in the central Appalachians, they cultivated a new fan base and simultaneously extended the reach and influence of the music industry into a part of the country that had previously been far more reliant on its own musical resources than it would ever be again. From the perspective of the big bands, these men made essential contributions to their success by creating new opportunities to perform directly for their fans along that part of "the road" that was the Mountain State.

CHAPTER EIGHT

The Big Bands' Audience in the Mountain State

We know where dances were held and who was responsible for getting the bands to those venues. But who danced to the music of the black name bands of the period in West Virginia, and what did they hear? First, we must examine the available evidence concerning the identity of the potential audience based on what can be determined about the larger African American population of the coalfields.

Dances not organized by a local promoter, such as George Morton or one of his associates, were put on by a variety of organizations. This included social clubs such as Les Precieuses, made up of women residing in McDowell County who sponsored a Colonial Garden party on May 7, 1937, in Kimball, a community located on U.S. Route 52 and the Norfolk & Western Railway approximately halfway between Bluefield and Welch. Edward Watkins and his Harlem Hotshots, a band based in Bluefield, provided the music (*PC* 5.15.37, 21). In February 1936 the Tuxedo Club of Charleston held a dance highlighted by "a 'Truckin' Contest' . . . to the winners of which cash prizes will be awarded." Jimmie Lunceford's Orchestra played that engagement, having been booked by one of the Kings of Amusement associated with George Morton (*PC* 1.25.36, 2/6). Alumni organizations associated with Bluefield State and West Virginia State Colleges put on dances. In the autumn months these were usually held in conjunction with football games. In July 1934 the Indianapolis-based band led by "Speed" Webb played a dance at the armory in Logan, seat of Logan County, that concluded a convention of a fledgling political organization, the Southern West Virginia Negro Democratic League. A report published in the *Logan Banner* described the crowd attending the dance as "huge" (*PC* 7.14.24, 1/5; *LB* 7.20.34, 20). It is safe to assume that many of the members of these various organizations constituted a portion of the black middle class of the Mountain State.

The Black Middle Class and the Promotion of Dances

Happily, it is possible to go beyond the level of social organizations to that of individuals, thanks in large part to evidence found within the enumerators' sheets of the U.S. Census of 1930. Additional information in some instances appears in one or another of the biannual city directories of major cities in West Virginia published by R. L. Polk of Pittsburgh. What follows is a series of thumbnail sketches of men and women previously mentioned in this study who actively participated in staging dances for black Mountaineers.

The first group to be considered are the five Kings of Amusement affiliated with George Morton, along with three of their associates located in smaller communities. The first documented collaboration of these individuals resulted in a series of benefit dances on behalf of black American Legion posts in the summer of 1935 for which Cab Calloway's band provided music (*PC* 3.30.35, 2/9). As noted earlier, three members of this consortium resided in Charleston.

The first was LeRoy Fonteneau, a native of Louisiana and age twenty-three in 1930 according to the census, which also indicated that he worked as an insurance agent and lived with his wife, Thelma, and two-year-old daughter, Audrey, in the home of Thelma's parents, Elliott and Elizabeth Dabney. Thelma had been born in Illinois, her parents in North Carolina and Virginia respectively, facts reminding us that many black Mountaineers had recently immigrated from elsewhere in the country. In 1936, according *Polk's Charleston City Directory*, Fonteneau clerked at a bookstore. By December 1938, sporting the nickname "Tex" and described in a report in the *Pittsburgh Courier* as an "energetic promoter and wide-awake business man," he opened the Alhambra Nightclub in the basement of the Ferguson Hotel at 1000 Washington Street, both establishments catering to African Americans. Cal Grear's Sweet Swing Orchestra was the club's house band for at least the first two months of operation (*PC* 12.17.38, 12). Fonteneau continued to manage the nightclub at least through November 1941, possibly longer (*PC* 11.15.41, 21).

The second Amusement King residing in Charleston was also a businessman. Since at least 1934, Dr. Thomas L. Mitchell was co-owner with

Leo M. Solomon of the M&S Pharmacy, 1000 Washington Street, next door to the Ferguson Hotel (*Polk's Charleston City Directory 1936*, 374). Previously, he had worked as a pharmacist for one George H. Willis, owner of the Gem Pharmacy, which had been located less than a block from the site of his future business at 912 Washington. Of C. W. Hart, the third of the Charleston group, little is known except that he was a clerk in the state auditor's office and thus a civil servant *(Polk's Charleston City Directory 1936,* 258).

The two remaining Amusement Kings resided in Welch and Bluefield respectively. Much like those of Fonteneau and Mitchell in Charleston, James Shelton's profession as a teacher in one of McDowell County's black public schools and James Martin's practice in dentistry in Bluefield enlarge our perspective on the African American middle class in the southern coalfields. Shelton, born in Kentucky in 1896 and thus thirty-four at the time of the 1930 census, resided in Welch, was married, and had two children. His wife was a native of the Mountain State (U.S. Bureau of the Census, "Fifteenth Census of the United States 1930—Population Schedule," West Virginia, MacDowell County, Enumerator District 24-23, Sheet 32A, lines 18–19). A dentist who had opened his practice in 1928 at 725½ Bland Street in Bluefield, James Ernest Martin, age 33 in 1930, was originally from Massachusetts (Rankin, 13). He and his wife, Bernice, born in 1903 in Virginia, lived over the business (1930 Census, Mercer County, Enumerator District 28-10, Sheet 18A, lines 20–21; *Polk's Bluefield City Directory 1936,* 149).

Three other individuals associated with the Amusement Kings but not included within the group were C. F. Shelton of Kimball, Sam Wade of Northfork, and Robert L. Robinson of Gary, communities east and south of Welch in McDowell County. Kimball and Northfork were not company towns but were surrounded by mining operations, each having its own resident labor force. On the other hand, Gary was a company town, its mines producing coal for United States Steel.

What Clarence F. Shelton, age 18 in 1930, did for a living could not be determined, but he was the son of James Shelton, Welch's Amusement King, and thus his ties to the group of promoters is clear. Sam Wade, 43, was employed as a teamster for an unidentified company in the 1930 census (1930 Census, MacDowell County, Enumerator District 24-41, Sheet 22B, line 38). Robert L. Robinson, 35, was a constable, the equivalent of a deputy sheriff in West Virginia law, for the Adkins Magisterial District of McDowell County (1930 Census, MacDowell County, Enumerator District

24-2, Sheet 26B, line 38). One who "keeps peace," which was how Constable Robinson described his work to the census enumerator, would surely know almost everyone in the vicinity of Gary and thus would be useful in promoting a dance to members of that community. Not knowing for whom Sam Wade worked, we are left to assume that his knowledge of the coal towns in the vicinity of Northfork and their residents enabled him to assist the Amusement Kings in promoting dances.

Three of the founders of the previously mentioned Les Precieuses women's club were included in the 1930 census which revealed that all three were teachers in one or another of McDowell County's black schools. Beatrice Crider of Kimball, 27 in 1930, was married to Douglas, 30, the owner of a clothes pressing shop. Incidentally, next door lived Samuel Crider, age 62 and apparently a widower, along with his daughter Ella, age 32, and two children whose ages were 10 and 8. That Mr. Crider was a justice of the peace is further evidence of the active role that black Mountaineers played in the social institutions of the state (1930 Census, MacDowell County, Enumerator District 24-21, Sheet 14A, lines 33–38). Ardelia Carter, 45, and her husband Bassett, 60, were both public schoolteachers in Kimball (1930 Census, MacDowell County, Enumerator District 24-21, Sheet 4B, lines 81–82). Lena Watkins, the youngest of the three at 23 supported her seventy-year-old father and fifty-eight-year-old mother as a teacher, the family residing in Northfork (1930 Census, MacDowell County, Enumerator District 24-43, Sheet 18A, lines 41–43).

Backgrounds of other fans of the black dance bands can also be sketched out from the 1930 census. Talitha G. Saunders, 30, a resident of the Winding Gulf company town in 1932 when she sang the praises of Noble Sissle in a letter the *Courier*, had previously lived in Mabscott, like Winding Gulf located in Raleigh County; her husband Robert, 33, was mining coal there as he would in Winding Gulf. The Saunders had a four-year-old daughter, Karen (*PC* 10.15.32, 2/1; 1930 Census, Raleigh County, Enumerator District 41-19, Sheet 3B, lines 98–100). Their move to Winding Gulf may have been prompted by closure of the Mabscott operation, perhaps because it had mined all the coal in the property it had leased.

Ernest Owens—who, as reported in the *Courier*, held a "radio party" for friends in his Fairmont home in September 1934 with music provided by broadcasts of bands led by Noble Sissle, Wayne King, and Claude Hopkins—shined shoes for a living at the time of the 1930 census when he was just 18 and, along with his older brother Floyd, a barber age 36, supported their mother. The family had moved to West Virginia from Tennessee

(1930 Census, Marion County, Enumerator District 25-7, Sheet 12B, lines 90–92). Richard Moore, another Fairmont resident and one of two men who the *Courier* reported had traveled to Charleston in August 1934 to hear Cab Calloway's band, was working as a chauffeur for a private family in 1930. Twenty-four years old, he lived with his father, a barber, his mother, a younger sister, as well as a lodger; the latter two individuals were teachers (1930 Census, Marion County, Enumerator District 25-8, Sheet 15B, lines 93–97).

Taken together, most of the people discussed thus far were members of the black middle class in the Mountain State: teachers, owners of small businesses, and employees of either state or local government. While these folks may not be entirely representative of the population as a whole, nevertheless the information associated with each contributes to our understanding of both the diversity of salaried employment available to African Americans in the coalfields and of the active role middle-class African Americans played in advancing the cause of big band jazz and dance music in West Virginia.

The Working-Class Black Community of Price Hill, West Virginia

By far the largest proportion of the audience for big band jazz and dance music among black Mountaineers were miners and their families: the working-class fans of the dance bands. Despite their numbers, however, these are the individuals least easily documented. They mostly exist as statistics in the *Annual Report of the* [West Virginia] *Department of Mines* through 1933. They stare out of photographs by "Red" Ribble and others hired to document the workers at various coal mines, though no captions attach names to faces. Apart from anecdotes of descendants concerning one or another individual, their lives are undocumented, save for census data.

Already discussed was the nature of the work of a typical miner's work during the Depression. Having argued that their relative prosperity following the implementation of the Bituminous Coal Code in the fall of 1933 created the economic conditions in which big band jazz could flourish in the coalfields of the Mountain State, it seems appropriate to examine what evidence there is that can shed light on the individual lives of some of those men. After all, it was their collective decision to devote discretionary income to attend dances that encouraged black bands to tour the state with considerable regularity.

In chapter 2 I discussed the connections between the work of the coal miner and local promoters, such as George Morton, in booking bands to play in the coalfields to the evidence of the earnings of one touring band, that led by Joe "King" Oliver, that validated the assertion by Herb Hall that black bands came regularly to West Virginia "because the mines were working . . . and everyone was employed."

While some readers may wonder at the reliability of an analysis of such a limited source of information as the census enumerator's sheets for the black residents of a single coal company town, there would seem to be little reason to suspect great variance in places of origin, age range, and family structure among the thousands of black miners at work in hundreds of mines scattered throughout the coalfields. Most came from the same states, Virginia primarily, and most had similar motivations for doing so: the promise of regular wages that would support a wife and one or more children in comparative comfort, especially when a mining family's standard of living was compared to that of the sharecropper's life that many left behind. For these reasons, I believe, we can gain insight into the lives of the working-class majority of the African American audience for the big bands in the Mountain State by looking at the black community embedded within the company town of Price Hill, West Virginia, located in northern Raleigh County.

There are several reasons for choosing this community. First, we have photographic evidence of the presence of black miners in the work force. Second, the community is less than two miles from Mount Hope, the location of both a National Guard armory and the gymnasium of DuBois High School, in both of which George Morton put on dances. Among the bands that played there were those led by Lil Hardin Armstrong (November 29, 1937), Count Basie (March 28, 1938), Hartley Toots (September 5, 1938, and April 10, 1939), and Jimmie Lunceford (March 27, 1939). The distance from Price Hill to Beckley was about eight miles. Beckley was the site of ten dances for which bands were booked by Morton, beginning with the first dance he ever promoted: the Earl "Fatha" Hines engagement of April 9, 1935. Thus, there would seem little reason to believe that those residents of Price Hill who wanted to attend dances faced significant obstacles to doing so. It is impossible to determine which individuals from this town went to dances or the number of dances they might have attended, but it is certainly reasonable to suppose that among those turning out to hear the bands booked by George Morton in Mount Hope and Beckley were residents of Price Hill. Who might they have been?

On April 4 and 5, 1930, Roscoe Williams, employed as an enumerator for the 1930 census, made his way along Oswald Road in Price Hill, stopping at each house to record by hand a variety of data about each resident: name, status within the household (head, wife, son or daughter, lodger, etc.), gender, age, race, marital status, place of birth, place of parents' births, whether employed or not, the occupation of the employed, and the industry in which that work was done.

As noted earlier and typical of company towns, the black population was more or less segregated from the whites. For some reason, Charlie Canko and his wife, natives of Czechoslovakia, resided in a house within the otherwise black neighborhood, perhaps a matter of convenience for the company which had a vacant house to rent at the time the Cankos needed housing. Apart from them, one sees immediately from Mr. Williams's documentation a succession of homes occupied by African Americans at the end of which the race of residents changes to white.

A total of forty-two black families resided along Oswald Road. Almost all of the men worked as miners, the exception being Lyman Leveret, a janitor in a public school. Almost all were married, and many supported not only their spouses but several children. Most of the men were in their thirties or forties, and most had been born in either West Virginia, Virginia, or North Carolina. The following seven miners and their families were in many respects representative of the black community of Price Hill, and therefore probably typical of the working-class African American Mountaineers who attended dances featuring the big bands of the period.

We begin with Major Green, age 38, a native of North Carolina, whose wife Ruby, age 30, was a native of West Virginia. The Greens had three young daughters: Annie (age 4), Minnie (3), and Mildred (1). Two houses away lived Sam Scott, age 40, originally from Virginia; his wife Roma, 24, also from the Old Dominion; and their six-year-old son, Hobart. A young, probably newlywed couple lived next door: Thomas and Lola Perkins, both from Virginia. He was 18, and she was 16. Odell and Rosa Byrd lived in the next house. He was from South Carolina, and she had been born in Virginia. Mr. Byrd was 42, his spouse 32. Their daughter, Mary, was ten years old. Next to the Byrds resided Price and Stella Massey, ages 50 and 49 respectively. Both were natives of Virginia (1930 Census, Raleigh County, Enumerator District 41-23, Sheet 4A, lines 31–45).

Coal company houses were not large. Down the road from the Byrds lived the Gains family, for whom space was surely at a premium. Walter,

36, and his wife Lucy, 30, he from Virginia, she from West Virginia, were rearing six children, three daughters: Virgie, Jettie, and Fannie, ages 14, 11, and 5, and three sons: Walter Jr., John, and Lawrence, ages 8, 7, and 2, in a house that may have had no more than four rooms (1930 Census, Raleigh County, Enumerator District 41-23, Sheet 3B, lines 91–98).

Henry and Estella Brooks, both in their 30s, had it a bit easier. In addition to their three children: Leroy, age 6, and twins Isadora and Henry [Jr.] who were not quite 2 on the day the census taker came to call, residing with them was Mr. Brooks's seventeen-year-old niece, Mary E. Brooks. Perhaps she was there to help with the twins (930 Census, Raleigh County, Enumerator District 41-23, Sheet 14A, lines 23–28). While more of the forty-one black miners and their families who lived in Price Hill could be discussed, these individuals seem representative of the entire group in terms of age as well as marital and family status.

Were any of these men among the thirteen black miners who appeared in Red Ribble's panoramic photo of the afternoon shift at the Price Hill Colliery Company's operation taken sometime in 1931? We may never know for certain, though the fact that both the census of 1930 and the photo of the following year occurred in the darkest days of the Depression when jobs were scarce and money was tight would support the idea that most, if not all, of the Price Hill miners documented in the census would have still been on the job the following year if they could help it, particularly those with families to feed and house. Judging from annual reports published by West Virginia's Department of Mines, the last year of the Price Hill operation was 1938; there are no references to it subsequently (*Annual Report of the Department of Mines: 1938*, 46–47, 86–87). With the labor agreements of 1933 and their subsequent renewals ensuring higher wages than previously, it is reasonable to suppose that many of these families remained there until operations ceased.

Like Red Ribble's photograph, this discussion provides but a snapshot of the African American world of the southern coalfields of the Mountain State. That world was populated by men and women of similar background who at the same time reveal a rather wide array of occupations and, implicitly, levels of education. What they obviously shared in common was their race, and many of them also shared an interest in social dancing. What remains to be explored in detail is the nature of their collective taste in dance music. As has been argued in earlier chapters, that taste embraced a variety of styles of dance music. The evidence that bands catered to that variety and the music that enabled them to do so is the topic of the next chapter.

CHAPTER NINE

The Dance Repertory Played in the Coal Fields

In what ways does the admittedly rough sample of the black population of the southern coalfields discussed in the previous chapter—by implication an equally rough sample of those likely to attend dances—shed light on the variety of music which the touring bands would perform? First of all, consider the age range in 1930 of the sample. The youngest of them was Lola Perkins of Price Hill. She was just 16, thus born around 1914, and was the wife of eighteen-year-old Thomas Perkins who mined coal. The oldest was the McDowell County Justice of the Peace, Samuel Crider, age 62, born around 1868.

Just as forty-six years separates the respective years of Perkins and Crider's birth, that same time period embraces a wide range of African American musical styles. Whereas Mr. Crider came of age before the advent of ragtime at the end of the nineteenth century, young Mrs. Perkins could have regarded jazz of the late 1920s as a well-established element of the American soundscape. The shared musical culture of these two would have been the variety of vernacular styles, both sacred and secular, that constituted the indigenous black musical culture of the Mountain State.

When we consider all thirty-two individuals discussed in the last chapter whose ages in 1930 were documented by the census enumerators (unfortunately, no data could be located for two of the Kings of Amusement: C. W. Hart or Thomas L. Mitchell, both of Charleston), the following facts come to light. First, the average age of this cohort is thirty-three years and five months. Second, the vast majority were in their thirties at the time of the census; the rest were distributed as follows: six were in their twenties, five in their forties, four in their teens, two in their sixties, and one was fifty years old.

What do these data suggest about the nature of the audience for big band dance music in the decade to come? First, it must be conceded that an arbitrary sample of people from 1930, some of whom we know to have been actively cultivating an audience for this music while others constituted its potential audience, is not necessarily predictive of that audience five and ten years later. It does suggest, nevertheless, that the musical tastes of black Mountaineers were probably broad, extending outside the realm of what has come to be defined as big band jazz, something that would appear to be even more likely as they heard a increasing variety of musical styles aired on network radio.

Moreover, as noted earlier, when we look at statements by black Mountaineers that found their way into various newspapers in the 1930s—especially the *Pittsburgh Courier* during the course of its band popularity contests and in comments send to the radio editor of that newspaper, whose weekly column informed readers of upcoming broadcasts by black bands—the extent of the variation in preferences for dance music becomes clearer.

In October 1932, as previously noted, Talitha G. Saunders let the *Courier* know that "Noble Sissle and his international orchestra are to my way of thinking superior to all the rest. He is my ideal and is appreciated most because of his ultra rhythmic syncopation that is so sweet and hot" (*PC* 10.15.32, 2/1). Her sentiments were echoed by Gladys Mike of Wheeling who wrote to say that "I think that Noble Sissle has the only Negro band on the radio that can compare with my great favorite, Guy Lombardo. His band has tone, harmony, volume, and sweetness; in fact, everything to make an excellent orchestra. He has certainly made a hit with me" (*PC* 10.29.32, 1/5). Members of two fraternal organizations on the campus of West Virginia State College held a Snow Fest on December 7, 1935, for which, according to a reporter for the student newspaper, the *Yellow Jacket*, "Elmer Anderson and his Rhythm Kings played sweet music for the lovely dancers" (*YJ* 12.21.35, 3).

In contrast, a letter sent to Allan Eckstein, radio editor of the *Courier*, staked out territory at some distance from the domain of sweet music. A self-described "regular radio maniac" wrote that, while he was always happy to hear the bands led by "Fatha" Hines, Don Redman, Cab Calloway, and Noble Sissle, "if you want to give me an idea of Paradise kindly let me have an occasional idea of the whereabouts of the incomparable Duke Ellington, the renowned Fletcher Henderson, and the one and only

McKinney's Cotton Pickers . . . these three constitute the radio world's idea of heaven" (*PC* 12/20/32, 2/1).

Hardly surprising should be the fact that music associated with social events attracting a variety of people would reflect a variety of stylistic preferences. At West Virginia State College, a dramatic club known as the Mimes "danced to the familiar tunes of Duke Ellington, Guy Lombardo, Chick Webb and many other popular bands" on December 16, 1938 (*YJ* 12.21.38, 3). One may infer that those "familiar tunes" were probably played on recordings. Previously mentioned was a radio party in Fairmont late in August 1934, hosted by Ernest Owens. As reported in the *Courier*, the broadcasts were of bands led respectively by Noble Sissle, Wayne King, and Claude Hopkins (*PC* 9.1.34, 2/6).

What are the implications for the music played for black Mountaineers by the black name bands? It seems clear that those bands must have played in a variety of styles ranging along a continuum from hot, uptempo jazz at one end to sweet, "mellow" dance music at the other. For reasons to be discussed below, it also appears probable that in the period under discussion, touring dance bands played their most diverse repertories on the road, including during engagements in West Virginia.

Consider the four types of settings in which dance bands performed in the 1930s and early 1940s: first, location jobs in northern big-city hotels and ballrooms; second, sponsored or sustaining radio programs often emanating from those hotels; third, the recording studio; and, finally, engagements played on tour. Each had its own set of expectations for the repertory performed, some most welcome by the musicians, others less so. Of the four, it seems certain that among the most inflexible were associated with hotel ballrooms and similar venues. There the constraints on repertory and style of performance reflected the time-tested musical preferences of regular patrons combined with the ambience of the establishment, which its management was committed to maintaining.

Consider the Roosevelt Grill in the Hotel Roosevelt in New York. Beginning in 1929, this venue became, and for several decades would remain, Guy Lombardo's home base. In his autobiography, *Auld Acquaintance*, the bandleader claimed that the success of his Royal Canadians lay in the fact that "our listeners recognized the melody because we didn't dress it up with fancy embellishments. . . . We were playing for the people who demanded the melody of their favorite songs and the beat that encouraged them to dance" (Lombardo 1975, 80). In addition, the Royal Canadians had established a reputation as a quiet band even before it went to New York, which, according to Lombardo, enabled patrons " to talk or whisper to each other as they danced. . . . It is difficult to offer an endearment if you have to compete with a loud orchestra" (Lombardo 1975, 40).

Such a formula proved highly successful, and the band's popularity with the patrons of the Roosevelt led to the expectation that, when Lombardo was on tour, any band that might substitute for the Royal Canadians would adhere to the same standards. Obviously these expectations would not have been consonant with the style of a jazz band the distinctive style of which depended on the "fancy embellishments" he decried, the product of innovative arrangements and individual players' improvisations. Also to be expected was that a jazz band would typically perform at a higher volume so that those improvised solos could be heard over a noisy crowd. Benny Goodman's band did not follow Lombardo's lead, the patrons at the Roosevelt did not welcome it, and it was quickly let go (Erenberg 1998, 4).

When the fit between the audience's preferences and a band is a good one, the band can expect to settle in for a long stand. One obvious example of such a good fit brought together the dancers who patronized the Savoy Ballroom in Harlem and the band led by drummer Chick Webb. The audience was young and mostly black; the music was hot; the Lindy Hop was the dance of choice. Lewis Erenberg observed: "Chick Webb, leader of the house band, gloried in his ability to work the dancers into a frenzy with 'Stompin' at the Savoy,' 'Don't Be That Way,' 'In the Groove at the Grove,' 'Undecided,' and others" (Erenberg 1998, 111). Simply put, by fulfilling his audience's expectations, Webb's band became the major force in creating the "Home for Happy Feet" that was the Savoy and would serve as its house band for five years as a consequence.

When considering the impact of radio, what must be borne in mind is that whether a broadcast originated in a venue suitably equipped for transmission (having a "radio wire," in other words) or in a broadcast studio, a band had to accept the constraints both of time and of commercial sponsors' expectations. A thirty-minute program probably included no more than eight arrangements, few much longer than three minutes, to allow time for commercial advertisements and announcements of each number. A fifteen-minute program would require half that number. An unsponsored sustaining program might allow somewhat greater discretion as to choice of music to perform, but as a band's self-interest dictated presenting listeners—its potential audience during subsequent local engagements and on tours—with as much music as possible to curry interest in its sound and style, there, too, arrangements would be short and the style varied.

In the recording studio, the Artist and Repertory (A&R) men or other recording company executives determined what was to be recorded, just as they would determine if and when a number would be released, in how many copies, and in what regions of the country. Black bands were presumed to be recording for the "race," meaning African American fans, and blues and jazz was to many in the recording business the self-evident music to record.

Well known is the determination of Andy Kirk to break out of that stylistic straitjacket when dealing with Jack Kapp of Decca Records in 1934. Kirk, whose Twelve Clouds of Joy also included crooner Pha Terrill, wanted to record a ballad. Kapp initially rejected the idea. "What's the matter with you? You've got something good going for you. Why do you want to do what the white boys are doing?" Kapp later backed down, and when "Until the Real Thing Comes Along" was released in 1936 it was a hit with both black and white audiences (Kirk 1989, 84–86).

Only a few black bands recorded in a variety of styles along the hot-to-sweet continuum, Kirk's being one example. One of the most frequently recorded black bands, presenting a varied repertory, touring extensively, and by all accounts with great success, was Jimmie Lunceford's Orchestra. Its success was surely due in part to its ability to gratify a variety of musical preferences. As previously noted, Lunceford's band came to West Virginia nineteen times between 1934 and 1942, far more than any other band in that period.

Before looking in detail at the live music played in West Virginia by touring bands beginning with Lunceford's, it is important to consider the fourth setting in which bands performed: engagements played on the road. Here I want to review the conditions encountered in the Mountain State. First, there were few permanent venues; most dances were staged in armories and other multi-use spaces. Each dance therefore was a product of the local booker's initiative, the diverse audience's musical tastes, and the repertory of the band that came to play. A vision of regular patronage by people whose musical preferences were well known, as would have been the case in the venues of the big cities, did not apply here. Second, the majority of black bands were playing for a percentage of the gate, not a fixed fee, and thus were obviously interested in attracting the largest crowd possible. In those instances where bands had been guaranteed a fixed fee, the local entrepreneur had a major interest in gratifying the tastes of as many attendees as possible to ensure a large attendance and thus more revenue.

Engagements on tours held the promise of a far greater return than did the location jobs in New York where bands were contracted for fixed weekly wages often so low they were in effect working at a loss. In "The Dance Band Business: A Study in Black and White," published in *Harper's Magazine* in June 1941, Irving Kolodin drew on the testimony of an unidentified bandleader in observing that:

> a struggling pianist can no more hope to make money by a Carnegie Hall recital than a bandleader can add directly to his savings by an engagement in a New York hotel. As one of them sadly remarked not long ago: "We opened at the Pennsylvania [Hotel] last fall with an $8,500 pay roll to meet. We got $2,500 a week from the hotel for the job that took most of the time." It was the total of his earnings from radio and recording contracts that made it possible for him to play the hotel job. (Kolodin 1941, 75)

The Pennsylvania Hotel welcomed only white bands, which also had far greater access to radio networks than did black ones. That the bandleader cited by Kolodin had one or more recording contracts put him in an elite company. Most black bands were paid a flat fee per side recorded, and a low one at that. The record companies cashed in on the proceeds of sales without paying royalties.

A third consideration is reflected in the demographic survey of black West Virginians presented earlier: a wide range in age, suggesting the probability that musical preferences would be as widely varied. This was obviously very different from the Savoy Ballroom, for instance, where teenagers and those in their early twenties appeared to dominate the dance floor, making it possible for bands to concentrate on playing swinging jazz arrangements, or, for that matter, the upscale white audience for Guy Lombardo's "Sweetest Music this Side of Heaven" at the Roosevelt Hotel.

Thanks to radio and newspaper publicity, many of the name bands that came to the Mountain State had already established reputations, thus accounting for the fact that hundreds of black West Virginians turned out for their dances, often traveling many miles to do so. What they expected to hear included the music they had already heard, but a four- to six-hour dance would have exhausted that repertory fairly quickly. What else was played and how did the bandleaders ensure maximum interest in part to hold on to those present and, perhaps, to attract latecomers?

It seems reasonable to suppose that just as a football team may plan out its first twenty plays as a way of testing the defensive ability of the opposition, so too bandleaders developed fixed set lists for the early part of an engagement to assess audience preferences. Those numbers surely represented various styles of dance music, some hot, some sweet, some somewhere in the middle, a fast Lindy Hop to get the younger audience out on the floor, a waltz for the older attendees, a ballad crooned by a band member for dancers and listeners of all ages. The measure of popularity would have been fairly obvious: the greater the number of patrons on the dance floor for a particular style of music, the greater the number of arrangements in that style as the evening wore on.

Discovering the types of music played by any particular band is not easy, nor is the evidence comprehensive to any extent. Most desirable would have been for a bandleader or sideman to go beyond general descriptions of a band's repertory to citing titles of arrangements associated with various styles of dance music. That such testimony is largely missing from the historical record is understandable: most bands whose members attracted the attention of scholars and critics were associated with jazz, and their contributions to the jazz tradition is what was of interest. Beyond the fact that attention has been focused on the evolution of big band jazz styles, the recordings documenting the work of these bands were in most instances recordings of jazz. As a consequence, perceptions of bands' musical endeavors not only focused on their cultivation of this one musical style but also reflect an unmistakable condescension by authors when dealing with evidence of a band's performances of "commercial music," whether recorded or not. In some instances, there is a sense that such an ensemble let down the side, so to speak, by failing to adhere exclusively to the highest standards of jazz expression.

Gunther Schuller was clearly ambivalent about the intrusion of the commercial into the domain of the artistic, that is, performances of sweet music by bands that otherwise played jazz and did a pretty good job of it. Consider observations made in connection with a discussion of the Erskine Hawkins Band in the chapter of *The Swing Era: The Development of Jazz 1930–1945* entitled "The Great Black Bands":

> But, as we have often seen on these pages, the temptations of commercial success were never far away in those days, nor are they today.

The fusion then of "sweet" and "hot" styles—"commercial" and "creative"—have been replaced in recent years by another fusion: pop/rock and jazz. And then as now, many musicians under the pressure of economics in what is—we must remind ourselves—essentially an "entertainment" field, succumbed to those commercial temptations. For many 1930s-40's bands a sweet trumpet solo or a couple of singers, or some novelty tunes were sometimes the difference between survival and demise. (Schuller 1989, 406)

Schuller's argument that economic pressures compelled some bands to play in styles that were not artistically rewarding is true (after all, eating is a hard habit for anyone to break, even a musician). What it fails to take into account is the possibility that bands that ultimately acquired significant reputations in the history of big band jazz may have also taken pleasure in their collective ability to perform a variety of styles and genres including sweet music and pride in being able to do so in a manner that appealed to the diverse tastes of their audience. Andy Kirk made plain that the Twelve Clouds of Joy was, fundamentally, a versatile dance band. "People were dance crazy in those days. And if you played the kind of music they liked to dance to, that's what mattered. As I've said, our band didn't stress jazz, though we played it. We emphasized dance music—romantic ballads and pop tunes and waltzes—Viennese as well as standard popular waltzes like 'Kiss Me Again' and 'Alice Blue Gown.' I loved to play waltzes. We were first and last a dance orchestra because people were dancing" (Kirk 1989, 61–62).

Studies of other black bands of the period confirm that many now understandably celebrated for their contributions to big band jazz, as documented by their recordings and personal testimonies, tended to resemble Kirk's definition of a "dance orchestra" when performing live, and nowhere would this be more true than on the road.

Consider the testimony of former members and observers of several black bands, all of which played in West Virginia for black audiences in the 1930s. Concerning Fletcher Henderson's orchestra in its final years, reed man Russell Procope recalled that it "played tangos, waltzes, foxtrots, college songs, current hits, excerpts from the classics in dance tempos, just about everything." Henderson biographer Jeffrey Magee noted that "for Procope that kind of versatility marked success" (Magee 2005, 138). In an interview with Stanley Dance in 1966, pianist/arranger Nat Pierce recalled hearing that Chick Webb "had a library of waltzes." Furthermore, he asserted that "It wasn't a crime to play a waltz then—not just a jazz waltz, but a regular waltz with a pretty melody" (Dance 1974, 343–44).

A territory band based in Indianapolis and later Cincinnati, Speed Webb's band returned several times to play for dances on the campus of West Virginia State College. A member in 1929 and 1930, trombonist Vic Dickenson remembered that "Seven guys arranged in that band, . . . and every week we had seven new arrangements. Of course, we played everything in the way of dance music in those days—waltzes, pop songs, everything" (Dance 1974, 303). Given that the socially conservative president of West Virginia State, John Davis, reportedly frowned on dancing, certainly of the more physical and demonstrative types such as the Lindy Hop, and given the fact that by the later 1930s Webb's interest in the band business was waning, it is logical to suppose that commercial stock arrangements of waltzes and pop songs in moderate tempos dominated his band's performances on campus and thus met "Prex" Davis's expectations (Belmear 2000; Scheidt 1965, 52).

Perhaps the clearest evidence of black bands' capacity to step outside the domain of jazz during dance dates was provided by none other than Duke Ellington himself during an engagement at the Crystal Ballroom in Fargo, North Dakota, on November 7, 1940, most of which was recorded by two local fans of the band, Jack Towers and Dick Burris. Not only did their initiative enable us to hear that band live, it also revealed Ellington's careful use of a thirty-minute sustaining radio broadcast early in the evening to showcase his music as well as well as the band's versatility, not only for listeners but also for those attending the dance itself.

The broadcast presented a total of seven arrangements, five by Ellington and his band members and two by other composers. After playing a portion of his "Sepia Panorama" as background music for the radio announcer's introduction of the band to listeners of Fargo's local station, KVOX, and to announce the first number, the band swung into its recently recorded, but not yet released, blues-based uptempo jazz number "Koko," a showcase for the timbres and talents of trombonists Juan Tizol and Lawrence Brown.

If "Koko" could be regarded as representing the "hot" jazz end of the spectrum of dance music styles, what followed took listeners to the other extreme. "There Shall Be No Night," composed in 1940 by Abner Silver with lyrics by Gladys Shelly, could be regarded as Ellington's take on Guy Lombardo's sweet style. The tempo is slow; the brass and reed sections play in close harmony and quietly; Jimmy Blanton's bass beats four-to-the-bar.

The solo passages by muted trumpet and, toward the end, Ben Webster's distinctive tenor saxophone are, at most, light paraphrases of the song's melodies. In other words, there were none of the "fancy embellishments" that Lombardo avoided in his band's arrangements. The sentimental lyrics were crooned by Herb Jeffries, who might be said to be the Ellington Orchestra's equivalent of Pha Terrill, Andy Kirk's singer whose recording of the ballad "Until the Real Thing Comes Along" was such an unexpected hit with black audiences.

Four Ellington compositions followed this ballad: "Pussy Willow," "Chatterbox," "Mood Indigo," and "Harlem Airshaft." Of these, "Mood Indigo" was the only piece in a slow tempo comparable to that of "There Shall Be No Night." The rest were mid- to uptempo fox-trot/Lindy Hop arrangements. Ivie Anderson then appeared to sing a chorus of a foreshortened arrangement in Ellington's style of "Ferryboat Serenade." After that "Warm Valley" served as background to the radio announcer's signing off "and returning [listeners] to our studios." Thereafter, the music continued through four sets, the dance ending around 1:00 a.m. on November 8.

Later that evening Jeffries returned to sing another pair of songs coupled into a medley. The recording captures only a portion of the second of these songs, the arrangement of which appeared to be on the sweet side, but considering the entire performance it seems apparent that the Fargo crowd did not need Ellington to step outside his own style to satisfy its musical tastes. The performance of "Mood Indigo" probably assured any doubters that if they wanted a slow, quiet number during which "to offer an endearment" à la Guy Lombardo, Ellington could accommodate them on his own aesthetic terms.

Surely his strategy for determining the best music to play for a particular audience, in operation at the dance in North Dakota, had been regularly used on the road for a number of years, including the three occasions on which he performed in West Virginia. The first occurred late in March 1935, and according to James West, Fairmont correspondent to the *Pittsburgh Courier*, "a large group of local dance lovers motored to Charleston to dance to the music of Duke Ellington and his famous orchestra" (*PC* 3.30.35, 2/7). On April 19 of the same year, on the evening following an engagement in Cincinnati, the band made its first appearance in the northern part of the Mountain State, playing at the Fairmont armory. The article in the *Courier* informing readers of this occasion claimed that "This affair looms as the 'biggest affair of the season' and it is expected that hundreds of people from surrounding towns will help to make of the affair a howling success" (*PC* 4.13.35, 2/8). On Christmas Eve 1937, Ellington returned to Charleston to play for a benefit dance sponsored by the 20th Century Athletic Club to raise funds to buy Christmas presents for disabled children in six counties in southern West Virginia. The *Courier*'s story also noted that the bandleader was entertained the previous night by, among others, LeRoy "Texas" Fonteneau. It will be recalled that Fonteneau was one of the Kings of Amusement who collaborated with George Morton in booking dances. That same article drew attention to the fact that the 20th Century Athletic Club was holding a New Year's Day dance on January 1, 1938, for which Chick Webb had been booked along with "the captivating songbird, Ella Fitzgerald" (*PC* 1.1.38, 2/12).

It is by virtue of the Fargo recordings that Ellington enters this narrative to demonstrate the requisite diversity of style that audiences on the road expected. There is no doubt that the bandleader who made such diversity a cornerstone of his style (or perhaps, under these circumstances, "styles") was Jimmie Lunceford.

In *Rhythm Is Our Business: Jimmie Lunceford and the Harlem Express*, Eddy Determeyer argued that "the ability to play romantic ballads next to novelty numbers and hard-swinging killer-dillers or flag-wavers put the Lunceford band in the vanguard with both the dancers and the listeners" (Determeyer 2006, 87). Two elements of this statement merit comment. The first is the implicit inclusion of several styles of music performed by Lunceford's band. In a passage from *The Swing Era*, Gunther Schuller reflected on the realities of life for black dance bands in the 1930s when it came to deciding what sort of music to play and what to avoid. In comparing Lunceford to Ellington and Basie in terms of balancing artistic and economic interests, he observed:

> They all made their peace with compromise of one kind or another. Thus the real and only valid criterion of judgment is *to what degree* economic and commercial pressures made inroads on artistic/aesthetic decisions—*not whether, but how much*. . . . In that regard I think the Lunceford band, at least in its early days and perhaps through the 1930s, could hold its own with any of its contemporaries [including Ellington and Basie]. As previously stated, the Lunceford formula—his and his soloists' and arrangers'—was to serve up a diversified musical menu for a variety of appetites. (Schuller 1989, 213)

Evidence of that "diversified musical menu" was discussed in chapter 6 in connection with Lunceford's first engagement in the Mountain State in September 1934 at the Fairmont armory. Seventeen recordings the band made in the first nine months of that year covered the spectrum from sweet to hot, slow to fast, quiet to loud. The band returned eighteen times prior to the shutting down of tours through West Virginia in the summer of 1942. There were four engagements in 1936, one in 1937, five in 1939, one in 1940, five in 1941, and the final pair toward the end of April 1942. Given the regularity of Lunceford's recordings throughout that period, it is easy to document the continuing creation of a diverse repertory.

Lunceford recordings beginning in the mid-thirties document arrangements of popular songs by Irving Berlin ("He Ain't Got Rhythm" and "Easter Parade"), Hoagy Carmichael ("Stardust"), and Cole Porter ("Miss Otis Regrets"), among many others. There were novelty numbers such as "The Merry Go Round Broke Down" and instrumental dance compositions including "For Dancers Only," "Uptown Blues," and "Lunceford Special." There were even some arrangements of art music for the band, including one of themes from Ludwig van Beethoven's Sonata for Piano, Opus 13, "Pathetique," by Chappie Willett, whom we previously encountered as a student bandleader at West Virginia State and then as the leader of Edward's Collegians after that band left Bluefield for Cincinnati and Philadelphia (Determeyer 2006, 277–91).

The link between recordings and the road for Lunceford was a close one, according to Eddy Determeyer; arrangements were "test-marketed" on tours before a decision was made to record them. As some of Lunceford's tours lasted several months, there were numerous opportunities to gauge the reactions of fans to a particular number. "Uptown Blues" was apparently introduced to fans at the Paramount Theater in New York sometime late in September 1939. It was not recorded until December of that year (Determeyer 2006, 79, 171).

Given his frequent trips through West Virginia, it is obvious that Lunceford enjoyed the same popularity in the Mountain State as elsewhere. Newspaper coverage provides evidence of the nature of that appeal and to whom within the black communities. On February 17, 1936, the day of its debut in Wheeling, "a number of West Virginia State co-eds and male college students will be included in the in the welcome reception committee to greet Jimmy [sic] and the boys when they arrive at the Wheeling Market Auditorium" (PC 2.15.36, 2/6). The presence of the West Virginia State students is remarkable because Wheeling is about 200 miles north of the West Virginia State campus. Moreover, the next night the band appeared in Charleston, less than twenty miles from campus.

So successful was its appearance in Charleston that the band returned on April 15 and was expected to draw several thousand to its dance. The unsigned article in the *Courier* announcing this dance noted that those who had attended the February engagement "were conquered by the music of the 'sweetest' band they had ever heard." Significantly, readers were informed of the band's popularity on various university campuses, perhaps a not-so-subtle outreach to middle-class blacks (*PC* 4.11.36, 2/10).

On July 23, 1937, Lunceford played a dance at the Vanity Fair Ballroom in Huntington, like the Charleston engagement a year earlier a single appearance in the state (*PC* 7.17.37, 20). Two years later, one can see both a further surge in his popularity as well as the efficiency of booker George Morton in organizing four dances to take place between March 25 and March 29, 1939, in Charleston, Mount Hope, Bluefield, and Fairmont. Reference was made in one of two *Courier* articles to the fact that Lunceford, a member of Kappa Alpha Psi at his alma mater Fisk University, would be greeted at both West Virginia State and Bluefield State Colleges by members of the local chapters of that fraternity. Indeed, the brothers at Bluefield State were reportedly going to discuss with Lunceford the possibility of his band playing for a future prom (*PC* 2.25.39, 21; 3.11.39, 20).

A third *Courier* story, datelined March 23 from Charleston, drew attention to the fact that, in advance of the show at the armory in Mount Hope, "Morton's Drug Store has already had its largest advance sale since Cab Calloway made his late appearance in the state." The drugstore in question was owned by George Morton's father. Attention was also drawn to the role of a "young college graduate and wide-awake hustler" named Yancy Whittaker who "joined Universal Promoters to bring [Lunceford] into Fairmont, W. Va at the Fairmont Armory" (*PC* 3.25.39, 20).

Beginning in 1940 the *Courier*'s coverage of big bands, including Lunceford's, was often reduced to a single column that listed the dates and destinations of a portion of various bands' tours. Largely absent was information that would shed light on the circumstances surrounding a dance, such as the name of the local promoter, anticipated size of the crowd, or mention of previous engagements and their impact. An early instance of this sort of reportage appeared in the issue of May 20, 1940, in which, on page 20, one encounters a column entitled "Lunceford's Route" which listed all known performances that month, including one held on May 30 at the Crystal Cavern Ballroom in Martinsburg, West Virginia, located in the state's eastern panhandle, far removed from the coalfields and quite possibly a dance for whites. Two days earlier, the band had performed in Providence, Rhode Island, and on May 31, it was performing the first of two engagements at Clemson College in South Carolina (*PC* 5.20.40, 20).

Similar coverage early in January 1941 revealed that the Lunceford band was scheduled to play five engagements in the Mountain State beginning in Huntington on February 6 and concluding in Wheeling on February 11. In between it played in Beckley, Charleston, and Bluefield on February 7, 8, and 10 respectively. While the band played two engagements in November 1942, the first on the 24th in Beckley and the second the next day in Huntington, the February 1941 series of engagements was its last extended visit to the Mountain State before World War II (*PC* 1.4.41, 18; 3.21.41, 20).

Examining Jimmie Lunceford's tours of West Virginia enables one to consider a number of related issues in terms of audience reception: the diversity of musical styles in which his band performed, the consequent large attendance at his dances, and the ways in which Lunceford's image was central to his appeal.

Concerning the diversity of styles performed by black bands when the situation warranted it, I drew attention both to contemporaneous characterizations of his style as well as to documentation provided by Lunceford's recordings. Andy Kirk emphasized that his band played "dance music" and "didn't stress jazz, though we played it" (Kirk 1989, 62). Duke Ellington appears to have been able to finesse the expectation of sweet music by composing ballads and ballad-like pieces that served the same purpose.

Lest the impression be created that in the Mountain State bands played no jazz, explicit evidence to the contrary appeared in connection with several engagements in the late 1930s. When Lunceford appeared in Charleston on February 18, 1936, the *Courier* reported: "An added attraction that night will be a 'Truckin's Contest' sponsored by the Tuxedo Club to the winners of which cash prizes will be awarded. Participants for the contest must register prior to February 18" (*PC*, 1.25.36, 2/6). Tiny Bradshaw's engagement at the Charleston armory on September 24, 1938, included a Lindy Hop contest. "Couples representing Charleston, Huntington, Parkersburg, Beckley, Mount Hope, Logan, Montgomery, Cabin Creek, and other smaller towns have been contacted and have consented to join in and see if they can't win one of the three cash prizes that are to be given away."

The article went on to suggest that any couple hoping to break into the entertainment business that also proved to be of above average talent might anticipate being hired by Bradshaw for subsequent engagements (*PC* 9.24.38, 20). Beyond the evidence that younger black Mountaineers were up on the dances of the day, this article provides further confirmation of the geographical range of audiences for this music. Several of the towns mentioned were at least an hour away from Charleston by automobile, Parkersburg more than three. That the promoters of this dance knew whom to contact when rounding up contestants is evidence of the regularity with which certain people traveled to Charleston for dances and demonstrates that some had already developed local reputations as good dancers.

A third description of a dance provides additional confirmation of interest in big band jazz but at the same time acknowledges a comparable interest in sweet music. Two Chapters of the Kappa Alpha Psi fraternity, one in Charleston, the other nearby in Institute, the home of West Virginia State College, cohosted an annual formal dance in Charleston at the Knights of Pythias Hall on March 25, 1938. Music was provided by two bands: the West Virginia State Collegians and Locklayer's Virginians. "The two orchestras were in contrast, the West Virginia Collegians playing snappy swing rhythms that gave pep and gaiety to the proceedings, and the Virginians playing the sweet, muted syncopations that is [*sic*] so pleasant to dance to" (*PC* 4.2.1938, 9). As noted previously, the president of West Virginia State frowned on dancing, but presumably as this dance took place off campus, the college band was not constrained in the music it performed.

There would seem little reason to doubt that the African American audience for dance music in West Virginia was representative of the larger black audience for big band jazz and dance music in the nation. Just as it embraced both working- and middle-class blacks, so too it embraced a variety of musical tastes, which challenges the conventional wisdom that blacks liked jazz more or less exclusively while whites preferred something sweeter. For black Mountaineers dance music was not "all jazz all the time"—and in saying this, I am arguing that their preferences were not significantly different from those of African Americans living in northern cities, nor for that matter of the American population in general, black and white. Because, in a sense, every dance venue in West Virginia attracted such a diverse audience, bands did not have the luxury of devoting themselves exclusively to a single style of dance music, even if their reputations would appear to have favored such narrow focus. On the one hand, whether or not broadcast performances by Noble Sissle's band reminded Wheeling resident Gladys Mike of her favorite orchestra, Guy Lombardo's

Royal Canadians, Sissle would have had to perform some uptempo swing to appeal to a significant portion of his audiences in Charleston, Huntington, and Welch when he toured to those cities in 1934. On the other hand (and we know this because the bandleader said it himself), at each of the ten engagements in West Virginia played by Andy Kirk's Twelve Clouds of Joy between October 1936 and July 1941, an array of dance music made up the program, and undoubtedly prominently featured was their sweet ballad, "Until the Real Thing Comes Along" (Kirk 1989, 88).

The evidence taken together also suggests that the black audience for big band jazz and dance music in the Mountain State included members of both the working and middle classes. Unlike the large northern cities where venues for entertainment existed in sufficient numbers to allow patrons to sort themselves out by shared levels of income, common forms of employment, and even age should they have chosen to do so, in West Virginia the armories, high school gymnasiums, and other improvised venues provided a common social ground for people who were economically and occupationally diverse. Teachers and miners, trackliners and doctors, civil servants and teamsters, along with their spouses or significant others assembled to waltz, fox-trot, and Lindy Hop, and, presumably, to watch others do the same.

It is easy to imagine couples from the company towns grouping themselves in one part of the venue, those from the larger communities elsewhere. No doubt people came in groups as well and naturally would sit and dance together. At the same time, such an occasion enabled those with friends or relatives residing elsewhere in the coalfields to meet for several hours to catch up on one another's news and discuss, if not solve, the problems of the world. Geraldine Belmear recalled that the four dances her father Samuel Carpenter booked in the mid-1930s attracted people from all social classes (Belmear 2000).

Dressed in their best to honor the occasion, to an outsider the day jobs of the dancers hardly would have been apparent. Undoubtedly, to the musicians for whom each engagement represented just another stop on what after a while may have seemed a perpetual tour, the black Mountaineers they entertained probably looked and acted little different from those making up the other audiences for whom they played on the road.

What bands may have found initially surprising were the sizes of audiences in a state that may have seemed to outsiders to be extremely rural with only a small population. Not only would that assumption have been quickly contradicted by the hundreds who turned out to see the touring bands, just as quickly invalidated would have been the corollary that as the state's population was presumably small, so too would be the night's wages. By 1935 when Herbert Hall, as baritone saxophonist and clarinetist in "Don Albert's Music: America's Favorite Swing Band," first came to Charleston, he and the rest of that band were introduced to the prosperity enjoyed by African Americans in West Virginia's coalfields. As he would note years later, this was not news to any of the bandleaders and their managers at the time. The industriousness of the miners and the local economies that prospered thanks to their labor would in turn have assured most bands that their night's work in the Mountain State would be better compensated than was the case elsewhere in the region.

CHAPTER TEN

The Party Winds Down

The coal industry provided the economic foundation for the culture of big band jazz and dance music in the Mountain State during the 1930s, and it would be that same industry that initiated its decline. Events following the start of World War II would complete that process.

It will be recalled that at the beginning of the 1930s much of the work associated with mining coal was done by hand. In chapter 1, the work of "hand loaders" was summarized by William Purvience Tams Jr. Tams also discussed the modification of that job description that resulted when mine operators acquired cutting machines that prepared the coal face for dynamiting by cutting into the bottom of a seam in far less time than a miner could by hand. In the words of labor historian Ronald L. Lewis, "the cutting machine did not displace the miner but rather converted him from a generalist to a specialized worker" (Lewis 1987, 167). Thus, while this equipment obviously enhanced productivity, it did not accomplish in dramatic fashion what mine owners wanted: a significant reduction in labor costs.

That goal seemed attainable beginning in 1935, when a piece of equipment that had been around since the early 1920s suddenly began to be acquired in considerable numbers, initially by many larger operations, subsequently by smaller ones: a mechanical loading machine developed by Joseph F. Joy. Joy had worked as a hand loader in mines in the vicinity of Cumberland, Maryland, beginning in 1898 at the age of fifteen, and had firsthand knowledge of the nature of this work and the time required to load mine cars with coal that had just been blown down from the seam. As its name suggests, the Joy loader was designed to take over the work of hand loaders. Operated by a single individual, it could scoop up coal and carry it via conveyer belt to waiting mine cars to be transported to the surface. Separate work spaces, "rooms," in which individual miners had worked to shoot down and load coal could now be replaced by larger exposures of the coal seam, and one operator could do the work formerly done by several miners. As Lewis also observed: "As the use of mechanical loaders spread throughout the industry during the 1930s and 1940s, the integrated factory system moved underground, transforming not only the production process but the nature of the work itself. With more machinery, coal mining became less labor intensive, and the number of machine operators, maintenance men, and service personnel increased, while the percentage of independent practical miners declined" (Lewis 1987, 167).

Investing in Joy loaders paid off handsomely for coal operators in increased productivity: "Between 1935 and 1947, coal loaded by machine in West Virginia grew from 2.1 million tons per year to 99.8 million tons, an increase of 4,900 percent" (Lewis 1987, 169). The same investment led to significant reductions in the labor force. Among Lewis's "independent practical miners," Tams's "hand loaders" by another name, it was the blacks who felt the impact first since they were discriminated against when the time came for mine superintendents to choose which men would be trained to use the modern equipment and which would be let go. Accounts of black miners being denied access to training are numerous. Others document the fact that, despite their seniority within a particular mine, African Americans were passed over in favor of their European-American co-workers when opportunities to operate the new machinery presented themselves. The intention to deny blacks the opportunity to learn to operate loaders and other equipment was often justified by superintendents and mine owners because they believed that blacks lacked the necessary intelligence to master the machinery or because they regarded such employment as a "white man's job." Even when confronted with evidence that a black miner had received the training necessary to operate the new mining machinery, rejection followed. In one operation, when a new superintendent took charge, the black miners who had constituted a majority of the equipment operators were summarily removed from those jobs and replaced by whites. The UMWA chose not to intervene on behalf of its black members in this or in other instances of similar injustice. After all, the white miners were also union members (Lewis 1987, 170).

The upsurge in mechanization combined with the denial of access to employment opportunities associated with this development initiated the steady decline of black employment in the West Virginia coalfields. Whereas there were 22,089 black miners (22.7 percent of the work force) in the Mountain State in 1930, that number dropped to 18,356 (17.3 percent of the work force) by 1940 (Barnum 1970, 28). The decline accelerated in the next decade, but that takes us beyond the scope of this study.

A survey of the number of dances presented to black Mountaineers in the period from 1939 to 1942 is only partially suggestive of the changing coal industry. In 1939 twenty dances for which touring bands provided music can be documented in the newspaper record, in 1940 only fifteen dances. Beyond the transformations wrought by mechanization of mining, it must be noted that in that year the nation slipped into recession, which had an adverse impact upon the state's mining industry. In 1941 there was a robust turnaround: traveling bands provided music for twenty-six dances. Unknown is whether there was a drop in attendance as black miners and their families departed the state, initiating a pattern of out-migration that would accelerate in the postwar period as further mechanization wiped out the jobs of thousands of miners of all races and ethnicities.

It is clear that employment practices in the coal industry would have eliminated most of the economic foundation for big band jazz and dance music in West Virginia eventually. Beyond the impact on their own livelihoods, it should also be borne in mind that the incomes of the thousands of black miners also supported many in the Mountain State's black middle class. The weakening of their economic circumstances did further damage to the prospects of touring bands. Yet, the deciding factors in bringing to an end the active cultivation of this music among black West Virginians were World War II and three federal policies arising from the war effort that were implemented by the middle of 1942. Their effect on this musical culture was devastating.

War-related problems for black bandleaders began to be observed as early as February 1942. In the February 14 issue of the *Pittsburgh Courier*, a story headlined "War Priorities Have Hit Les Hite" reported that the bandleader "was unable to find a new or suitable tire to replace a completely worn one on his bus." The story continued: "Like every big band, Hite's crew relies on the bus form of transportation to cover the jump from one engagement to another, the cost of rail traveling being much more expensive" (*PC* 2.14.42, 20). The reporter overreached a bit—Duke Ellington traveled by train routinely while on tour and had for a number of years—but the fact was that every band (apart from Ellington's) that toured West Virginia did so by bus.

Two weeks later the *Courier* printed the following report under the headline "War Curb Effective On Musical Instruments": "One of the most effective curtailments to hit the music profession came into being here this week with the War Production Board ordering a two-month curb on the use of critical metals and plastics in the making of musical instruments.

Transportation Snag Hits Theatre World

Curtailment of Traveling Facilities Practically Dooms Small Bands—Even the Count Has Had His Troubles.

By BILLY ROWE
(Theatrical Editor)

NEW YORK CITY, June 4—The curtailment of transportation facilities which went into effect June 1 has one nite dance promoters tearing their hair and gambling on short odds. The new law also takes telling effect on bands in all brackets of success as it calls for the immediate confiscation of chartered buses the main mode of traveling of every aggregation in the country.

HITS SWING KING

Caught short here just before the law took effect, Count Basie, leader of America's No. 1 band, almost didn't leave town to fill a session at the Howard theatre in Washington. However after much string pulling and pleading the "King of Swing" set out on the longest and most complete tour of the country scheduled to drop him off in Hollywood the latter end of July.

NO ADVANCE IN BOOKING

Geared to meet the new situation, bookers in various sections of the country are eliminating the heretofore long-advance booking of bands for dance engagements. Such a move has been deemed advisable to avoid being caught short when a band is either grounded by the snatching of a bus shortage of gas or the absence of rideable tires.

NOT TO OPEN

Max Kearson promoter using the Mecca temple in Scranton Pa and Rochester N. Y. has announced that he will not open his usual summer stand Fernbrook park in Dallas Pa. Like Kearson many of the seasoned promoters are more or less on the panicky side and will book only sure things and use halls that are easy to get to.

WILL KILL SMALL BANDS

The new transportation problem coupled with many others which yes indeed will take a heavy toll in the huge band business, will kill many of the small bands. Here last week Joe Glaser, Moe Gale and Harold Oxley, bookers and managers of the best known colored bands announced that from now until the end of the war they will concentrate on location for each of their bands. Glaser has set Hampton for a turn at the Casa Manana. Oxley has Lunceford slated for the Trianon on the Coast, while Gale has Hawkins at the Savoy with several of his other attractions to follow.

Already weighted down with gas rubber metal instruments and now transportation curtailment the profession is fighting for national survival.

UNION IN FIGHT

Joined by every theatrical union in the country, the American Federation of Musicians has petitioned the government for a priority rating with the theme uppermost that most musicians and performers are not only essential to the morale of the public but the fighting forces as well. In the present drive for all out dollars for the purchase of war bonds the big and small name bands have played a most important part to say nothing of their aid to the USO program. "Willard Alexander personal manager of Count Basie. Something should be done agreed everybody but what as priority has struck and nobody is screaming indeed."

Fig. 10.1. Report by Billy Rowe, theatrical editor of the *Pittsburgh Courier*, on the devastating impact on black dance bands of the rationing of rubber and gasoline as well as the confiscation of chartered buses by the federal government, June 6, 1942. (*Pittsburgh Courier* Archives)

The new order came about by the by great war demands which needs such metals for planes, weapons, and ships" (PC 2.28.42, 20).

On June 1, 1942, the Office of Defense Transportation (ODT) implemented its policies regarding rationing of both rubber and gasoline. The *Courier*'s theatrical editor, Billy Rowe, reported two consequences (see Fig. 10.1). "The curtailment of transportation facilities that went into effect June 1 has one nite [sic] dance promoters tearing their hair and gambling on short odds." With only a few exceptions throughout the entire period of this study, every dance in West Virginia was a "one nite" engagement. Rowe went on: "The new law also takes telling effect on bands in all brackets of success as it calls for the immediate confiscation of chartered buses, the main mode of traveling of every aggregation in the country." Later in the article, he summarized the consequences of these policies for big bands. "The new transportation problem coupled with many others which will take a heavy toll in the huge band business will kill many of the small bands" (PC 6.6.42, 21).

The managers of the most famous bands, including Joe Glaser, Moe Gale, and Harold Oxley, immediately went to work lining up "location jobs," long-term engagements in hotels and commercial dance venues for the bands they had under contract. Many bands went out of business. Later, the ODT agreed that bands could travel by train from one military base to another to play for the troops and, when doing so, sandwich in engagements for civilians where possible. West Virginia did not then, nor does it now, have a military base of any sort; any wartime engagements played in the state could only occur when bands traversed the entire state in order to travel from one base to another.

By September a small measure of relief was granted by the ODT to black bands, when it agreed that five buses would be allocated for the exclusive use of "colored outfits, who find their most lucrative territory in the south, but who are not able to travel to these points via rail because of the jim-crow conditions. Even when they have been able to travel on the trains, the have often found that many small towns are not accessible by these means" (PC 9.5.42, 21). Presumably, the "jim-crow" conditions referred not only to limited seating for black passengers on many trains but also to the lack of space for instruments, suitcases, and other band equipment in the baggage cars.

The constraints imposed on touring bands obviously had a comparable impact on black Mountaineers who in the past traveled by car to a dance held in a nearby (or not so nearby) town. The wartime ration of four gallons of gasoline per week did not allow for a lot of recreational driving. As can be easily imagined, the big band culture for most black communities was reduced to what could be heard on the radio. Even production of radio receivers for civilian use was also sharply reduced, as was the availability of shellac, essential at the time in the manufacturing of recordings (PC 8.15.42, 20). For all of these reasons, it is fair to say that the summer of 1942 was the period in which the lively musical culture of big band jazz and dance music in black West Virginia established in the early 1930s came to an end.

Conclusions

This has been a study of a remarkable and previously unexamined series of developments in the history of American music. Like all such developments, these were contingent on a set of preconditions the impact of which could not have been anticipated: the geology of West Virginia that created the coalfields, the post–Civil War industrial and technological developments associated with railroading and coal mining, issues of public policy at both the state and federal levels that created a favorable social environment for black Mountaineers, and African American musical traditions and aesthetic values that made it easy to embrace big band jazz and other dance musics once these arrived in the Mountain State.

Large quantities of high-quality bituminous coal were prerequisite, as was the construction of railroads to export that coal to the nation and abroad. The discovery of West Virginia's vast coal reserves—preceded by post–Civil War emancipation of enslaved blacks and their discovery of the economic limitations of agricultural life as sharecroppers in Virginia, the Carolinas, and elsewhere in the Old South—encouraged steady migration to the Mountain State by African Americans to build railroads and mine coal. Beyond that, West Virginia's state constitution ensured resident males of all races the right to vote. The concentration of black Mountaineers in certain counties gave them a degree of political influence in the state not seen in most parts of the country, north or south.

Bringing their own musical traditions with them, the African Americans living in the coalfields preserved much of the oral tradition of their home states and quickly adopted new practices where these proved useful. Despite formidable terrain, the Mountain State did not impose obstacles to traveling tent shows in the early twentieth century, further enriching the black music of the coalfields and keeping it up to date.

That the mines needed electricity and brought it to most of their company towns meant that residents, both black and white, could listen to music on the radio. By the 1930s radio broadcasts increasingly featured big band dance music, including jazz. A large percentage of the black population of West Virginia appears to have had more or less easy access to radios and thus to the emerging national culture of music.

Despite all of these conditions favorable to local cultivation of big band dance music, the principal factor that energized the musical developments at the heart of this study was the Bituminous Coal Code of 1933, with its empowering of the United Mine Workers of America, and the union's commitment to equal pay for equal work for African Americans. With the stabilization of the mining industry and the rise in wages came a sense of economic security, on the part of African American miners and those who provided them services among the black middle class, that was reflected in their enthusiastic support of this musical culture.

Taken together, these forces distinguished the black musical history of the Mountain State from that of states further south and west having significant African American populations. What West Virginia's blacks shared with their brothers and sisters in the Deep South were numbers and a rural life. They did not have to share (or, more accurately, have to endure) the economic exploitation and hostile, at times even terrifying, social environment of the southern states. In arguing this position, I am not suggesting that black Mountaineers found "Jerusalem in West Virginia's green and pleasant land," to paraphrase a line from William Blake's poem. Life was hardly perfect. However, even though segregated in public education and denied services in a variety of public businesses, they had a degree of agency, opportunity, and, from late in 1933 to the end of the decade, a degree of economic prosperity that was hard to find elsewhere.

Within this social context, regular visits by name bands to black West Virginia takes on an added meaning. Surely, no matter how bad things might have been in the larger world, the combination of the music performed, the artistry of the musicians performing it, and the social environment created, albeit temporarily, in the gymnasium of a black high school, within a national guard armory, or in a nightclub rented for the occasion affirmed the values and interests of all who were present.

The dances represented a sanctuary in which one was temporarily free of the burden not only of the day's work but also the annoyances and inconveniences resulting from living in a segregated society of unequal opportunities. Furthermore, those dances were major social occasions, with at least two generations in attendance. No doubt, even as the music was playing, folks got caught up on each others' news, courting by members of the younger generation took place under the watchful eyes of their parents, and solutions to the problems of the world were proposed and debated. Simply put, those dances provided a public space for the authentic expression of what it meant to be a human being on one's own terms, and the music gave voice to that humanity. The more frequently the bands came, the more frequent the creation of this social environment, something that black Mountaineers valued highly, judging by the size of the crowds.[1]

As a consequence, touring black bands as often as possible made certain that West Virginia was one of the important stops on their travels. The road, as shown in this study, was where lots of money was to be earned. Herbert Hall spoke of the highly favorable opinion bandleaders had of the audience for their music found among black Mountaineers. Paul Barnes's gig book corroborates Hall's memories.

Beyond the seeming improbability of West Virginia being a magnet for African American dance bands during the years of the Great Depression, there is something almost miraculous in the fact that it was. All of the preconditions, like pieces of a puzzle, had to fit together to ensure this outcome. One "piece" was millions of years old, others dated from the late nineteenth century, and the last and in some respects most crucial was created through the cobbling together of public policies to energize America's failing economy within the first one hundred days of Franklin Delano Roosevelt's presidency. The contingent nature of history is vividly illustrated by these developments. And almost as quickly as those pieces came together in 1933, they were pulled apart in 1942 by forces well beyond the power of black West Virginians to control.

A subject that permeated this discussion of the music performed for black Mountaineers concerns connections between social class and stylistic preferences. The available evidence suggests these were independent variables in West Virginia. While upper-class whites in New York may have preferred the sweet sound of Guy Lombardo's band at the Roosevelt Grill, and working-class blacks further uptown "naturally" took to the Lindy Hop and other modern dances performed to hot, loud jazz, this study demonstrates that assumptions about class-based tastes are at best overly simple and at worst prompted by unsupported assumptions about relationships between the race and social status of an audience and the choice of music it preferred to hear.

Lewis Erenberg discussed the effect of the onset of the Depression and its impact on popular music in the United States in his monograph *Swingin' the Dream: Big Band Jazz and the Rebirth of American Culture*. He argued that, by the early 1930s, the jazz of the 1920s was dismissed as symbolic of the crass materialism and overindulgence that characterized that decade, and that, accordingly, jazz bands (at least in white America) were compelled either to modify their styles or to go out of business. "As hotter jazz groups disbanded and live entertainment shrank drastically, sweet (melodic) bands took over the commercial air waves, content to comply with radio's insistence on inoffensiveness and the audience's desire for soothing sounds" (Erenberg 1998, 17–18).

Erenberg's attention was focused on developments in urban America, principally New York City, but the desire for soothing sounds was not limited to audiences residing in Gotham, as demonstrated by the continuing and favorable references by black Mountaineers to sweet music in reports and correspondence concerning black dance bands that performed in West Virginia. As counterintuitive as this may seem, the popularity of sweet music had an inescapable logic based on the realities of day-to-day life in the coalfields for the same reasons that certain types of sentimental, nostalgic country music appealed to white folks further west and south in the same period.

In the preface to his study of country music and its relationship to the white southern working class, Bill C. Malone discussed his roots in east Texas and his family's circumstances that attracted them to the "fantasy and escapism" that defined certain genres of country music in the 1930s: "Living in Smith County, Texas, during the Great Depression, and struggling to scratch a living from our cotton farm, was all the realism our family needed. Therefore, we seldom sought realism in our music but instead relished and cherished its capacity for deliverance" (Malone 2002, 7–8).

One may observe that there was at least as much "realism" to be encountered both within a coal mine and within the adjacent company town. Coal mining was hazardous and dirty work. Accidents easily crippled and killed, and none was more common than the roof fall following the shooting down of coal but prior to the propping of the newly exposed roof. As attractive as it was, good pay was no protection against such catastrophes. Cheaply constructed, company houses were close together and small. Personal privacy in many instances was limited; next-door neighbors were quite possibly only a few feet away. Amenities were few.

Coal mining is a dirty business not only in the mines but in the immediate vicinity as well. Probably at least once a day, if not at the end of every shift, loaded coal hopper cars were hitched up to a steam locomotive to be hauled away. The engines were noisy; their smokestacks belched smoke and ash; their whistles at crossings could be heard for miles. Those engines and those cars filled with dusty coal often passed within a few feet of company houses in the steep-sided, V-shaped valleys of the coalfield counties.

Keeping a house clean was undoubtedly a continuing and at times a seemingly futile struggle for the miners' wives. Freshly washed laundry hanging on the line to dry would also have been compromised. The produce in the family garden could also be covered with a fine coating of coal dust. Under such circumstances, who would not welcome a program of quiet, soothing music broadcast from some faraway venue suggesting that somewhere life was more pleasant and relaxed?

Added to that was the fact that, as Guy Lombardo noted, when William Paley purchased what would be known as the Columbia Broadcasting System, "one of his first moves was to bring live music to his affiliated stations, which were obligated to play whatever programs emanated from New York if he so ordered. He decided that the Royal Canadians' broadcasts from the Roosevelt, though nonsponsored, would be carried by the eastern stations in the network" (Lombardo 1975, 94). Among those stations was WOBU in Charleston, which at night could reach all over the southern part of the state and beyond. As a result, the Royal Canadians' sweet music undoubtedly became part of the soundscape of the coalfields, a source of entertainment for black listeners seeking some escape from the realities of coal camp life, and a baseline by which to measure the style and quality of black dance bands that toured West Virginia.

An apparent interest in sweet music that crossed class boundaries was accompanied by a similarly broad-based interest in big band jazz. Just as young people at the Savoy Ballroom were drawn to Chick Webb's big band swing, so too were college students in West Virginia drawn to similar styles played by various bands. A theme running through newspaper coverage of dances in Charleston, not twenty miles from the campus of West Virginia State College, concerned collegiate identity: the attendance of college students was noted, as was the role of college alumni associations in sponsoring dances. That Jimmie Lunceford was a college graduate as were most, if not all, of his sidemen was commented on in numerous stories of his engagements in the Mountain State. To propose that perhaps this represents the boundary dividing middle- and working-class identity is to overlook the fact that dances were open to all. Attendance estimates in the hundreds, if not thousands, imply a wide variety of backgrounds and occupations among black Mountaineers. There simply were not enough college students in any one location to populate the dance floor in the numbers reported in the press. Jazz must have been as appealing as sweet music to the socio-economically diverse audiences for the black bands.

Another fact challenges notions of class difference and, by implication, social distancing among black Mountaineers. For many African Americans, higher education was a common aspiration, if not for themselves, for their children. Every one of the informants for this study graduated from either Bluefield State College or West Virginia State College prior to or, because of military service, just after World War II. Without exception, they represented the first generation of college-educated members of their families. With the exception of George Morton, the fathers of these informants either mined coal or worked for the railroad. Their achievements exemplify Booker T. Washington's vision of black self-reliance and "uplift," and rightly so. At the same time, their aspirations for upward social mobility differ little from those of contemporary European immigrant families throughout the nation.

A subject that merits some attention concerns the movements of those who became black Mountaineers beginning in the late 1860s and continuing into the 1930s. A central narrative of African American history in the twentieth century is that of the Great Migration of blacks from the rural South to the urban North beginning in the period of World War I and continuing into the 1950s at least. Its importance to the history of African American cannot be denied, but it is my belief that for several reasons the history that I have outlined is not part of that narrative.

First of all, the immigration of black Virginians and North and South Carolinians began within five years of the end of the Civil War, during the period of Reconstruction, when freed men, women, and children were on the move throughout the South. That the promise of a better life in West Virginia attracted these former slaves well before the post-Reconstruction resurgence of white political and social domination places their migration well before twentieth-century population shifts.

That the arrival of blacks continued unabated until the 1930s, as shown by the continuing rise in their numbers reflected in census data, is more likely to reflect the persuasive powers of those who had already established themselves in the Mountain State and then went back to tell their families and friends about the opportunities to be found there. Surely such conversations began in the early 1870s when, as Jedidiah Hotchkiss noted in his discussion of the blacks who built the Chesapeake & Ohio Railway, "The contractors had but one complaint to make—that the colored men *would* go 'home' for Christmas. Home to them meant Eastern Virginia and we were told that many of them returned joyfully to the old plantations where formerly they were slaves and where ... they are still made welcome on holidays" (Hotchkiss 1873, 289). Winter is obviously a period of comparative inactivity in agriculture. It is easy to imagine that during that season, having heard of the prospects for a better life in the Mountain State, many black Virginians or Carolinians decided that the time had come to pull up stakes and try another form of work, particularly if their previous summer's crop had been poor or the owner of a farm on which they were sharecropping had shortchanged them one too many times at the end of the growing season.

But what to make of the end of the period, when the Great Migration was well under way? Does the emigration of black Mountaineers who lost their jobs to the Joy Loading Machine and discriminatory practices by mine operators represent a part of that story? Perhaps, but unlike the migrants from the Deep South who made their way to northern cities and the promise of a comparatively better life both economically and socially, black West Virginians appeared to have been forced from better paying jobs in the mines to poorer ones in the heavy industries of the North. They gained no greater political power, on the contrary the kind of influence exerted by African Americans in the legislature of West Virginia was nonexistent in northern states. Finally, while immigration to the Mountain State represented a change from agricultural to industrial labor, the common denominator was a rural life, where the sort of recreational opportunities (hunting, fishing, gardening) known in the home place could be maintained in the company towns, and where, even if the company housing was densely packed, the outdoors was not far away.

If much of the life of black Mountaineers was defined by the rural setting in which most lived, the arrival of big band dance music added to the quality of their lives while, in a sense, connecting them to the northern cities in which that music originated. At the same time, this audience blended it into their already established musical culture and absorbed it into their daily lives. While perhaps emblematic of urban, industrial life in the North, in the Mountain State it was more of an ornament to life in the coalfields.[2]

Given the focus of this study on the black musical experience in the Mountain State, the reader may reasonably wonder about black–white interactions regarding big band dance music, since whites were attracted to this music to such an extent that by the late 1930s it had become the prevailing popular musical style of the nation. The newspaper record indicates that the principle of racial segregation defined most of those encounters.

In a few instances, a band might perform on one occasion for a black audience and within a few weeks circle back to the same community to play a dance for whites, or vice versa. As noted in chapter 2, King Oliver's band regularly played separate engagements for black and white dancers in various West Virginia communities.

There were occasions when the interest of members of one race in a band playing for the other led to a curious compromise: whites would be admitted as "spectators" to a black dance and vice versa. Don Redman's band played for a "colored" dance at the armory in Fairmont on October 4, 1934. According to an article in the local newspaper, "Because of Redman's local popularity among the white folks, arrangements have been made to seat approximately 100 spectators in the balcony" (*WV* 10.3.34, 5). In at least one instance, such an occasion led to a subsequent engagement for the band. On February 15, 1934, Noble Sissle played for whites in Wheeling because, according to a report in the *Pittsburgh Courier*, "when Sissle and his Sizzling Orchestra played in Wheeling several months at a colored dance, more than 500 white people stormed the balcony and raved over his music. At the dance in Wheeling, colored spectators will be given an opportunity to hear Sissle again" (*PC* 2.3.34, 2/6).

Not every white dance was so accommodating. A social organization, the Dice Club, advertised a dance for which Duke Ellington was booked to play at the armory in Charleston on April 16, 1935. At the bottom of the advertisement were the words "For White People Only" (*CDM* 3.24.35, 2/2). One wonders if this were not a preemptive strike against black Mountaineers showing up at the door to ask if they could watch. The newspaper record of the period reveals no comparable declarations by promoters of black dances.

In sum, although the color line proved to be occasionally porous, it was never challenged by members of either race. Racial segregation of the dance floor was a given, but we may never know if some of those spectators in the balcony did not seize the opportunity to do a little dancing of their own while looking over the crowd for whom the music was intended.

Today, Price Hill, West Virginia, may be found on a detailed map of Raleigh County, but no road sign identifies it. If one did not know its history, the collection of aging mobile homes, a couple of churches, and a sewage treatment plant would be presumed to be an extension of the neighboring town of Mount Hope. The railroad line that served the mine was taken up long ago and only here and there can its roadbed be detected.

Oswald Road, on which resided the black miners and their families, is now heavily wooded, revealing nothing of its past. All that is to be seen is a creek on one side and a small stream red with iron oxide presumably from an old mine on the other. The steep side of the valley comes within four or five feet from that stream. Locating the site of the company housing for the African American community of Price Hill is virtually impossible, though about twenty feet up from the road, it does appear that someone had carved out level land. Perhaps that was where the housing was situated, though absent the information from the 1930 census there would have been no reason for a stranger even to anticipate finding such a location in the settlement today, a reality replicated widely throughout the coalfields of the Mountain State.

The current condition of Price Hill serves as a metaphor for the musical developments discussed in this study. One may find documents of this part of American musical history, and one may listen to the recordings of the big bands who brought jazz and other dance styles to the black West Virginians of the state's coalfields. But just as the evidence of day-to-day life during the 1930s and early 1940s in those coalfields—the mines, the railroad lines, the company houses—have vanished and their locations have returned to a state of nature, so too has this once flourishing musical environment disappeared, leaving behind only a distant memory of what had been.

Notes

Introduction

1. It is important to note that while rural blacks were migrating from Virginia and the Carolinas to West Virginia, a parallel migration of rural whites was occurring within those three states during the period from the 1880s to the 1920s. Their destination was the burgeoning textile industry. As evidence of that development, Patrick Huber notes in the Introduction to *Linthead Stomp: The Creation of Country Music in the Piedmont South* (Chapel Hill: University of North Carolina Press, 2008) that in North Carolina, whereas there were 49 textile mills employing more than 3,300 workers in 1880, by the mid-1920s there were 556 mills with a total workforce of more than 97,500 workers. Significant is the fact that 98 percent of those workers were white. Except for menial jobs, blacks were excluded from this workforce. This may explain the migration of African Americans from the Piedmont to West Virginia: it represented an opportunity for economic progress denied them in their home states.

2. The 1933 report confirmed that those counties having the largest number of black residents also included the largest numbers of black miners: Fayette, 2,932; Kanawha, 908; Logan, 2,440; McDowell, 5,566; Mercer, 833; Mingo, 573; and Raleigh, 3,426 ("Nationalities of Persons. . . ." *Annual Report 1933*, 114–17). That there were, literally, "tens of thousands of southern blacks" residing in West Virginia in this period stands in stark contrast to the more recent past. The decline in the state's African American population accompanied an overall decline in the number of West Virginians is explained by the fact that as coal companies turned increasingly to mechanizing their operations, the need for labor declined precipitously. Black miners were among the first to be laid off, but by the 1950s miners of all ethnicities were let go with increasing frequency throughout the entire industry. As noted by Ronald L. Lewis, "Between 1950 and 1970, the white work force fell [nationally] from 483,818 to 128,375 men, a decline of 73.5 percent. The effect on blacks was even more devastating as their total plunged from 30,042 to 3,673, a reduction of 87.8 percent in twenty years" (Lewis, 1987, 180). Absent alternative job opportunities in the state, miners both black and white left for the industrial centers of the North. The departure of African American miners and their families explains the "whitening" of the state's population, leading to its current image in the popular imagination.

3. Jedidiah Hotchkiss drew attention to one new operation prompted by the arrival of the C&O: "at Cannelton, the railroad has already given a stimulus to a mining operation conducted . . . on a very large scale." Cannelton is located on Fullpush Fork,

a tributary of the Kanawha, about ten miles north of Montgomery in Fayette County (Hotchkiss 1873, 289).

4. Work songs performed by blacks at work on the railroads of West Virginia were recorded and transcribed by Cortez D. Reece in "A study of selected folksongs collected mainly in southern West Virginia," PhD diss., University of Southern California, 1955.

5. The cultural transformation resulting from the rise of the coal industry may also be observed in the emergence of new musical styles resulting from the blending of practices associated with the several distinct populations from which came the workforce for the mines, interactions representing those "widely varying trajectories of change and cross-fertilization" that existed within the cultural spaces that were company towns where "a variety of musical practices coexist[ed]." One example of this cross-fertilization in the central Appalachians is that blend of diverse folk traditions known as bluegrass. The now well-established instrumentation of bluegrass bands clearly illustrates this cultural fusion. The fiddle, double bass, and mandolin are of Italian origin (as were many of the European-immigrant miners in West Virginia's coalfields); although the mandolin only recently had been introduced, violins and basses had been part of American musical culture since the late seventeenth or early eighteenth century. The guitar was Spanish, but while ubiquitous in the South and Southwest regions of the country only came to the mountains by way of the Sears Roebuck mail-order catalogue following World War I (*NYT* 10.10.1999, 20). The banjo is of West African ancestry. The presence of improvisation in many bluegrass performances also reflects influences of black musical traditions of America, particularly that of the blues.

6. Because there were only three black families in Cassville, Cranford recalls that they were not segregated from the white residents, either native or foreign-born. The family encountered racial segregation when it traveled to nearby Morgantown, the county seat.

7. In the period following World War I, according to Price Van Meter Fishback, while black agricultural workers (that is, sharecroppers) in the South earned on average between $.75 and $1.00 a day in the mid-1920s and unskilled black factory workers earned around $2.50 per day, African American coal miners in central Appalachia earned between $3.20 and $7.40 per eight-hour shift ("Employment Conditions of Blacks in the Coal Industry, 1900–1930," Ph.D. diss., University of Washington, 1983, 147–69).

8. While racially segregated public education became symbolic of racial oppression in the former Confederacy, it cannot be denied that in the North similar discrimination was practiced, though with greater subtlety. Allowing blacks to live only in certain neighborhoods in northern towns and cities and then drawing boundaries defining school districts in such a way that white and black children did not attend the same schools accomplished the same end.

9. Kenneth Gray, a generation younger than Ray Williams, recalled that in the late 1940s there were four black high schools in McDowell County: Elkhorn, Kimball (in the town named for Frederick Kimball, the financier of the Norfolk & Western Railway that runs through it), Gary District, and his own alma mater: Excelsior.

Chapter One

1. One place this phenomenon can be observed is along U.S. Highway 52, a road that traverses the state from east to west through the southern coalfields, entering the state at Bluefield, exiting it at Huntington. In eastern McDowell County, one community follows another so closely that often only a road sign indicates that one has left one settlement and entered another.

2. "Smokeless coal" was one of several terms referring to the type of bituminous (soft) coal found throughout southern West Virginia. Other terms include "metallurgical" because of its use in steel making, "steam," or "low sulphur" coal.

Chapter Two

1. The two volumes are now part of the collection of the Hogan Jazz Archive, Tulane University, New Orleans. Portions of the gig book relevant to Joe Oliver's life appeared in transcription in Walter C. Allen and Brian Rust's *King Joe Oliver* first published in 1955 and reissued in a revised edition entitled simply *King Oliver* by Laurie Wright in 1987. That transcription does not present all entries in their entirety, however, and in a number of instances it contains errors as well.

2. Herbert Hall noted that maintenance of the first bus that the Don Albert Orchestra acquired in 1931 was of such importance that "that was taken care of first so we could get to the next town . . . and what's left, then we divide[d] it" (Hall 1980; Wilkinson 2001, 74).

3. As uncertain as income based on a percentage of the gate may seem, it should also be noted that black bands under national management saw only a very small percentage of the money they earned for a guaranteed wage. Much later in life Andy Kirk, one of Joe Glaser's bandleaders, reflected on this state of affairs. "People may wonder if we were exploited by agents. We all were. In contracts. The bookers and managers had their own lawyers who were ours too. That didn't make any sense. Glaser got his cut, the territory booker [e.g. George Morton] got his cut, the ballroom or location got their cut. We had what was left. But we were happy to be playing, so we didn't think too much about the money" (Kirk 1989, 93–94).

Chapter Three

1. Schuller's discussion of big bands in the 1920s in the sixth chapter of *Early Jazz: Its Roots and Musical Development* focuses on recordings, which is understandable since his study is grounded in recordings of this music. He noted: "As jazz expands in the 1920s, it becomes increasingly difficult to sort out the many strands of . . . regional-social characteristics. At one level, it is self-evident that the sudden wide dissemination of records (and radio) broke down regional differences. A musician in Kansas City did not have to travel to Chicago or New York to know what was being played in those cities. He could hear it on records, and he could be influenced by what

he heard (if he was so inclined)" (242). In West Virginia, recordings were not as easily available as were radios; it was the latter medium that widely disseminated the sound of the big bands in the Mountain State.

Chapter Four

1. Les Precieuses Club was founded in 1931 by seven women with the purpose of promoting "civic and social development," according to Mrs. Nakomis Shelton in an article on the history of black McDowell County published at some point late in the 1950s in the *Welch Daily News*. Such development included, at least by the 1950s, the funding of scholarship, support for the Red Cross and the Home for the Aged, the location of which was not indicated (*WDN*, date unknown).

2. I interviewed Lester Clifford at his home in Piedmont on two occasions: June 27 and July 11, 2001. Additionally, I had a short telephone conversation with him on July 20 of the same year. The description of the Midnighters' history is based entirely on those interviews.

3. The titles were selected from Table 3, "Jazz Standards in Order of Publication," of Richard Crawford and Jeffrey Magee's *Jazz Standards on Record, 1900–1942: A Core Repertory*, xii–xiii.

4. Best known of such college bands was the 'Bama State Collegians, originally from Alabama State University. Led by trumpet player Erskine Hawkins, the band had a style that was alternately sweet and hot that ultimately appealed to dancers more than to fans of jazz. Gunther Schuller wrote that it had a "single-minded function as a superior dance band" (1989, 412). In doing so, he was damning it with faint praise.

Chapter Seven

1. The West Virginia newspapers documenting the dances held in 1934 are the *Beckley Post-Herald, Bluefield Daily Telegraph, Charleston Daily Mail, Charleston Gazette, Fairmont Times, Fairmont Times–West Virginian, Fairmont West Virginian, Huntington Advertiser, Logan Banner, Welch Daily News*, and the *West Virginia Weekly*.

Chapter Ten

1. In the introduction to his study, *Swinging the Machine: Modernity, Technology, and African-American Culture between the World Wars*, Joel Dinnerstein situates public dances in a larger cultural context: "The social function of nearly all African American musical practice before 1945 was to create a public forum that provided the following: social bonding through music and dance, an opportunity to create an individual style within a collective form, and a dense rhythmic wave that imparts 'participatory consciousness' to the audience" (7–8).

2. As its subtitle suggests, Dinnerstein's *Swinging the Machine* argues for a close connection between jazz-related dance and the impact of machines on American life: "big-band swing, tap dance, and the lindy hop were public models of humanized machine aesthetics" (12). He goes on to assert that "as machines speeded up hands, hearts, and minds individuals had to engage these new aesthetics on the body" (13). Epitomizing such a connection was Duke Ellington's virtuosic, high-speed composition from 1930, "Daybreak Express." It seems plausible that a connection between the demands of assembly-line labor and an up-tempo dance that empowered the dancers to make their own moves may have been at work in the factories of the urban North. Not so in the coalfields of West Virginia. Mining was not assembly line work; each miner set his own tempo. The trains moved slowly on the constantly curving tracks that climbed or descended long and in places steep grades. I suspect the popularity of the Lindy Hop among black Mountaineers had far more to do with the simple fact that it was an up-to-date, big-city dance that permitted individual expression, provided an opportunity to demonstrate creativity in collaboration with a partner, and in the final analysis was just plain fun to dance, rather than being a conscious projection of larger cultural forces.

Works Cited

Ambler, Charles H., and Festus Summers. 1958. *West Virginia: The Mountain State.* 2nd ed. Englewood Cliffs: Prentice-Hall.
Baratz, Milton S. 1955. *The Union and the Coal Industry: Yale Studies in Economics 4.* New Haven: Yale University Press.
Barnes, Paul. 1933–1952. Unpublished personal diary. William Ransom Hogan Jazz Archive, Tulane University, New Orleans, Louisiana.
Barnum, Darold T. 1970. *The Racial Policies of American Industry, Report No. 14.* Philadelphia: Wharton School of Finance and Commerce, University of Pennsylvania.
Bureau of Negro Welfare and Statistics. 1933. *Fifth Biennial Report of the Bureau of Negro Welfare and Statistics 1929–1932.* Charleston, WV.
Byerly, Don W., and John J. Renton. 2006. "Geology." *Encyclopedia of Appalachia,* ed. Rudy Abramson and Jean Haskell. Knoxville: University of Tennessee Press.
Corbin, David Alan. 1981. *Life, Work, and Rebellion in the Coal Fields: The Southern West Virginia Miners, 1880–1922.* Urbana: University of Illinois Press.
Crabtree, Mark. *Cirkut Panoramic Photos by Ruffus E. "Red" Ribble.* homepage.mac.com/crabtree/ribble.htm (accessed June 21, 2010).
Crawford, Richard, and Jeffrey Magee. 1992. *Jazz Standards on Record, 1900–1942: A Core Repertory.* Chicago: Center for Black Music Research, Columbia College Chicago.
Dance, Stanley. 1974. *The World of Swing.* New York: Charles Scribner's Sons.
Determeyer, Eddy. 2006. *Rhythm Is Our Business: Jimmie Lunceford and the Harlem Express.* Ann Arbor: University of Michigan Press.
Dinnerstein, Joel. 2003. *Swinging the Machine: Modernity, Technology, and African-American Culture between the World Wars.* Amherst: University of Massachusetts Press.
Dubovsky, Melvyn, and Warren Van Tine. 1977. *John L. Lewis: A Biography.* New York: Quadrangle.
Eller, Ronald D. *Mountain Road: A Study of the Construction of the Chesapeake and Ohio Railroad in Southern West Virginia, 1867–1873.* M.A. thesis, University of North Carolina.
Erenberg, Lewis A. 1998. *Swingin' the Dream: Big Band Jazz and the Rebirth of American Culture.* Chicago: University of Chicago Press.
Fishback, Price Van Meter. 1983. *Employment Conditions of Blacks in the Coal Industry, 1900–1930.* Ph.D. diss., University of Washington.

Franklin, John Hope. and Alfred A. Moss Jr. 1988. *From Slavery to Freedom: A History of Negro Americans.* 5th ed. New York: Alfred A. Knopf.

Gates, Henry Louis, Jr. 1994. *Colored People: A Memoir.* New York: Alfred A. Knopf.

Gleason, Ralph J. 1975; 1999. Excerpt from *Celebrating the Duke* in *Reading Jazz: A Gathering of Autobiography, Reportage, and Criticism from 1919 to Now.* Ed. Robert Gottlieb. New York: Vintage. 494–500.

Hennessey, Thomas. 1994. *From Jazz to Swing: African-American Jazz Musicians and their Music, 1890–1935.* Detroit: Wayne State University Press.

Hotchkiss, Jedidiah. 1873. "New Ways in the Old Dominion: The Chesapeake and Ohio Railroad—II." *Scribner's Monthly* 5, no. 2 (January): 273–92.

Huber, Patrick. 2008. *Linthead Stomp: The Creation of Country Music in the Piedmont South.* Chapel Hill: University of North Carolina Press.

Joly, Marcel. 1988. "Barnes, Polo." *New Grove Dictionary of Jazz.* New York: St. Martin's.

Kirk, Andy. 1989. *Twenty Years on Wheels,* as told to Amy Lee. Ann Arbor: University of Michigan Press.

Kline, Michael. 1987. "Something to Give: Nat Reese's Early Life and Music." *Goldenseal* 13/4 (Winter): 9–18.

Kolodin, Irving. 1941. "The Dance Band Business: A Study in Black and White." *Harper's Magazine* 183/1 (June): 72–82.

Lambie, Joseph T. 1954. *From Mine to Market: The History of Coal Transportation on the Norfolk and Western Railway.* New York: New York University Press.

Laing, James T. 1933. *The Negro Miner in West Virginia.* Ph.D. diss., Ohio State University.

Lewis, Ronald L. 1987. *Black Coal Miners in America: Race, Class, and Community Conflict, 1780–1980.* Lexington: University Press of Kentucky.

———. 1989. "From Peasant to Proletarian: The Migration of Southern Blacks to the Central Appalachian Coalfields." *Journal of Southern History* 50/1 (February): 77–102.

———. 1999. "Beyond Isolation and Homogeneity: Diversity and the History of Appalachia." *Confronting Appalachian Stereotypes: Back Talk from an American Region.* University Press of Kentucky. 21–43.

Lomax, Alan. 1990. *Appalachian Journey* (VHS). Series: *American Patchwork.* Alexandria, VA: PBS Video.

Lombardo, Guy, with Jack Altshul. 1975. *Auld Acquaintance.* Garden City: Doubleday.

Lord, Tom. 1995. *The Jazz Discography.* Vol. 13. West Vancouver, BC: Lord Music Reference.

Magee, Jeffrey. 2005. *The Uncrowned King of Swing: Fletcher Henderson and Big Band Jazz.* New York: Oxford University Press.

Malone, Bill C. 2002. *Don't Get Above Your Raisin': Country Music and the Southern Working Class.* Urbana: University of Illinois Press.

McCarthy, Albert. 1964. "Jimmie Lunceford: A Reply." *Jazz Panorama.* Ed. Martin Williams. New York: Collier. 136–38.

———. 1974. *Big Band Jazz.* New York: G. P. Putnam's Sons.

McPhee, John. 1998. *Annals of the Former World.* New York: Farrar, Straus, and Giroux.

McQuitty, Mose. [n.d.] Unpublished Route Book, property of Alex Albright, East Carolina University, Greenville, NC.

Meador, Michael M. 1987. "Viola Clark." *Goldenseal* 13/4 (Winter): 28–30.

National Recovery Administration. 1933. Bituminous Coal Code. Washington, DC: Government Printing Office.

Northrup, Herbert R. 1944. *Organized Labor and the Negro*. New York: Harper.

Owston, James M. 1989. *Heterodyning in the Hills: The WOBU Story*. jeff560.tripod.com/wchs1.html (accessed June 21, 2010).

Pearson, Barry Lee. 1990. *Virginia Piedmont Blues: The Lives and Art of Two Virginia Bluesmen*. Philadelphia: University of Pennsylvania Press.

Posey, Thomas E. 1934. *The Negro Citizen of West Virginia*. Institute, WV: Press of West Virginia State College.

Rankin, John R. 1984. "Blacks in Bluefield: Past and Present." *Mercer County History*. Princeton: Mercer County Historical Society. 11–14.

Ridgway, Thomas S. 1872. "Report of the Iron, Coal, and Other Minerals Along the Route of the Chesapeake and Ohio Railroad." *Commercial and Financial Chronicle* 15 (September 21, 1872): 387–88. Qtd. in Ronald D. Eller, *Mountain Road: A Study of the Construction of the Chesapeake and Ohio Railroad in Southern West Virginia, 1867–1873*. M.A. thesis, University of North Carolina.

Rural Electrification Administration. 1940. *Rural Electrification in West Virginia, June 30, 1939. 1939 Report of the Rural Electrification Administration*. Washington, DC: Government Printing Office.

Russell, Ross. 1971. *Jazz Style in Kansas City and the Southwest*. Berkeley: University of California Press.

Satchmo. 1989. Prod. Tony Byron, dir. Gary Giddins with Kendrick Simmons. Masters of American Music series, no. 2. CMV Enterprises videocassette, 87 min.

Scheidt, Duncan. 1965. "Speed Webb." *Sounds and Fury* September-October (1/2): 46–52.

Schuller, Gunther. 1989. *The Swing Era: The Development of Jazz, 1930–1945*. New York: Oxford University Press.

Stowe, David W. 1994. *Swing Changes: Big-Band Jazz in New Deal America*. Cambridge: Harvard University Press.

Straw, Will. 1991. "Systems of Articulation, Logics of Change: Communities and Scenes in Popular Music." *Cultural Studies* 5/3 (October): 368–88.

Tams, William P., Jr. 1963. *The Smokeless Coal Fields of West Virginia: A Brief History*. Morgantown: West Virginia University Press.

Taylor, Alrutheus A. 1926. *The Negro in the Reconstruction of Virginia*. New York: Association for the Study of Negro Life and History.

Thomas, Jerry Bruce. 1998. *An Appalachian New Deal: West Virginia in the Great Depression*. Lexington: University Press of Kentucky.

Tribe, Ivan M. 1984. *Mountaineer Jamboree: Country Music in West Virginia*. Lexington: University Press of Kentucky.

Trotter, Joe William Jr. 1990. *Coal, Class, and Color: Blacks in Southern West Virginia, 1915–1932*. Urbana: University of Illinois Press.

U.S. Bureau of the Census. 1941. *Sixteenth Census of the United States 1940. Population Second Series: Characteristics of the Population of West Virginia*. Prepared under the supervision of Dr. Leon E. Truesdell. Washington, DC: Government Printing Office.

U.S. Congress. Senate. 1925. *Report of the United States Coal Commission*. Sen. Doc. 195, 68th Congress, 2nd session. Washington, DC: Government Printing Office.

West Virginia Department of Mines. 1931. *Annual Report of the* [West Virginia] *Department of Mines, 1931*. Charleston, WV.

———. 1933. Nationalities of Persons Employed at the Mines and Coke Ovens by Counties. *Annual Report of the* [West Virginia] *Department of Mines, 1933*. Charleston, WV.

———. 1941. Comparative Statement of the Number of Men Employed, Men Killed, and the Production of Coal from 1883 to 1941. *Annual Report of the* [West Virginia] *Department of Mines, 1941*. Charleston, WV.

Wilkinson, Christopher. 2001. *Jazz on the Road: Don Albert's Musical Life*. Berkeley: University of California Press.

Williams, John Alexander. 2002. *Appalachia: A History*. Chapel Hill: University of North Carolina Press.

Wriggle, John. 2007. "Chappie Willet, Frank Fairfax, and Phil Edwards' Collegians: From West Virginia to Philadelphia." *Black Music Research Journal* Spring (27/1): 1–22.

Newspapers

Abbreviations used to cite these publications in the main text are given in parentheses.

Beckley Observer (BO)
Bluefield Daily Telegraph (BDT)
Charleston Daily Mail (CDM)
Chicago Defender (CD)
Cincinnati Enquirer (CE)
Pittsburgh Courier (PC)
New York Times (NYT)
News Observer (NO)
Twin State News Observer (TSNO)
Welch Daily News (WDN)
West Virginian (Fairmont, WV) *(WV)*
Williamson Daily News (WillDN)

Interviews

Belmear, Geraldine Carpenter. 2000. Interview with the author. Morgantown, WV. May 30.

Cranford, Marcus, Hughie Mills, John M. Watson, Ellis Ray Williams, and Christine Neal Williams. 2008. Interview with the author. Morgantown, WV. October 14. Cited as Cranford et al.

Clifford, Lester. 2001. Interview with the author. Piedmont, WV. July 11.

Flippen, Francis Morton and J. Bryan. 2005. Interview with the author. Silver Spring, MD. October 8.

Glover, June. 2005. Interview with the author. Williamson, WV. June 15.

Hall, Herbert. 1980. Interview with Sterlin Holmesly. February 23. Research Library, Institute of Texan Cultures, San Antonio, Texas.

Mack, Thomas H. 2005. Interview with the author. Bluefield, WV. July 14.

Nallen, Hazel. 2001. Telephone interview with the author. May 14.

Wilder, Joe. 2008. Telephone interview with the author. June 7.

Williams, E. Ray and Christine N. 2005. Interview with the author. Welch, WV. July 13.

Index

African Americans in West Virginia: as coal miners, 6–7, 24, 29; educational opportunities for, 27; as members of the middle class, 26–27; migration patterns of, 5, 12–13, 14–15, 24; political benefits, 24–26; as railroad workers, 12–14, 23–24
Akron, Ohio, 94, 139
Alabama, 24
Albert, Don, 3, 69–70, 88, 164
Alhambra Night Club, 45, 141
Alleghenian Orogeny. See West Virginia: geologic history of
Allegheny Mountains, 9
Allegheny plateau, 9
Alpha Kappa Alpha, 73, 119
Alpha Phi Alpha, 73, 119
Amusement Kings, 129–30, 140–43, 148, 158
Anderson, Elmer, and his Rhythm Kings, 119, 149
Appalachian Agreement. See Bituminous Coal Code
Arkansas, 3
Armstrong, Lil Hardin, 145
Armstrong, Louis, 80, 88, 96, 99, 127, 132
Ashland, Kentucky, 53, 92
Associated Booking Artists, 46, 132
Audience reception. See Musical taste of black audiences

Bailey, Pearl, 76
Baldwin-Felts Detective Agency, 29
Baltimore & Ohio Railroad, 10, 74, 75, 113, 138
Band popularity contest. See *Pittsburgh Courier:* Most Popular Dance Band contest of
Barnes, Paul D. "Polo," 4, 48; gig book of, 48–50, 53, 54–56, 57–58, 67, 70, 106
Barnes, Walter, and his Royal Creolians, 45, 91, 92, 97, 125
Basie, William "Count," and his Orchestra, 57, 62, 69, 136, 139, 145
Bears Club, 45, 96
Beckley, West Virginia, 16, 23, 26, 44, 66, 72, 82, 89, 95, 100, 109, 128, 131, 133, 136, 145, 161
Belton, C. S., and his Society Syncopators, 91, 94–95, 99
Berlin, Irving, 84, 159
Billups, Eddie, 82
Biloxi, Mississippi, 54
Bittner, Van Amberg, 30
Bituminous Coal Code, 30–31, 43, 46, 51, 67, 88, 144; impact on coal industry, 30–31, 102, 106, 171
Black Mountaineers. See African Americans in West Virginia
Bluefield, West Virginia, 16, 17, 22, 25, 26, 29, 72, 83, 95, 99, 109, 131, 133, 136, 140, 142, 159, 160, 161
Bluefield State College, 73, 81, 83, 104, 140, 160, 175
Bradshaw, Myron "Tiny," and his Orchestra, 132, 136, 161
Bramwell, West Virginia, 17
Brooks, Henry, 147
Buckhannon, West Virginia, 27
Byrd, Odell, 146

Cabell County, 45
Cabin Creek, West Virginia, 161

Calloway, Blanche, and her Orchestra, 45–46, 91, 94, 99
Calloway, Cab, and his Orchestra, 66, 68, 88, 99, 107, 111, 112, 121, 125, 128, 131, 136, 141, 144, 149
Campus Nighthawks, 45, 82
Campus Revelers, 70, 82, 84, 107, 113
Capehart, Hugh J., 26, 133
Capehart Anti-Lynch Law, 26
Carmichael, Hoagy, 79, 81, 159
Carpenter, Samuel, 45–46, 130, 137–39, 163
Carter, Ardelia, 143
Carter, Benny, 70, 111
Cassville, West Virginia, 22
Celestin, Oscar "Papa," 48
Charleston, West Virginia, 4, 23, 26, 45, 65, 70, 82, 86, 95, 100, 104, 107, 109, 129, 130, 133, 136, 140, 141, 148, 157, 158, 160, 161, 162, 174
Charlottesville, Virginia, 136
Chesapeake & Ohio Railway (C&O), 10–13, 14, 24, 36, 175
Chicago, Illinois, 87, 94, 96, 108, 111
Chicago Defender, 97
Chula Vista, California, 64
Cincinnati, Ohio, 12, 51, 64, 86, 88, 95, 98, 100, 104, 157, 159
Cincinnati Enquirer, 98
Circuses. *See* Musical Life in Black West Virginia before the 1930s
Clark, Viola, 73
Clarksburg, West Virginia, 77, 83, 113, 138
Clemson College, 161
Cleveland, Ohio, 87, 94
Clifford, Lester, 74, 77, 79, 118
Clifford, Mack, 76
Coal camps. *See* Company Towns
Coal mining: description of the work involved in, 38–40, 43; economic benefits of, 24, 43; impact of mechanization, 165–66; safety issues of, 40–42; size of black workforce in, 6–7
Coalwood, West Virginia, 19
College dance bands, 81–83

Columbia Broadcasting System (CBS), 65, 174
Columbus, Ohio, 94, 132
"Commonwealth" principle, 53–54, 79
Company towns, 15, 18, 19, 21, 31, 35–36, 44, 62–63, 66, 118, 143, 173
Cotton Club, Harlem, New York, 111, 121
"Cotton Club Parade," 111
County seats. *See individual places*
Crider, Beatrice, 143
Crider, Samuel, 143, 148
Crystal Caverns Ballroom, Martinsburg, West Virginia, 161
Cumberland, Maryland, 72, 75, 113, 138

Dallas, Texas, 70
Dalton, Quenton, 46
Dances: promotion by local bands of, 77; social function of, 171–72
Davis, John W., 119, 156
Decca Records, 152
Delta Sigma Theta, 73
Detroit, Michigan, 87
DuBois, W. E. B., 73, 82
Dubois High School, 45, 82, 133, 145

Eckstein, Allen E., 65, 66, 70, 149
Edwards, Philip H., 83, 91
Edwards's Collegians, 82, 83–84, 88, 95, 97–100, 120, 159
Electricity, availability of, in West Virginia, 62–63
Elkhorn, West Virginia, 78, 113
Elkins, West Virginia, 78, 113
Elks Rest, 45, 72, 78, 138
Ellington, Edward Kennedy "Duke," 57, 62, 66, 69, 79, 84, 88, 99, 110, 111, 115, 121, 149, 157, 161, 167, 177; broadcast from the Crystal Ballroom, Fargo, North Dakota, 156–57
Ellington, Ruth, and her Orchestra, 46, 139
Embry, Jordan, 91, 92, 104

Fairfax, Frank, 84
Fairmont, West Virginia, 4, 23, 26, 45–

46, 61, 65, 72, 74, 77, 78, 86, 96, 100, 106, 107, 110, 113, 115, 117, 119, 121, 125, 128, 130, 133, 137, 138, 157, 159, 160, 177
Fargo, North Dakota, 156–58
Fayette County, West Virginia, 11
Ferguson Hotel, 45, 111
Fitzgerald, Ella, 57, 136, 158
Fisk University, 27, 160
Florida, 56
Fonteneau, Leroy "Tex," 130, 141, 158
Fox Trot, 22, 163

Gains, Walter, 146–47
Gale, Moe, 132, 136, 169
Garnett High School, 70
Gary, West Virginia, 17, 19, 27, 104, 131
Gates, Henry Louis, Jr., 75
Georgia, 56
Gershwin, George and Ira, 79, 85
Gilmore, James, 74, 77, 79, 88
Gilmore's Midnighters, 74, 76–79, 84, 113; repertory of, 79–80, 115, 118, 120
Glaser, Joe, 46, 53, 89, 112, 126, 132, 136, 169
Goodman, Benny, 65, 79, 110, 121, 125, 126, 151
Grafton, West Virginia, 138
Grear, Cal, and his Sweet Swing Orchestra, 79, 84, 88, 141
Great Depression: on black miners, 29; impact on coal industry, 29
Great Migration, 175–76
Green, Major, 146
Greenbrier County, West Virginia, 26
Greystone Ballroom, Cincinnati, Ohio, 84, 88, 95, 98
Grider, Joseph, 70, 82
Griffith, D. W., *The Birth of a Nation*, law prohibiting showing in West Virginia, 26
Guffey-Snyder Act, 31
Guffey-Vinson Act, 31

Halifax, Nova Scotia, 64
Hall, Herbert, 34, 47–48, 57, 67, 85, 100, 145, 163, 164

Hampton, Lionel, and his Orchestra, 25, 132
Harlan, Kentucky, 53
Harlem Hotshots. *See* Watkins, Edward
Harrison County, West Virginia, 6, 113, 137
Hart, C. W., 130, 141, 148
Havana, Cuba, 64
Hawkins, Erskine, and his Orchestra, 57, 136, 154
Henderson, Fletcher, and his Orchestra, 66, 68–69, 72, 76, 99, 104, 110, 111, 112, 125, 149, 156
Hines, Earl "Fatha," and his Grand Terrace Orchestra, 66, 91, 92, 128, 131, 145, 149
Hinton, West Virginia, 131
Hite, Les, 167
Holden, West Virginia, 20
Holmesly, Sterlin, 3
Hopkins, Claude, 23, 70, 98, 107, 143, 149
Hopkinsville, Kentucky, 50
Hotchkiss, Jedediah, 12, 16, 175
Hotels owned by black West Virginians, 133
Huntington, Collis Potter, 10
Huntington, West Virginia, 12, 17, 45, 46, 50–51, 54, 56, 65, 70, 86, 95, 100, 106, 108, 125, 131, 160, 161, 163

"I Got Rhythm," 79–80
Iaeger, West Virginia, 17
Illinois, 50
Indiana, 50
Indianapolis, Indiana, 37, 87
Institute, West Virginia, 66, 162
International Sweethearts of Rhythm, 131
Itmann, West Virginia, 16, 19, 21
Ivy Leaf Club, 119

Jackson, James, 45
Jacksonville, Florida, 104
James, Harry, 80
Jenkinjones, West Virginia, 18
Jenkins, Kentucky, 53

"Jim Crow" (railroad passenger) car, 25
Joy, Joseph F., 165
Joy Loading Machine, 165–66, 176

Kanawha County, West Virginia, 5, 6, 11, 136
Kansas City, Missouri, 99
Kapp, Jack, 152
Kappa Alpha Psi, 160, 162
Kappa Kappa Psi, 83
Kaye, Sammy, and his Orchestra, 65
KDKA (Pittsburgh, Pennsylvania, radio station), 64, 65
Kennedy, John F., 3
Kentucky, 3, 7, 8, 9, 11, 14, 44, 51, 53, 95
Keyser, West Virginia, 78, 138
Keystone, West Virginia, 17, 72, 131
Kimball, Frederick J., 13, 14
Kimball, West Virginia, 17, 131, 140, 143
King, Wayne, 23, 143, 149
Kings of Amusement. *See* Amusement Kings
Kirk, Andy, and his Twelve Clouds of Joy, 4, 57, 62, 68, 132, 139, 152, 155, 161, 163
Kodak #8 Cirkut Outfit (camera), 36

Lanes, Maude Wanzer, 70
Lee, Clarence, 137
Les Precieuses Club, 72, 73, 140, 143
Lewis, John L., 30
Lewis, Willie, 111
Lexington, Kentucky, 53
Lindy (hop), 22, 151, 154, 156, 161, 163
Locklayer's Virginians, 162
Logan, West Virginia, 26, 109, 128, 131, 136, 140, 154, 161
Logan Banner, 65
Logan County, West Virginia, 20, 30, 45, 65, 109, 140
Lomax, Alan, 21
Lombardo, Guy, and his Royal Canadians, 79, 118, 149, 150–51, 153, 157, 162, 172, 174
Los Angeles, California, 125, 126
Louisiana, 56

Louisville, Kentucky, 108
Lunceford, Jimmie, and the Harlem Express, 4, 57, 62, 69, 107–8, 109–13, 115, 120, 136, 137, 138, 140, 145, 152, 158–61, 174; recordings by, 113–14, 116–18, 125, 159; repertory played, 115–18, 120, 158, 161
Lunceford, Joan, 4

Mabscott, West Virginia, 143
Marion County, West Virginia, 6, 113, 137
Market Auditorium, 107, 159
Marrow, Vernon, 46
Martin, James Ernest, 130, 142
Maryland, 74, 113
Massey, Price, 146
Massey, Sylvester, 46, 51, 84
Maybeury, West Virginia, 17
Maysville, Kentucky, 53
McConnell, Ross, 50, 51, 106
McDowell County, West Virginia, 6, 14, 16, 17, 18, 19, 24, 26, 27, 30, 44, 64, 72, 99, 104, 133, 136, 140
McKinney's Cotton Pickers, 66, 76, 149
McQuity, Mose, 16
Mechanization of coal mining. *See* Coal mining: impact of mechanization
Mercer County, West Virginia, 14, 30, 109
Merman, Ethel, 79
Miami, Florida, 46, 132
Michigan, 50
Mike, Gladys, 118, 162
Millinder, Lucky, and his Band, 83, 111
Mills, Irving, 111, 112, 120, 121
Mills Blue Rhythm Band, 94, 99
Mineral County, West Virginia, 74
Mingo County, West Virginia, 14, 21, 30, 64
Minstrel shows, 16
Mississippi, 56
Mitchell, Thomas L., 130, 141–42
Monongalia County, West Virginia, 6, 22, 113, 137
Montgomery, West Virginia, 131, 161

Moore, Richard, 107, 144
Morgantown, West Virginia, 77, 113, 138
Morris, William, 112
Morrow, Vernon, 46, 137
Morton, Edward LeRoy, 27, 128, 160
Morton, Ferdinand "Jelly Roll," 48
Morton, George, 27, 46, 89, 126, 128–36, 138, 139, 140, 141, 145, 146, 158, 160
Moten, Bennie, and his Kansas City Orchestra, 61, 88, 94, 99
Mount Hope, West Virginia, 36, 45, 82, 131, 133, 136, 145, 160, 177
Mullins, West Virginia, 16, 17, 78
Musical life in black West Virginia before the 1930s, 176: blues, 16, 18–19; circuses, 16; commercial music including popular songs, 23–24; in company towns, 15, 22–23; in county seats, 15, 23; gospel, 16, 19–20; parade bands, 19; piano "professors," 21; square dancing, 22–23; string bands, 19; tent shows, 16–17, 18; work songs, 16
Musical taste of black audiences, 116, 161, 162–63

National Guard armories. *See* West Virginia National Guard, armories of
National Industrial Recovery Act, 28, 30
National Recovery Administration (NRA), 30, 31, 43
Nelson, Charles "Turk," 137
New Dardenella Girls, 92
New Orleans, Louisiana, 48, 51, 69, 99, 104
New York, New York, 99, 104, 105, 111, 115, 126, 128, 138
Newberry, South Carolina, 27
Norfolk & Western Railway (N&W), 9, 10, 14, 15, 16, 17, 25, 51, 141
North Carolina, 15, 16, 20, 56, 95
Northfork, West Virginia, 142
Nunn, William G., 136

Office of Defense Transportation, 168
Ohio, 8, 9, 11, 15, 51, 92

Oliver, Joe "King," and his Victor Recording Orchestra, 4, 48, 51, 56, 57, 70, 79, 88, 106, 120, 121, 125, 133, 138, 145, 177
Oliver, [Melvin James] "Sy," 115
Omega Psi Phi, 83
Original Diamond Band, 48
Owens, Ernest, 23, 143, 150
Oxley, Harold, 112, 136, 169

Palomar Ballroom, 125
Parker, Virginia "Peppy," 72, 88
Parkersburg, West Virginia, 10, 65, 113, 161, 162
Pennsylvania, 8, 92
"Percentage dates," 53, 79, 152
Perkins, Lola, 146, 148
Perkins, Thomas, 146, 148
Philadelphia, Pennsylvania, 82, 84, 99, 159
Pianos and parlor music, 23
Piedmont, West Virginia, 74–75, 86, 113, 138
Piedmont City Band, 76
Pittsburgh, Pennsylvania, 12, 51, 94, 128, 137, 138
Pittsburgh Courier, 4, 61, 65, 66, 83, 89, 97, 99, 128, 133, 135, 137, 138; Most Popular Dance Band contest of, 97, 98–100, 118, 149
Plessy vs. Ferguson (1896), 24
Pocahontas, Virginia, 17
Pocahontas coalfield, 14, 16
Poore, Richard, 70
Porter, Cole, 115, 159
Price Hill, West Virginia, 36, 144, 145–47, 177–78
Price Hill Colliery Company, 36, 45, 147
Promotion of dances, 133
Providence, Rhode Island, 161
Public Works Administration, 30
Purnell, William "Keg," 70

Radio, 19, 23, 58, 62–65, 97, 99, 100, 109, 113, 126, 149, 151, 153, 170
"Radio Highlights." *See* Eckstein, Allen E.

Railroads in West Virginia. *See individual railroads*
Raleigh County, West Virginia, 6, 14, 27, 44, 109, 137, 143, 145
Raschel, Jimmie, and his New Orleans Ramblers, 104
Recordings and phonographs, 18, 19, 23, 110, 111–12, 126, 149
Redman, Don, 66, 69, 70, 72, 107, 111, 125, 149, 177
Redman, Louis, and his Bellhops, 72
Rena, Henry "Kid," 48
Ribble, Rufus E. "Red," 36, 144, 147
Richmond, Virginia, 136
Riley's Nighthawks, 66, 82
Robinson, Robert L., 131, 142
Rockwell-O'Keefe, 46, 89, 132
Rogers, Henry Huddleston, 14
Roosevelt, Franklin Delano, administration of, 7, 28, 30, 102, 172
Roosevelt Grill, Hotel Roosevelt, 150, 174
Rose Garden Inn, 73, 133
Russell, Charles "Inky," and His Orchestra, 88

Saunders, Charles, 137, 139
Saunders, Talitha G., 66, 118, 143, 149
Savoy Ballroom, Harlem, New York City, 94, 151, 153, 174
Scott, Cecil, and his Orchestra, 125
Scott, Sam, 146
Shaw, Arvell, 127
Shelton, Clarence F., 131, 142
Shelton, James A., 130, 131, 142
Silas Green from New Orleans. *See* Musical life in black West Virginia before the 1930s: tent shows
Sissle, Noble, and his Orchestra, 4, 23, 45, 65, 66, 99, 108–10, 119, 121, 125, 137, 139, 143, 149, 162, 177
Smith, Bessie, 17
Smith, Bobby, and his Collegians, 105
Snelson, Floyd, 98
Social classes of black West Virginians, 163, 172, 174–75
South Carolina, 15, 16, 20, 27, 56

"Stardust," 79
Stepin Fetchit Review, 84
Stewart, "Smiling" Billy, and his Floridians, 104
Stock arrangements, 68–69, 70, 79
Summers County, West Virginia, 18
Sunset Royal Serenaders, 46, 125
Sweet music vs. hot jazz, 79, 86, 116, 149, 150–51, 153, 162–63, 172–73

Tams, William Purvience, 35, 38–43, 165, 166
Tate, Erskine, and his Vendome Theater Orchestra, 45, 96–97
Taylor County, West Virginia, 138
Tennessee, 3, 44, 95
Tent shows. *See* Musical life in black West Virginia
Terrell, Pha, 152, 157
Territory bands, 68, 86–87, 122
Toledo, Ohio, 87
Toots, Hartley, and his Orchestra, 132, 145
Trent, Alphonso, 46, 51, 84
Tuxedo Club, 140

Uniontown, Pennsylvania, 113
United Mine Workers of America (UMWA), 7, 24, 28–29, 30, 31, 43, 46, 67, 102, 171; Local 17 of, 30
Universal Promoters, 132, 136, 137, 160
Utica, New York, 73

Vanity Fair Ballroom, 45, 46, 108, 132, 160
Vendome Theater, 96
Virginia, 3, 7, 13, 16, 21, 24, 44, 50, 56, 87
Virginian Railway, 10, 14–15
Vivian, West Virginia, 17

Wade, Sam, 142
Waller, Thomas "Fats," 85, 115
War, West Virginia, 17
War Production Board, 167
Washington, Booker T., 175

Washington, Chester "Chet," 128
Watkins, Edward, and his Serenaders, 72–73, 140
Watkins, Harry, 72, 83
Watkins, Lena, 143
"Wave Lengths." *See* Eckstein, Allen E.
WBRW (Welch, West Virginia, radio station), 65
WBTH (Williamson, West Virginia, radio station), 65
WCSH (Charleston, West Virginia, radio station), 65
Webb, Lawrence Arthur "Speed," and his Orchestra, 20, 45, 92, 125, 140, 156
Webb, William Henry "Chick," and His Chicks, 57, 94, 132, 149, 151, 155–56, 158, 174
Welch, West Virginia, 26, 44, 64, 104, 108, 109, 128, 131, 133, 140, 142, 156
West, James A., 46, 128, 130, 137, 157
West Palm Beach, Florida, 95, 99
West Virginia, 3, 11, 14; constitution of 1872, 25; geologic history of, 7–9, 40–41; growth of black population, 5–6; topography of, 92. *See also individual counties and communities*
West Virginia National Guard, 29; armories of, 45, 46, 95, 96, 107, 108, 109, 129, 131, 133, 137–38, 139, 145, 157, 159, 160
West Virginia Pulp and Paper Company, 74, 77
West Virginia State College, 27, 46, 66, 70, 73, 81, 83, 91, 100, 104, 105, 120, 128, 140, 149, 156, 160, 162, 174
West Virginia State College Club, 45, 108
West Virginia State Collegians, 82, 83, 162
West Virginia State Scrollers, 83, 119
Weston, West Virginia, 113
Wheeling, West Virginia, 17, 19, 65, 92, 94, 100, 104, 107, 108, 109, 149, 160, 161, 177
WHIS (Bluefield, West Virginia, radio station), 72

White audiences for black bands in West Virginia, 78, 108, 176–77
White Sulphur Springs, West Virginia, 136
Whittaker, Yancy, 137, 160
Whyte, Zach, and his Chocolate Beau Brummels, 94, 104, 139
Wilberforce College, 83
Wilder, Joe, 25
Wilder, Virginia, 27
Willet, Francis "Chappie," 70, 82, 84, 91, 120, 159
Williams, Roscoe, 146
Williamson, West Virginia, 15, 16, 17, 21, 50, 64, 106, 131
Winding Gulf, West Virginia, 66, 118, 143
Winding Gulf coalfield, 14, 16
WLOG (Logan, West Virginia, radio station), 65
WLW (Cincinnati, Ohio, radio station), 61, 64, 65, 84, 95, 98, 100
WMMN (Fairmont, West Virginia, radio station), 128, 129
WOBU (Charleston, West Virginia, radio station), 64, 65, 66, 70, 82, 83, 174
World War II, impact on dance bands, 167–69. *See* Office of Defense Transportation; War Production Board
WPAR (Parkersburg, West Virginia, radio station), 65
WSAZ (Huntington, West Virginia, radio station), 65
WWVA (Wheeling, West Virginia, radio station), 65
Wyoming County, West Virginia, 14, 16, 30, 78

Yellow Jacket, 66, 83, 149

www.ingramcontent.com/pod-product-compliance
Lightning Source LLC
Chambersburg PA
CBHW030623230426
43661CB00053B/2118